MANAGERIAL DECISIONS WITH THE MICROCOMPUTER

In memory of
Maria Lorantos

MANAGERIAL DECISIONS WITH THE MICROCOMPUTER

John Bridge
Cardiff Business School

PHILIP ALLAN
New York London Toronto Sydney Tokyo

First published 1989 by
Philip Allan,
66 Wood Lane End, Hemel Hempstead,
Hertfordshire, HP2 4RG
A division of
Simon & Schuster International Group

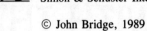

Printed and bound in Great Britain by
BPCC Wheatons Ltd, Exeter

Library of Congress Cataloging-in-Publication Data

Bridge, John, 1947–
    Managerial decisions with the microcomputer / John Bridge.
        p.   cm.
    ISBN 0-86003-547-6. — ISBN 0-86003-649-9 (pbk.)
    1. Management — Data processing. 2. Decision-making — Data
processing. 3. Lotus 1-2-3 (Computer program) 4. Microcomputers —
Programming.   I. Title.
HD30.2.B75   1989
658.4'03'00285416 — dc19   88-39367
                                                                   CIP

British Library Cataloguing in Publication Data

Bridge, John
    Managerial decisions with the microcomputer.
    1. Management. Decision making. Applications of
microcomputer systems
    I. Title
    658.4'03'0285416

    ISBN 0-86003-547-6
    ISBN 0-86003-649-9 (pbk)

1 2 3 4 5   93 92 91 90 89

CONTENTS

PREFACE   viii

Chapter 1 MANAGEMENT DECISION AND THE
           SPREADSHEET   1

           1.1 The Nature of Management   1
           1.2 Decision Support System Applications   4
           1.3 The Process of Evaluation   8
           1.4 Origins and Properties of Spreadsheets   9
           1.5 Cells, Numbers, Labels and Screen Display   10
           1.6 Formulae   13
           1.7 Functions Available in Spreadsheets   15
           1.8 Saving and Retrieving Files   16
           1.9 Facilities for Preparing Tables and Graphs   17
           1.10 Maintaining Order in Spreadsheet Modelling   19
           Appendix: Lotus 1-2-3 Release 3.0   20

Chapter 2 SENSITIVITY ANALYSIS AND REGRESSION
           USING DATA COMMANDS   23

           2.1 Data Table 1   23
           2.2 Data Table 2   25
           2.3 Sensitivity Analysis in Investment Appraisal   26
           2.4 Goal Seeking or Backward Iteration   28
           2.5 Data Regress   30
           2.6 The Two-Variable Linear Model   32
           2.7 Multiple Regression   36
           2.8 Other Data Commands   37
           Appendix: A Template for Linear Regression   38

Chapter 3   INVESTMENT APPRAISAL   **44**

    3.1   Characteristics of Investment   44
    3.2   Discounted Cash Flow   45
    3.3   DCF Methods of Appraisal   49
    3.4   Choice of Appraisal Method   52
    3.5   Special Cases with IRR   55
    3.6   Rent or Buy?   58
    3.7   Variations on the Basic Discounting Approaches   60
    3.8   Traditional Methods of Appraisal   62
    3.9   Writing-Down Allowances and Taxation   65
    3.10   Sensitivity Analysis   68
    3.11   Advanced Topics   71
    3.12   Risk and Uncertainty in Investment Appraisal   76
    Appendix: A Note on Portfolio Theory   80

Chapter 4   DEMAND ANALYSIS AND ESTIMATION   **85**

    4.1   Determinants of Demand   85
    4.2   Marketing Concepts   87
    4.3   Multivariate Demand Functions and Elasticity   88
    4.4   Elasticity and Logarithmic Functions   91
    4.5   Extensions to the Elasticity Concept   96
    4.6   Problems of Econometrics   98
    Appendix: Illustration of Autocorrelation and its
                  Correction   102

Chapter 5   DEMAND FORECASTING   **106**

    5.1   Prediction Using Statistical Methods   106
    5.2   Multiple Regression in Forecasting Using Minitab   113
    5.3   Moving Averages in Time-Series Analysis   118
    5.4   Error Measurement in Forecasting, and Exponential
          Smoothing   122
    5.5   External Forecasts and Indicators   128
    5.6   Impact of the Product Life Cycle   129

Chapter 6   COST AND PRICE RELATIONSHIPS   **136**

    6.1   Cost−Volume−Profit Analysis   136
    6.2   CVP and Economic Theory   140
    6.3   Cost-Based Pricing Models   146
    6.4   Target Rate of Return (TRR) Pricing   148

6.5 Modified Cost-Plus Procedure 1: Processing Charge
     to Reflect Opportunity Cost   151
6.6 Modified Cost-Plus Procedure 2: Marginal Cost and
     Elasticity   156
6.7 A Pragmatic Approach to Pricing   158
6.8 Value or Utility Pricing   160
6.9 The Product Life Cycle   163
6.10 Experience Effects   164

Chapter 7 LINEAR PROGRAMMING   **170**

7.1 Background and Applications   170
7.2 The Product-Mix Problem   171
7.3 The Graphical Method   175
7.4 Sensitivity Analysis   178
7.5 Spreadsheets in Linear Programming   179
7.6 Data Matrix Commands in Linear Programming   184
7.7 Media Selection   187
7.8 Multi-Period Capital Rationing   190

Chapter 8 ISSUES IN PUBLIC SECTOR ANALYSIS   **197**

8.1 Cost–Benefit Analysis   197
8.2 The Choice of Discount Rate   201
8.3 Option Appraisal   202
8.4 Indicators and Qualitative Factors in Benefit
     Assessment   203
8.5 Note on the Delphi Method   206
8.6 Analysis of Costs and Benefits   207
8.7 Specialised Software Applications   209

ANSWERS   **220**

AUTHOR INDEX   **224**

SUBJECT INDEX   **226**

PREFACE

In recent years there has been a tremendous expansion in the use of micro-computers in business schools and management departments of universities and polytechnics. The spreadsheet package has made an important contribution to teaching through the medium of the microcomputer — particularly for courses in finance, quantitative methods, and economics. In business, it now provides decision support across a broad spectrum of managerial applications.

The arrival of Lotus 1-2-3™ [1] further increased the popularity of spreadsheet software, both in business practice and in teaching, since it provided a wide range of functions, data handling routines and graphics in an integrated package. This package is regarded as *the* standard, to the extent that an ability to import Lotus files or to interface directly with Lotus 1-2-3 is seen as a highly desirable attribute in related products.

Many textbooks in managerial economics, business finance, and quantitative methods now make reference to spreadsheet applications of the techniques which those disciplines encompass. However, sometimes the material is relegated to a brief appendix, or to an accompanying teacher's manual. Although there is no shortage of reference books on Lotus 1-2-3, many of which do an excellent job in teaching the novice how to use the product without the assistance of an instructor, there are few texts geared to the teaching of specific subject areas through the spreadsheet medium.

This was the problem which I faced in the teaching of managerial economics — broadly defined to include topics such as linear programming and investment appraisal, both in commercial and in public service contexts. It no longer seemed relevant to teach my students how to solve problems manually, yet there remained a need to develop an awareness of the principles and concepts on which my course had traditionally been based.

---

1. Lotus 1-2-3 and Symphony are registered trademarks of Lotus Development Corporation.

This book, which has emerged to meet the need, does not aim to teach micro-computing from first principles. However, the level of prior knowledge required is minimal. A session on system details and keyboard facilities, followed by instruction on Lotus 1-2-3, through the tutorials provided by Lotus with the package, should be sufficient. The use of Lotus 'macros' is not covered in this book, because the facility is well documented elsewhere, and it contributes little to the understanding of the structure of the problems which appear in the text.

Despite the versatility of the spreadsheet medium, it has been necessary to expand the coverage of the book to include some references to statistical soft-ware, routines for linear programming, and software to facilitate the planning of health services. With regard to the latter, it is software which runs in conjunc-tion with another Lotus product, namely Symphony, to which reference is made. Likewise, products which interface with Lotus 1-2-3 and/or Symphony, or which are specifically designed to run alongside or within their environments (add-ons and add-ins), are those which have been chosen in most of the other applications.[2]

The major exception to this emphasis on compatibility with the Lotus standard is the description of a program (for linear programming), written in BASIC, by D. Whitaker in his book 'OR on the Micro'. I am grateful to John Wiley & Sons Ltd. for their permission to reproduce, in modified form, the material in Chapter 7 which was derived from Whitaker's program.

Of the available statistical software, it is Minitab™ which has been chosen to show how regression can be extended beyond the level of analysis permitted by Lotus 1-2-3. The latest 'Standard' microcomputer version of the product (Release 6.1) comes complete with a Lotus interface, to facilitate the transfer of worksheets between the packages, and so give access to the wide range of statistical procedures available in Minitab. The present volume, however, is restricted to the regres-sion facilities of the product.

I am grateful to Minitab Inc., 3081 Enterprise Drive, State College, PA 16801, USA (Telephone 814/238-3280, Telex 881612) for the services given through their Author Assistance Programme. Minitab is a registered trademark.

I should further add that DHSS material is Crown Copyright, and although the illustrative material which I prepared for Chapter 8 was not extracted from any publication, DHSS data from the computer files was inevitably displayed in the performance indicator graphs.

I am indebted to my colleagues at the Cardiff Business School for their helpful comments on the draft manuscript. They include Gerald Harbour, Mark Goode, Steve Hill, Dick Edwards, and Malcolm Morgan. From the DHSS, valuable comments on Chapter 8 were offered by Paul Forte, Rob Moore, and Warren Brown. Robert Ingram of Lotus Developments checked my references to Lotus Release 3.0 in the Appendix to Chapter 1. The notes of an independent reader, acting for the publisher, were also of great value in improving the manuscript.

---

2. These products include Goal Solutions and What's *Best!*, which are registered trademarks of Enfin Software Corporation and General Optimization Inc. respectively.

I thank all these individuals for their contributions but, needless to say, any deficiencies which remain are my responsibility alone.

Although each worksheet and program illustration has been carefully checked, neither the author nor the publisher will be held liable for any problems which arise in application. It is the user's responsibility to check that the results are accurate and valid in the context of the decisions being taken.

Finally, a few words about system requirements are in order. The minimum internal memory (RAM) to support Lotus 1-2-3 Release 2.0 or 2.01 is 256K. The IBM PC, or a compatible, with two double-sided, double-density diskette drives using PCDOS versions 2.0, 2.1, 3.0 or 3.1, is required to run the software. If the IBM PC/AT is used, DOS 3.0 or 3.1 is required. The software automatically uses the 8087 or 8027 mathematics coprocessor, if fitted, and this is a highly desirable accessory to speed up computational time.

Minitab, standard microcomputer version 6.1, is more demanding in RAM, with 512K stipulated as a minimum. Although a computer with two double-sided, double-density diskette drives is theoretically capable of running Minitab, a hard disk installation of 10 Megabytes or more is recommended, as is a mathematics coprocessor.

Other applications require still more RAM and disk storage capacity. For instance, the Balance of Care System, which runs in conjunction with Symphony, really needs 1000K RAM, and the system's files will rapidly use up space on a 10 Megabyte hard disk. My own computer (an Olivetti M21 with MSDOS 2.11) has 640K RAM, one diskette drive, a 20 Megabyte hard disk and 8087 mathematics coprocessor.

John Bridge
Cardiff Business School

MANAGEMENT DECISION AND THE SPREADSHEET

1.1 The Nature of Management

Management is frequently defined in terms of the functions which managers perform. Management functions have been classified as decision making, planning and control, organising and staffing, communicating and directing.[1]

Although computers have found their way into virtually every aspect of management, in business and most other types of organisation the most obvious applications are in decision making, planning, and control.

Decision Making is frequently singled out as the primary function of management, since it is usually an integral part of the other activities listed above. A decision is a conscious choice from various options, and the process of decision making is usually seen as involving some, or all, of the following steps: objective setting; problem definition; generation of alternatives; evaluation of options; and CHOICE.

This book's main concern is with analytical approaches to decision making, particularly those approaches which lend themselves to computer solution.

Planning is essentially a forward-looking or 'anticipatory'[2] form of decision making to which many analytical techniques may be applied. Inevitably, forecasting is an important part of planning, and a variety of techniques is available to assist at that stage of the process. At the highest level of planning, an organisation's strategy is developed. A strategy may be defined as:

> the pattern or plan that integrates an organisation's major goals, policies, and action sequences into a cohesive whole.　　　　　　　　(Quinn 1980, p. 7)

Strategic decisions include such matters as new product development, acquisi-

---

1. As described by Massie (1987, p. 5).
2. As described by Ackoff (1970).

tion and merger, expansion and investment at home and overseas. The information which is needed is largely external to the organisation, and tends to be specific to the problem under consideration.

Control is the process by which actual resource utilisation and organisational performance are compared with objectives, to enable corrective action to be taken by management. It includes budgetary and cost control, and monitoring of achievement by reviewing sales, market share, divisional profit performance etc.

Management Systems

Control requires appropriate information to measure performance, so as to identify when 'variances' occur, and to indicate when the remedial adjustments to system input have had the desired effect in eliminating such variances. This adjustment process involves feedback, either in a closed-loop or open-loop system. The latter is illustrated in Figure 1.1 which includes a 'management process' in the control system to interpret 'organisational problems', and determine appropriate action.

Simple control systems, such as thermostats and mechanical regulators, can function without human intervention. Such closed-loop systems have their parallel in business organisations, in the form of stock control and credit control systems which, within prescribed limits, can operate without the management process. This is by-passed with an automatic correction mechanism as shown in Figure 1.1.

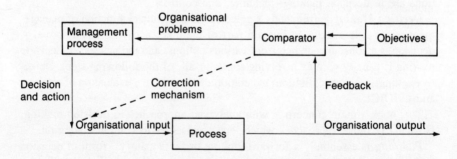

Figure 1.1   Control System

Control is particularly important in the context of decisions at the operational level in all departments and functions of a business. In place of separate information systems, which were once commonly maintained for each operational department — sales, marketing, production, finance, and personnel — the modern view of a management information system (MIS) is of an extensive mainframe computer-based *integrated* system for the collection, storage, and retrieval of data.

Although an MIS is neither restricted to the control function nor to decisions at the operational level, it tends to be most effective for decisions which are repetitive, or which are clearly structured: e.g. budgeting procedures and periodic reviews.

Another type of management system which co-exists with the MIS is the decision support system (DSS). Its place is defined by Keen and Scott Morton (1978) in terms of the middle ground between the extremes of 'structured' and 'unstructured' tasks.

Some tasks cannot be modelled effectively, because they are heavily subjective, the decision mechanisms are poorly understood, and supporting data is absent or scarce. Many decisions in the personnel function, such as hiring and firing, fall into this category, and computerised systems have little to offer.

The well understood 'structured' tasks such as cost control and payroll administration are served by the organisation's MIS, but there is a need for a computer-based system which complements the MIS in lending support to the decision process at both operational and strategic levels, particularly in those 'semi-structured' problems where the application of judgement is an essential part of making a choice.

In describing a problem as 'semi-structured', McCosh and Scott Morton (1977, p. 12) mean that one or more phases of the decision process –

intelligence: obtaining data to define the problem
design: generating solutions to the problem
choice: evaluating and selecting the best[3]

– are unstructured, with the consequence that managerial judgement is a vital element of the decision.

This semi-structured area of decision making, appropriate to the DSS approach, is such that:

... the manager alone and the system alone cannot make as good a decision as the two in combination ...

(McCosh and Scott Morton 1977, p. 12)

A DSS may be based on microcomputers, used independently, or linked to the main computer network of an organisation, with each manager having access to a terminal or a 'work-station'. Data from the MIS may be accessed when needed: for instance, sales data maintained in the MIS database, which records transactions in terms of price, quantity, territory and date, may be accessed when short-term sales forecasts are to be prepared. However, for many purposes, especially in strategic decision making, data specific to the task will often be required, and the historical data from the MIS will only provide a limited perspective.

One advantage which microcomputer systems have over traditional mainframe arrangements is that the analysis and decision can be brought closer together. Complex problems no longer have to be channelled through a centralised manage-

---

3. Intelligence, design, and choice follows the classification of Simon (1960).

ment science or operational research department before a model may be prepared for computer solution. User-friendly software on microcomputers facilitates the decentralisation of problem solving, and expertise tends to be applied in the departments where it can be most effective.

The decision process becomes interactive in character, with the results of a preliminary analysis providing feedback to the manager, who can experiment with modifications to the original proposals, refine his options, and revise his calculations where necessary. He continues in this vein until he has a short list of the most promising options, with an evaluation of each.

1.2   Decision Support System Applications

An empirically based classification of DSS applications developed by Alter (1980) comprises seven distinct types: file-drawer systems; representational models; data-analysis systems; accounting models, analysis—information systems; optimisation models; and suggestion models. Of these, the ones that will feature in the present text are primarily: accounting models; analysis— information systems and optimisation models.

Accounting Models

A break-even chart, or Cost-Volume-Profit (CVP) chart, is one of the simplest accounting models. Its main purpose is to show how cost and revenue behave in relation to the volume of activity.

The output and sales volume at which costs will just be covered may be identified (break-even output/sales), and a projection of profits or losses for positions either side of that point may be given. The device may also be used to determine the consequences of different prices and cost levels on profits. The data on which the chart is based is set out in Table 1.1(a).

In Figure 1.2 the break-even point occurs at around 235,000 units of production, where the revenue and cost lines intersect, so that the firm will just be able to cover its outgoings at that level. Its expected level of production (and sales) is 400,000 units, based on a sales forecast, which gives it a 'margin of safety' of 165,000.

Questions which might be asked subsequent to this CVP analysis include:

1. How reliable is the forecast of 400,000 units sold annually?

2. Will it be possible to maintain a price of £2.70, or should the price be modified?

3. Is it worthwhile spending money on capital equipment to enable the firm to produce at this level?

Table 1.1(a) Revenue, Costs, and Profit

	A	B	C	D	E	F	G	H
1								
2								
3								
4	revenue							
5	*******							
6								(£ 000's)
7	price	2.70						
8	quantity	400	thousand			total revenue		1080
9						*************		
10								
11	variable costs			TVC	(£ 000's)			
12	**************			***				
13								
14	material	0.75		300				
15	labour	0.50		200				
16	var O/H	0.30		120				
17		----		---				
18		1.55	sum	620		gross profit		460
19		----		---		***********		
20								
21	fixed costs			TFC	(£ 000's)			
22	***********			***				
23								
24	fixed O/H (production)			150				
25	selling			50				
26	admin			70				
27				---				
28			sum	270		net profit		190
29				---		**********		===
30								

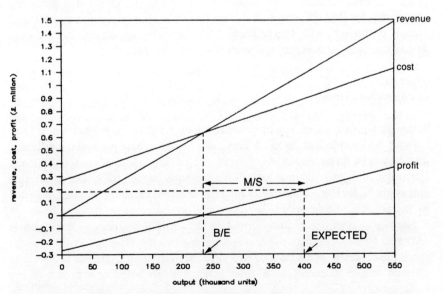

Note: The broken lines, arrows and labels were added after the Lotus graph had been printed.

Figure 1.2 Break-Even Chart

4. Suppose that the firm is presently in the sports goods business, and the units of production at the moment are all footballs of the same type: should it extend its product range, should it diversify into other forms of leisure goods, or clothing, or something completely different?

To explore these and other issues, different forms of analysis will be invoked, although it may be possible to relate these to the accounting model developed here in order to gauge the impact on profitability of varying assumptions and different options.

Analysis—Information Systems

To help determine whether the assumption about sales potential is plausible, some analysis of demand conditions and market trends would be required. Data on past sales and prices charged, period by period, should be available in most firms, even if the information systems are rudimentary. From an MIS, detailed information on sales achieved over time will be available for use in the context of a DSS, based on a spreadsheet or a statistical package to enable further analysis to take place, in support of sales forecasting, pricing, and 'marketing mix' decisions.

Time-series models involving regression analysis, trend analysis, and detection of seasonal variations, can be devised. Additionally, information generated specifically for the DSS, based on market research, opinion surveys and external economic forecasts, will often be utilised. The topics of demand analysis and sales forecasting will be covered in Chapters 4 and 5 respectively.

Optimisation Models

Although the firm in our example is already engaged in the production of footballs, it is possible that its machinery, labour resources, marketing skills and distribution facilities, could be deployed in the manufacture of related products. For instance, a product mix comprising footballs, tennis balls, and swimming aids might be seen as a means of ironing out seasonal variations in sales, detected in the analysis of time-series data described in the previous paragraph.

The question of optimisation in the product mix then arises — how should resources be allocated between these products when the existing factory is working at full capacity? What balance will yield the highest profits overall? This kind of issue will be discussed in Chapter 7 which deals with linear programming techniques.

The firm will also have to allocate investment funds between competing projects. Sometimes the decisions will reflect an intention to expand in the same line

Table 1.1(b) Investment Appraisal

	I	J	K	L	M	N	O	P
1								
2								
3								
4			1989	1990	1991	1992	1993	1994
5								
6	investment		-680			-200		
7								
8	revenue			1080	1139	1202	1268	1338
9	growth	5.5%						
10								
11	var costs			620	654	690	728	768
12	fix costs			270	270	270	270	270
13	===							
14	net cash flow		-680	190	215	42	270	300
15	===							
16								
17	discount rate							
18		9.0%						
19								
20	NPV	94.2				IRR	13.79%	

of business, but the strategic issues of diversification and acquisition of other businesses also involve investment.

The accounting model serves as the basis for profit computations and for cash flow projections when an investment appraisal is undertaken. In Table 1.1(b) the previous analysis is extended to project the opening revenue of 1,080 (thousand pounds) at a 5.5% growth rate, and to compute the 'net cash flows' over a six-year period after allowing for capital expenditures of £680,000 and £200,000 in 1989 and 1992 respectively.

The first question to be asked is whether the project taken in isolation is worthwhile. This involves discounted cash flow (DCF) appraisal if optimal investment rules are to be followed, although the concept of the 'payback period' may be applied as a rough-and-ready rule by some firms.

Otherwise, within DCF, the net present value (NPV) or internal rate of return (IRR) computations are advocated to determine acceptability. Although these will not be discussed in detail until Chapter 3, the results displayed in Table 1.1(b) for NPV and IRR[4] show that the expenditure is worthwhile (NPV is positive, and IRR exceeds the assumed discount rate of 9%).

If several different kinds of expansion are contemplated, for example, the production of exercise cycles, or weight-training equipment, while capital funds are limited, the *optimal allocation* of capital can also be determined (Chapter 3: investment appraisal and Chapter 7: linear programming).

---

4. Tables 1.1(a) and 1.1(b) are part of the same microcomputer spreadsheet display. The latter table is one screen to the right of the initial display, with revenue projections being made in row 8, so as to line up with the initial revenue computation in cell H8 of Table 1.1(a).

Another type of DSS application features what Alter calls *suggestion models*. Although these are not encountered as frequently as those discussed above, brief reference will be made to models which fall into this category. For instance, 'value' or 'utility' pricing, discussed in Chapter 6, offers a suggested price for each product manufactured by a firm based on a formula which gives weight to each significant characteristic. It is particularly valuable for firms which manufacture a large number of product versions, based on a given theme, but with a wide range of optional features and extras. Microcomputers with all the variations of memory, disk drives, graphics cards, monochrome or colour displays, etc., could well be priced using this approach.

1.3   The Process of Evaluation

The evaluation stage of the decision-making process is mapped out in Figure 1.3. The unordered set of alternatives A1, A2 etc. represents the feasible options which have been prepared in response to an operational problem or strategic opportunity. Each option is to be evaluated in terms of cost and effectiveness.

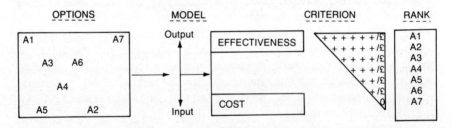

Figure 1.3   The Evaluation Process

In order to perform this evaluation, it is desirable to construct models which enable the impact of causal relationships to be explored: for instance, a statistical analysis of sales data might suggest that sales revenue is related to advertising expenditure, but with diminishing marginal effectiveness. The estimated relationship then serves as a model which can help to compare the cost of advertising at various levels with the anticipated benefits.

The models need to include the major variables which influence the issues under consideration, and be accessible to the user, so that changes in inputs to the model may be effected easily and the changes in the model's output may be observed readily. Results expressed in cost and effectiveness measures may then be compared for each option, by applying appropriate criteria (e.g. return on investment) and an assessment of which is best in meeting the criteria can then be made.

One of the most useful software packages available for a business user of the microcomputer is the spreadsheet. Although individual programs may still be acquired for specialist purposes — e.g. statistical analysis, project analysis, cost accounting — the spreadsheet provides a general-purpose modelling device, the potential of which has expanded in recent years following the incorporation of database and graphics facilities into the most popular packages.

Although it has these multi-purpose qualities, the special contribution of the microcomputer spreadsheet is that it enables *sensitivity analysis* to be performed efficiently. Spreadsheet packages are extensively promoted for this facility — usually described as 'what if?' analysis. This latter term is perhaps more explicit than the concept of 'sensitivity' analysis.

The basic principle behind these notions is that decisions are taken under conditions of imperfect knowledge, and that one can only identify a choice as desirable or optimal if particular conditions are anticipated. Under different assumptions, the spreadsheet is able to recalculate the results of the analysis, and indicate whether another option might be preferred. Options which retain their high rank in the face of parameter changes (i.e. are relatively 'insensitive') are obviously preferable to choices which are highly sensitive to such changes.

1.4 Origins and Properties of Spreadsheets

The spreadsheet is designed specifically to facilitate the recalculation which is needed whenever a model is revised in any way. The spreadsheet approach was originally used in manual exercises for instructional purposes at the Harvard Business School.[5] Business models were constructed on vertically ruled paper (called a spreadsheet), with various inputs listed in the left margin — e.g. selling price, growth in volume etc. — and their impact period by period was shown sequentially in the columns of the sheet.

Whilst this provided a convenient format in which to trace the consequences of variations in the inputs, considerable recalculation was involved, and the need for computerisation was apparent. The computer-based spreadsheet emerged in the form of *Visicalc*™ (developed by Software Arts) in 1979. It was available for use with the Apple II microcomputer and, subsequently, with several other machines.

The spreadsheet is sometimes viewed as a package for decision support in *financial* planning. Finlay (1985, Chapter 11) treats it as such, but he points to the need for modelling exercises which include all relevant resources, and involvement by managers from other decision areas. In an article by the same author (1983), it was suggested that financial packages have the potential ' to increase significantly the effective application of quantitative techniques by company management in many areas'.

This prediction has certainly come to pass so far as spreadsheet applications are concerned. Despite their obvious use in the construction of accounting models,

---

5. As described by de Pace (1984, pp. 84—5).

they are also widely used for the analysis of production issues and for sales and marketing purposes.

In fact, the spreadsheet may be used for any application in which relationships between numerical values are established. Each figure is entered in a specific cell which is identified by its row number and column letter, giving it a unique 'address'. Although only about 20 rows and 10 columns may appear on the screen at any time, several thousand cells (depending on the hardware and software capacities) may be available for modelling purposes. The spreadsheet *Lotus 1-2-3*™, release 2.0 and above, offers 256 columns and 8192 rows in a given worksheet.

A complex matrix of relationships may be established using formulae to express the dependency of the value in one cell to the value in another. In turn, further cells will feature in the pattern of interdependencies which are established. Ultimately, a change in one input cell can have a ripple effect (which takes place almost instantaneously) to cause changes in hundreds of other cells, and on the final output in which one is interested.

The microcomputer spreadsheet is designed to facilitate recalculation for any change in parameter values. The manner of modelling should be such that each of the key variables is identified separately in a particular cell of the worksheet in use.[6]

1.5 Cells, Numbers, Labels and Screen Display

(a) Cells

The basic working unit of the spreadsheet is the cell, which is identified by an 'address' (column letter and row number). Normally, when starting with a blank worksheet, the screen cursor is positioned at cell address A1. The usual way of moving from cell to cell is through the arrow keys, or the Page Up and Page Down keys. An alternative method which is useful when moving around a large worksheet is to use 'GOTO', which is performed by pressing function key f5 in Lotus 1-2-3. The cell may be used to hold numbers, text, formulae, or functions, each of which is now described in turn:

(b) Numbers

Numbers are entered into a cell simply by moving the cursor to the required address and typing the appropriate figures. Each spreadsheet package normally offers choices as to the format in which figures will appear on the screen. For example,

---

6. The term 'worksheet' refers to a particular spreadsheet application, and usually a separate file will be constructed and saved for each of these.

the Lotus worksheets which have been used so far in this chapter are mainly in 'fixed' format with up to two decimal places, although 'percentage' format has been selected where appropriate.

The 'general' format is the default setting which will be maintained unless the appropriate command is given to present an alternative format. There are no commas after the thousands in general format, negative values contain a minus sign, and as many decimal places appear as necessary subject to column-width limits. The latter are variable, but are initially set at 9 characters, which will accommodate a number such as 638.1407, which allows for 7 figures plus the decimal point, plus a space between numbers in adjacent columns.

In Tables 1.2(a) and (b), which are shown as screen displays, the original worksheets are modified so that most of the entries are now in 'comma' format.

Table 1.2(a)   Revenue, Costs, and Profit

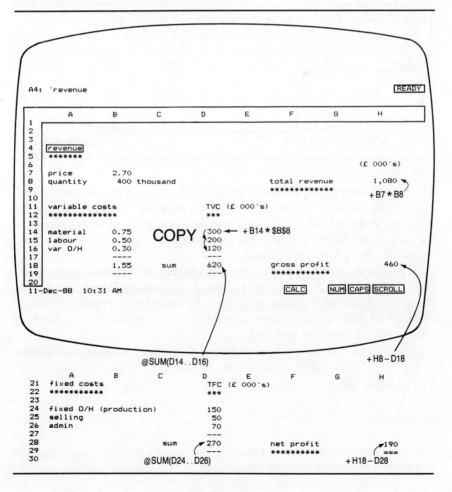

Table 1.2(b) Investment Appraisal

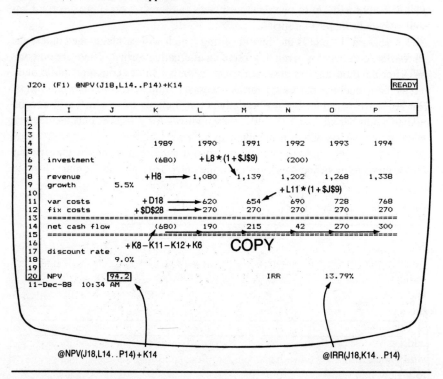

$$@NPV(J18,L14..P14)+K14 \qquad\qquad\qquad @IRR(J18,K14..P14)$$

The comma appears after thousands, and negative values are indicated in brackets. The *complete* displays are given in these tables, including certain peripheral items which are described below. The cell formulae, once entered, do not appear on the main screen display, of course, but are indicated with arrows, as are the 'copy' commands, for the reader's benefit.

To change the format of a range in the worksheet, the command sequence is: **/RF** (the forward slash starting the command, followed by **R**ange **F**ormat). To change the format of the whole worksheet, the command sequence begins with **/WG** (**W**orksheet **G**lobal), before choosing Format. In either case a menu of choices for the format is provided.

Within the worksheet one needs a means of labelling the rows and columns – e.g., time period, sales, fixed cost etc. – and of providing headings – e.g. Project Appraisal.

(c) Labels

Text or *label* entries are made in Lotus 1-2-3 by moving the cursor to the required cell address and typing the appropriate word(s). When an entry is complete, the

'ENTER' or 'RETURN' key is pressed, and the cursor can be moved to another cell as soon as the word 'READY' appears at the top right of the screen. If an entry starts with a letter of the alphabet, it will be interpreted as a label entry and will start at the left of the cell unless a label-prefix character is specified, or the default is changed. The prefixes are: ′ for alignment at the left edge of the cell; ″ for alignment at the right edge of the cell; and ^ for centering in the cell.

A backslash may also serve as the first character of a label entry, and any character which follows is repeated so as to fill the cell. Thus \= creates a cell appearing as =========, which is a useful device for underlining, or separating the contents of a worksheet, particularly when copied across a range of cells. The underscoring included to separate the net cash flow from the other items in Table 1.2(b) was prepared in this manner.

(d) Screen Display − Mode Indicators and Other Items

Moving back to the portion of the worksheet displayed in Table 1.2(a), it can be seen that the cursor is currently positioned at cell A4. This cell *address* is indicated above the worksheet at the top left of the screen followed by a colon, and a description of the cell contents which is a left-aligned label indicated by the single apostrophe which precedes the word 'revenue'.

The entries above the worksheet form the 'control panel', starting with the cell address as described, then the mode indicator (showing 'READY' at the top right, which means that the entry has been completed and that the cursor can be moved to a new cell address if required).

If there are second and third lines in the control panel (not in use here), these will display menu items or instructions when a new mode is entered (e.g. 'FILES' or 'POINT' mode), and characteristics of the menu choice. At the bottom left is the date and time and, at the bottom right, indicators to warn the user when recalculation, 'CALC,'[7] is needed, or that 'NUM LOCK', 'CAPS LOCK', or 'SCROLL LOCK' keyboard controls are in use.

Also shown in Table 1.2(a), for completeness, are rows 21 to 30 which would be lying off-screen when the main part of the worksheet was printed.

1.6 Formulae

A worksheet can simply be used to display an array of numbers − e.g. a summary of annual sales returns, or a cash flow statement, although in all but the most elementary worksheets there will be relationships between the cells which contain the figures. A *formula* enables such relationships to be specified.

---

7. 'CALC' will appear when needed if the automatic recalculation of Lotus 1-2-3 has been over-ridden by the command for manual recalculation which is **/WGRM** (Worksheet, Global, Recalculation, Manual).

The simplest formula in Table 1.2(a) is that for total revenue which equals price multiplied by quantity. Cell H8 is used to display the total revenue, and in Lotus 1-2-3 the formula is typed in as +B7*B8. The output of the formula 1,080 appears at cell address H8 after the formula has been ENTERED.

In Table 1.2(b) the value shown in cell M8 is 1,139, but again it is the output of a formula which comprises the year 1990 sales revenue plus 5.5% annual growth. The formula in cell M8 is +L8+L8*J9 or alternatively +L8*(1+J9).

Note that the formulae require a plus sign to commence the entry, otherwise they would begin with a letter such as H or L which would be interpreted as a label. (Some other spreadsheets use the 'equal' = sign to indicate that a formula is to be entered.)

Multiplication, using the * sign, takes precedence over addition, so that in the first of the alternative formulae for cell M8, the product L8*L9 is calculated before the result is added to L8.

In order to override the precedence ordering of operators (in Lotus 1-2-3 this is exponentiation [^]; multiplication, division [* /]; addition, subtraction [+ −]; in descending order), it is necessary to use brackets. So in the above variant of the formula, +L8*(1+J9), the contents of the bracket are computed before multiplication with L8. Without the bracket, L8 would have been multiplied by 1 and then added to J9, which would have been completely inappropriate.

To illustrate the precedence of operators, suppose that we had in the first row of a worksheet the following:

	A	B	C	D	E	F	G
row 1	1.2	2	4	2	3	8	

In cell G1 we enter the formula:

$$+A1\wedge B1*C1+D1*E1-F1$$

Exponentiation takes place first, so 1.2 is squared (raised to the power 2 indicated in cell B1) yielding 1.44. Multiplication follows, with this result being multiplied by 4 (cell C1) to give 5.76.

D1 and E1 are also multiplied to give 6.

Finally, addition and subtraction take place, with 5.76 being added to 6, and the number 8 in cell F1 being subtracted.

The result of 3.76 will appear in cell G1.

None of the intermediate stages in the computation are apparent to the user as the computation proceeds − they have been included just to demonstrate the precedence ordering.

Copying Formulae

When a formula has been used to express a relationship between cells, it is often necessary to replicate the same relationship elsewhere in the worksheet. For example, in Table 1.2(b), having established that the net cash flow is the sales revenue, less fixed and variable costs, less capital outlay, a similar formula will be required for each entry in row 14.

Copying facilities are provided to enable formulae to be placed in the appropriate cells without having to re-type the entries in each position. The command sequence for copying begins with /C after which the user is prompted for the source cell(s) and destination cell(s).

When the copying operation takes place, the software does not simply replicate term by term, but will make adjustments for the relative position of the cells, unless instructed otherwise.

Thus, whilst cell K14 contains the formula $+K8-K11-K12+K6$, it will appear as $+L8-L11-L12+L6$ when this is copied to cell L14, and likewise for M14 to P14. This will give a set of net cash flows in row 14 of Table 1.2(b) from a single formula copied along that row.

The growing sales revenue figures in row 8 of Table 1.2 (b), however, are treated rather differently. Although we wish to add a percentage growth rate successively to L8, M8, etc. until we reach P8, the model assumes that a particular growth rate (in cell J9) will persist. This means that the copying procedure needs to ensure that cell J9 remains fixed in the formula whilst tracking across the row from L8 to P8.

Thus cell M8 holds the formula $+L8*(1+J9)$, and we want N8 to hold the formula $+M8*(1+J9)$. The usual copying procedure would yield $+M8*(1+K9)$, however, i.e. K9 instead of J9, because of the relative cell locations.

The problem may be overcome in Lotus 1-2-3 by making cell J9 an *absolute* cell address in the formula for M8, appearing thus: $+L8*(1+\$J\$9)$, the two 'dollar' characters being typed in directly, or activated with function key f4 (if in POINT mode). When this formula is copied, the $\$J\$9$ will remain fixed in the formula, regardless of the relative cell locations. Some cell references will be part absolute (by either row or column), and part relative.

If a cell address in a formula has inadvertently been entered as relative when it should be absolute, the editing facility (function key f2 in Lotus 1-2-3) can be invoked. This enables a formula (or label) to be altered without re-typing the whole entry. Having entered EDIT mode, the arrow keys are used to move to the part of the formula which needs to be amended, and function key f4 can be used to change from relative to absolute, to mixed, by pressing this key once, or several times until the desired form of cell address appears.

1.7 Functions Available in Spreadsheets

Although formulae may be used to obtain statistics such as mean, variance, and standard deviation, or financial values for present value or compound interest, most spreadsheets offer a variety of *functions* which save considerable effort in model building.

Functions are entered in Lotus 1-2-3 by typing the @ sign followed by the function required and the range of cells involved. For example, suppose we wish to add the values in column D of Table 1.2(a) for variable costs. They appear in cells D14, D15 and D16. The total is to be given in cell D18. Instead of using the formula: +D14+D15+D16, we could use the function: @SUM(D14..D16). The desired range for summation is indicated in the brackets.

Examples of functions available in Lotus 1-2-3 are:

Mathematical — @EXP, @LOG, @LN (exponent, logarithm, and natural logarithm).

Statistical — @SUM, @MIN, @MAX, @AVG, which are self-explanatory, @VAR, @STD (variance and standard deviation).

Financial — @NPV, @IRR, @FV (net present value, internal rate of return, and future value).

To see a financial function in use, we can refer back to Table 1.2(b). The cell address where the cursor is positioned is indicated at the top left of the display (first line of the worksheet's control panel).

At this stage the cursor was at J20, in which use of the @NPV function was made. Inside the bracket can be seen J18,L14..P14. These are the discount rate (J18) and the range over which discounting is to take place (L14..P14). The bracket which appears after J20 — showing (F1) — denotes a 'fixed' entry with a given number of decimal places, namely 1.

There are many other mathematical, statistical, and financial functions which have not been mentioned here. There are also logical, string, date and time functions and various 'special' functions which are detailed in the reference manual. Although most spreadsheets have similar functions available, which are often indicated by the @ sign, some functions may not be available in every case (e.g. @IRR does not appear in all packages), and the particular form of entry must be learned for the package in question.

1.8 Saving and Retrieving Files

When a worksheet has been prepared, in order to preserve it for future reference, it is necessary to Save it to file. The command sequence is /FS. Files are Retrieved through the sequence /FR.

The file extension for Lotus 1-2-3 release 2.0 and above is **WK1** and for earlier versions **WKS**.

It is good practice to save every time a set of relationships has been specified, or a series of data has been entered, even if each of these only occupies a small portion of the worksheet. Although it may interrupt creative thinking while moving around the worksheet, it avoids the danger of losing valuable time and effort in the event of accidental erasure or power failure.

1.9   Facilities for Preparing Tables and Graphs

Tables for Printing

If one wishes to print the contents of the screen including the row and column identifiers, the control panel, and other peripheral entries, the procedure is simply to press the PRT SC key (shifted) when a printer is connected.

More usually, for presentation, the identifying row and column references of the worksheet will be omitted, and appropriate headings chosen. In order to print such a table, a choice has to be made between directing the output straight to the printer, or to save it as a file which may subsequently be word-processed and incorporated into a document. The command sequence starts with:

/PPR   or   **/PFR**

i.e. Print Printer, or Print File, followed by the Range.

Next, the range of the worksheet is indicated, either by typing in the cell address at the top left corner followed by the bottom right corner of the range − e.g. B3..G14 − or point mode may be used to highlight the range required for printing. The sequence for direct printing continues with:

A   for Align (the paper in the printer)
G   for Go
P   for Page (if more printing is to follow)
Q   for Quit when printing is completed

The alignment and page commands are omitted if a *file* is being created, and the operator will be prompted for a file name − the default file extension being **.PRN**.

Preparing Graphs

Although the graphics part of the Lotus package permits a variety of displays − including bar charts and pie diagrams − in the main we shall be using 'XY' graphs, or 'LINE' graphs. Figure 1.2, displayed earlier in the chapter, is an example of a 'line' graph. (The main difference between these two types of graph is that the XY graph displays numeric values on both axes, whereas the line graph may have other data displayed on the X-axis: for example, the months of the year. In this case numeric output values have been chosen for the X-range, and there is little difference in the appearance of the graph in one form or the other.)

/G is the command to enter the graphics facility. This is followed by **T** to indicate the Type of graph, and **X** to prepare an XY graph (or **L** to prepare a line graph). The data ranges are then selected. **X** will be typed to indicate the range of data to feature on the horizontal (X axis). Several lines or scatters of symbols may then be prepared by designating **A, B, C, D, E** and **F** ranges — i.e. up to six data ranges.

V enables the graph to be Viewed when in the graphics facility. Options for choosing the format (lines or symbols or both) are available from an Options menu (keystroke **O**, followed by **F** for format).

Table 1.3 Worksheet Area for Break-Even Chart

	A	B	C	D	E	F	G	H
61								
62	output	revenue	cost	profit				
63								
64	0	0	270	−270 ◄── +B64 − C64				
65	50	135	347.5	−212.5				
66	100	270	425	−155				
67	150	405	502.5	−97.5				
68	200	540	580	−40				
69	250	675	657.5	17.5				
70	300	810	735	75				
71	350	945	812.5	132.5				
72	400	1080	890	190				
73	450	1215	967.5	247.5				
74	500	1350	1045	305				
75	550	1485	1122.5	362.5				
76								
77								
78								
79								
80								

+A64 ∗ $B$7   + $D$28 + $B$18 ∗ A64

Table 1.3 was used to prepare Figure 1.2, displayed in section 1.2 above. It has been constructed within the same worksheet as the previous tabulations, and is based on the same data. To prepare the graph, the X-range will be A64..A75. The first, second, and third data ranges will be B64..B75, C64..C75 and D64..D75.

Each of the data ranges may be typed in as upper and lower cell addresses, or indicated in point mode. Alternatively, if a range is likely to be invoked repeatedly in copying, printing or graphing, it may be useful to name it before entering the graphics facility. To do this, the command sequence is /**RNC** (Range Name Create). Once a range has been defined and named, it can be recalled from a list by pressing function key 3, whenever the user is prompted for a range.

A graph may be saved for subsequent printing by choosing 'Save' from the Graphics menu. One is then prompted for a name, with the file extension .PIC automatically added. The Printgraph part of the Lotus package is invoked from the Lotus access menu, the appropriate file is selected for printing, and the graph is produced with the aid of a suitable graphics printer. Many dot-matrix printers will produce line graphs of reasonable quality.

When one has prepared the graph and has Quit (**Q**) the graphics facility, the graph may be viewed on the screen by pressing function key 10. If the worksheet file is saved, after a graph has been prepared, the screen display is always available on retrieval of the file, when this function key is used. This applies regardless of whether a separate .PIC file has been saved for printing purposes.

1.10 Maintaining Order in Spreadsheet Modelling

The spreadsheet's ability to handle a complex matrix of interrelationships is only a virtue if the entries are correct and the logic is consistent. The plausibility of any solution is enhanced if it is known to have been derived by computer, yet it is only too easy for major flaws to enter a worksheet and render the computations completely invalid.

For instance, a growth rate of 5.5% is usually entered as .055 in the worksheet. If the figure 5.5 is entered into a cell in percentage format, this will come out as 550%, making a huge difference to any projections based on this figure. In this instance it should rapidly become apparent that an error has occurred, provided that the operator applies common sense.[8]

Apart from the application of common sense, there are systematic principles which can help to minimise error. In particular, the use of labels is strongly recommended to keep track of the relationships which are being established. These should be added at each stage, rather than waiting until the worksheet is complete and ready for printing.

If an erroneous entry is copied to other locations in the worksheet, it will replicate, and compound the problem. Before copying any formula or function, it should be checked carefully. Having ensured that the worksheet has been saved, simple single digit numbers can be entered in the cells which feature in any complex formula, and the result checked for consistency. The worksheet can then be retrieved and the copying procedure set into motion.

In tabulations where subtotals are aggregated, a useful cross-check is to ensure that the row and column aggregates produce the same figure. Thus two sets of totals will be produced − normally at the bottom right corner of the worksheet.

A sensible precaution to prevent a formula being altered, typically through a number being typed in inadvertently, is to *protect* it. This operation is performed as follows in Lotus 1-2-3:

/WGPE is typed to invoke Worksheet Global Protection Enable.

---

8. Useful common sense principles are expounded in articles by Grushcow (1987) and Schofield (1987). These cover most of the points made in this section, and offer several other useful hints as well.

/RU is used to Unprotect a Range, followed by the cell addresses defining the range, for those areas of the worksheet in which cell variations are to be permitted.

Finally, to prevent loss of the model in whole or in part, it is essential to save the file after every major modification. Once completed, a backup copy of the worksheet file should be kept, either on a separate diskette, or in another sub-directory of a hard disk.

APPENDIX: Lotus 1-2-3 Release 3.0

This book was completed before Lotus 1-2-3 Release 3.0 was issued, and the contents were checked to ensure compatibility as far as was possible without actually using the new version. All worksheets in the present volume were created using Release 2.0 or 2.01 and, as the Lotus information sheet for Release 3.0 states: 'The product will be compatible (file and macro) with all previous releases of 1-2-3, and will read and write Release 2.0 files directly.'

The main characteristics of the new product which have been publicised are:

3-dimensional worksheets;

multiple files in memory;

linking of formulae with files on disk as well as in memory;

files can support multiple worksheets, with 256 being available in total, each containing 256 columns by 8,192 rows;

an *optimal* recalculation feature increases the speed of computation by restricting the cells involved in the recalculation to those which are dependent on what has been changed; *background* recalculation allows the user to continue working in the spreadsheet;

graphics facilities have been enhanced to provide a wider range of graph types, and graphs may be printed from the menu. Text and graphs may be printed on the same page.

Although there is no guarantee that the existing versions of add-in/add-on products featuring in this book (Goal Solutions and **What's***Best*!) will function correctly with Release 3.0, it is anticipated that software houses will modify their existing products where necessary to create versions which will function with the new release of 1-2-3.

Apart from the inconvenience associated with upgrading Lotus 1-2-3, and possibly the auxiliary packages too, it would appear, therefore, that the new version will offer increased flexibility to this package in all the applications which feature in this text.

Exercises

1. A cell in a Lotus 1-2-3 worksheet contains the formula:

   3.5^2*2.3/5+4*3−2.5^3

   What does this represent in conventional arithmetic, and what is the result?

2. You are selling tickets for a disco with buffet at £7.50. The hire of premises and the disco will cost £300 for the event, and a catering firm has agreed to provide a buffet at £3.75 per head, for up to 150 persons.

   (a) Set up a worksheet to calculate the profit on the event if the maximum 150 tickets are sold.
   (b) How many tickets need to be sold in order to break even?
   (c) Save the worksheet for further use in the first example at the end of Chapter 2.

3. Calculate the average sales achieved by a sales force of 14 employees whose returns for the week are:

   10, 8, 12, 9, 6, 12, 15, 7, 16, 4, 10, 11, 8, 7 units, using a worksheet column, or row, as follows:

   (a) Find the total with a formula which adds the contents of all the cells together, then divide by 14.
   (b) Use the function @SUM and divide by 14.
   (c) Use the function @AVG.

4. Compute the variance and standard deviation of the sales returns given in exercise 3 using the functions @VAR and @STD. Find the square root of the variance using @SQRT.

5. In cells A2 to F2 of a worksheet, set out the cash flows of an investment which starts with an outflow of cash (negative) of £15,000, following by inflows (positive) of £3,000, £6,000, £10,000, £4,000 and £2,000, in time sequence at annual intervals.

   (a) Use the function @NPV(0.1,B2..F2)+A2 to find the investment's Net Present Value, discounting at 10% (i.e. 0.1).
   (b) Compute the Internal Rate of Return for the investment using the function @IRR(0.1,A2..F2). Express your result in percentage format to 2 decimal places.
   (c) Raise the discount rate of 10% (that is, the 0.1 inside the bracket) in part (a) of this exercise to 21%, and show how this affects the NPV.
   (d) Save your worksheet for exercise 2 at the end of the next chapter.

References and Further Reading

Ackoff, R.L. (1970) *A Concept of Corporate Planning*, Wiley.
Alter, S. (1980) *Decision Support Systems: Current Practice and Continuing Challenges*, Addison-Wesley.
Finlay, P.N. (1983) 'How to manage non-financially with packages', *Management Today*, May, pp. 39—44.
Finlay, P.N. (1985) *Mathematical Modelling in Business Decision-Making*, Croom Helm.
Grushcow, J. (1987) 'Avoiding spreadsheet slip-ups', *Lotus*, September.
Keen, P.G.W. and Scott-Morton, M.S. (1978) *Decision Support Systems: An Organisational Perspective*, Addison-Wesley.
McCosh, A. and Scott-Morton, M.S. (1977) *Management Decision Support Systems*, Macmillan.
Massie, J.L. (1987) *Essentials of Management*, 4th edn, Prentice-Hall.
de Pace, M. (1984) *The IBM Personal Computer*, Granada, London.
Quinn, J.B. (1980) *Strategies for Change*, Richard D. Irwin.
Schofield, J. (1987) 'Beware of spreadsheets', *Management Today*, February, pp. 39—40.
Simon, H.A. (1960) *The New Science of Management Decision*, Harper and Row. (Revised edition: Prentice-Hall, 1977.)

Books about Lotus 1-2-3

Ewing, D.P. and Associates (1987) *Using 1-2-3 — Special Edition*, QUE Corporation.
Lunsford, E.M. and Antoniak, P. (1988) *Power User's Guide to 1-2-3*, Sybex.
Mylus, R. (1987) *Illustrated Lotus 1-2-3*, Wordware Publishing Inc.

See also References in Chapter 2 to Cain and Cain, Jackson, Jorgensen, and Cretien.

Chapter 2

SENSITIVITY ANALYSIS AND REGRESSION USING DATA COMMANDS

2.1 Data Table 1

The purpose of this section is to demonstrate how the data table commands of Lotus 1-2-3 can assist in sensitivity analysis. If the user wishes to test the sensitivity of *several* outputs to changes in just *one* variable, then Data Table 1 should be used.

The cost—volume—profit example which featured in the previous chapter is reconsidered here in Table 2.1. Also shown is a completed data table (Table 2.2) in which the impact of variations in the quantity sold on *revenue*, *variable cost* and *net profit* is explored.

Instead of accepting, without question, the original assumption that 400 (thousand) footballs would be sold in the first year of operation, sensitivity analysis is conducted to examine the consequences of selling as few as 300, or as many as 500 (thousand) units. To start, a blank area of the worksheet is selected, and the first part of the procedure is to mark out the boundaries of the data table as follows:

Set the cells C35, D35 and E35 equal to H8, D18 and H28 respectively. In Table 2.2 the formula for each is presented in 'text' format, appearing as +H8 for revenue, rather than the numeric value contained in that cell; similarly, +D18 and +H28 for variable cost and net profit. The variations in quantity are set vertically in cells B36 B37 ... up to B40. Vertical placement is required for the *input* of the sensitivity analysis, whereas the *output* cells are set horizontally, across a row.

Table 2.1 Revenue, Costs, and Profit

	A	B	C	D	E	F	G	H
1	.			.				
2								
3								
4	revenue							
5	*******							
6								(£ 000's)
7	price	2.70						
8	quantity	400	thousand			total revenue		1,080
9						*************		
10								
11	variable costs				TVC (£ 000's)			
12	**************				***			
13								
14	material	0.75			300			
15	labour	0.50			200			
16	var O/H	0.30			120			
17		----			---			
18		1.55	sum		620	gross profit		460
19		----			---	'	************		
20								
21	fixed costs				TFC (£ 000's)			
22	***********				***			
23								
24	fixed O/H (production)				150			
25	selling				50			
26	admin				70			
27					---			
28			sum		270	net profit		190
29					---	**********		===
30								

Table 2.2 Data Table 1

	A	B	C	D	E	F	G	H
30								
31								
32	DATA TABLE 1 - Sensitivity of revenue, cost and profit to quantity sold							
33								
34			revenue	var cost	net profit			
35		q	+H8	+D18	+H28			
36		u	300	810.000	465.000	75.000		
37		a	350	945.000	542.500	132.500		
38		n	400	1080.000	620.000	190.000		
39		t	450	1215.000	697.500	247.500		
40		i	500	1350.000	775.000	305.000		
41		t						
42		y						
43								
44	all figures in the range C36 to E40 are £ 000's							
45								

At this stage the cells in the range C36 to E40 are all blank.

The sequence is then: **/DT1**

Range is: B35 . . E40 (including the cell address of the blank top-left corner cell)

Input cell is B8 which holds the original quantity

The array of figures from C36 to E40 appears soon after pressing ENTER

Note that at the original output of 400, the net profit is £190 (both figures in thousands), as originally specified. At the extremes of the data table's quantity range 300 to 500, net profit varies between £75 and £305 (thousand). If one refers back to the break-even chart of Figure 1.2 and to Table 1.3, the projections at various outputs can be seen to be consistent with the figures in the data table.

The data table's main advantage over other forms of data manipulation is that it permits analysis of the impact of *any* input change − e.g. selling price or labour cost − on a specified output which is related through a formula or function − e.g. sales revenue, total variable cost, or net profit.

2.2   Data Table 2

This facility allows for testing the sensitivity of a *single* output to variations in two input cells. In Table 2.3, the output is net profit which appears in cell H28 of the cost−volume−profit worksheet. Input 1 is labour cost, for which variations are set out vertically from cells B51 to B56. Input 2 here is the selling price, the range of which is set out across row 50 of the worksheet.

Table 2.3   Date Table 2

	A	B	C	D	E	F	G	H
47	DATA TABLE	2 − Sensitivity of profit to selling price and labour cost						
48								
49					price			
50		+H28		2.10	2.30	2.50	2.70	2.90
51	1	0.40	−10.000	70.000	150.000	230.000	310.000	
52	a	0.45	−30.000	50.000	130.000	210.000	290.000	
53	b	0.50	−50.000	30.000	110.000	190.000	270.000	
54	o	0.55	−70.000	10.000	90.000	170.000	250.000	
55	u	0.60	−90.000	−10.000	70.000	150.000	230.000	
56	r	0.65	−110.000	−30.000	50.000	130.000	210.000	
57								
58	all figures in the range C51 to G56 are net profit (£ 000's)							
59								
60								

Prior to issuing the data table commands, the chosen area of the worksheet will be blank, apart from the range of input variations selected by the user and the cell address of the chosen output. Unlike Data Table 1 which contains a blank top-left corner cell, the initial cell of the Data Table 2 range refers to the address of the output cell which has been chosen. In this illustration, the relevant cell for net profit is H28, so the formula +H28 is typed into cell B50 (in 'text' format here, although a numeric form is perfectly acceptable if preferred).

The command to start is **/DT2**

followed by Range B50..G56

Input 1 is B15 (labour cost)

Input 2 is B7 (price)

The full array of figures appears after pressing ENTER

2.3 Sensitivity Analysis in Investment Appraisal

The net profit of £190,000 calculated at the original set of assumed values forms
the starting position for the subsequent investment appraisal. In the net profit
calculation, depreciation has been deliberately omitted, and the stated net profit
differs from what would customarily be reported in accounting profit statements.

Table 2.4(a) Investment Appraisal

	I	J	K	L	M	N	O	P
1								
2								
3								
4			1989	1990	1991	1992	1993	1994
5								
6	investment		-680			-200		
7								
8	revenue			1080	1139	1202	1268	1338
9	growth	5.5%						
10								
11	var costs			620	654	690	728	768
12	fix costs			270	270	270	270	270
13	==
14	net cash flow		-680	190	215	42	270	300
15	==
16								
17	discount rate							
18		9.0%						
19								
20	NPV	94.2				IRR	13.79%	

Table 2.4(b) Sensitivity Analysis on Investment Appraisal

	I	J	K	L	M	N	O	P
34					price			
35		+J20	2.30	2.50	2.70	2.90	3.10	
36	g	3.5%	-640.5	-308.8	23.0	354.7	686.5	
37	r	4.5%	-617.5	-279.6	58.3	396.2	734.1	
38	o	5.5%	-594.1	-249.9	94.2	438.4	782.5	
39	w	6.5%	-570.2	-219.7	130.9	481.4	831.9	
40	t	7.5%	-545.9	-188.8	168.2	525.2	882.2	
41	h	8.5%	-521.1	-157.4	206.2	569.8	933.4	
42								
43								
44		all figures in the range K36 to O41 are NPV.						
45								

The reason for this omission is that the *full* capital outlays appear in the appraisal (in cells K6 and N6 of Table 2.4(a)), and any allowance for depreciation would result in double counting. The usual term for net profit calculated without deduction for depreciation is 'cash flow'. The values which remain, after calculating cash outflows such as capital expenditures and taxes, are the 'net cash flows'.

The subject of investment appraisal will be covered in greater depth in Chapter 3. For the moment the reader is asked to accept that two of the financial functions available in Lotus 1-2-3, namely @NPV and @IRR, provide useful outputs on which to focus in such an appraisal. The principal features of the investment appraisal presented in Table 2.4(a) are:[1]

Row 6   Two items of capital expenditure are listed — for the years 1989 and 1992. These are placed in the appropriate time periods.

Row 8   The initial revenue in cell L8 is given by the formula +H8 thus providing a direct link with the original revenue computation on the left side of the worksheet.

M8 through to P8 incorporate the growth rate selected in cell J9. For example, the formula for M8 is:

+L8*(1+$J$9) which may be copied across the row

($J$9 being an absolute cell address to facilitate transmission of a given rate of growth by copying)

Row 11 The initial variable cost is again taken from the estimates prepared on the left side of the worksheet. L11 holds the formula +D18.

For M11 we build in the growth rate by typing: +L11*(1+$J$9) or by copying M8 to M11.

Copying as far as P11 provides the remaining entries for row 11.

Row 12 All the fixed costs are constant and given by +$D$28.

Row 14 The net cash flow is revenue less variable cost less fixed cost, plus investment (provided that the latter is entered with a minus sign, as displayed in cell K6, *viz* −680.

Thus cell N14 contains the formula: +N8−N11−N12+N6; typically this would be copied from a comparable entry in K14. Similarly for all other net cash flows shown.

---

1. Reference back to Table 1.2(b) is advised for readers who need further guidance with the worksheet formulae and functions.

Cell J20   This uses the @NPV function to compute the project's net present value at any chosen discount rate. The latter in cell J18 should be the (opportunity) cost of capital to the company, which will be related to long-term interest rates prevailing in the economy.

The function will appear as follows here:

@NPV(J18,L14..P14)+K14

Cell O20   The required functional form here is:

@IRR(J18,K14..P14)

(J18 serves as a 'guessed' rate of return in this instance rather than as a cost of capital)

In Table 2.4(b), Data Table 2 is used to determine the impact of changes in two variables (growth and selling price) on a *single* output cell (NPV for the project). At a growth rate of 5.5%, and a price of £2.70, the original NPV of 94.2 (£000s) is confirmed. The investment would be seen as unprofitable if the NPV were to fall to zero, and the data table shows that this would happen at a price of £2.30 or £2.50. Provided that the £2.70 price level is attainable, the prospects improve as the growth rate increases.

It would, of course, be entirely sensible to use Data Table 1 for other sensitivity tests − e.g. for evaluating the effect of different growth rates on **both** NPV and IRR.

2.4   Goal Seeking or Backward Iteration

Another way of examining sensitivity issues is to pose the question: how much would an input in the model have to change in order to achieve a 'goal' output figure? For example, we might ask how small the initial quantity sold would have to be for a zero NPV to result. This goal-seeking or 'backward iteration' facility is not provided directly by Lotus 1-2-3, although some other packages do have such a capability (e.g. Framework II and Supercalc 4).[2]

If a major part of sensitivity analysis is to take this form, it may affect the choice of spreadsheet package, although, as used here, it is possible to attach an inexpensive add-in package for Lotus 1-2-3 called *Goal Solutions*[TM].[3]

In Table 2.5(a), the 'Goal Solutions Form' is illustrated. This appears after

---

2. Remenyi and Nugus (1988, Chapter 7) provide a macro-driven routine for backward iteration in Lotus 1-2-3.
3. Trade mark of Enfin Software Corporation. It is described as an add-*in* because, once installed, it may be invoked at any time from within a Lotus 1-2-3 session, using ALT f10.

Table 2.5(a) Backward Iteration

Goal Cell	Target	Goal Solutions Form Achieved	Variable Cell	Required
A J20	0	0.00	B8	380.95
B				
C				
D				
E				

the required operations have been undertaken by the user, and it summarises the selections made and the solution provided. The cell address J20 for NPV is the 'Goal Cell' − this being the first item requested when the goal-seeking procedure is invoked. The 'target' value for cell J20 is set at zero, in this instance, and B8 is the 'variable' cell − containing the quantity (refer back to Table 2.1).

The other headings in the goal solutions form display the output of the procedure. The target of zero is 'achieved' as 0.00, which is accurate to two decimal places (further iterations might be necessary if greater accuracy is required). The 'required' value for B8 (the variable cell containing quantity sold) is computed to be 380.95. This value may be placed automatically in cell B8 from the function key menu, which designates function key 2 for this purpose.

The whole worksheet will then be recalculated, and the investment appraisal area will now appear as in Table 2.5(b).

All the revenue and variable cost figures have fallen in line with the initial output reduction (the value in cell B8 having been reduced from 400 to 381, but off-screen at this juncture). NPV has fallen to zero in line with the 'goal' selected. Also observe that IRR is now 9%, which is exactly the same as the discount rate. An explanation for this will be given in Chapter 3.

Table 2.5(b) Target Achieved

	I	J	K	L	M	N	O	P
1								
2								
3								
4			1989	1990	1991	1992	1993	1994
5								
6	investment		−680			−200		
7								
8	revenue			1029	1085	1145	1208	1274
9	growth	5.5%						
10								
11	var costs			590	623	657	693	731
12	fix costs			270	270	270	270	270
13	===
14	net cash flow		−680	168	192	18	244	273
15	===
16								
17	discount rate							
18		9.0%						
19								
20	NPV	0.0				IRR	9.00%	

Note that in setting up the worksheet for this purpose, it was necessary for NPV to be related, through a function, to the net cash flows in row 14. These cash flows were related, in turn, to the cells for revenue and cost through a simple formula. Finally, the revenues and variable costs were based on formulae which contained cell address B8 for the quantity sold. It was possible, therefore, for the model to explore the impact of changes in quantity on the viability of the project as measured by its NPV.

Readers without the goal-seeking facility may check that a quantity of 380.95 (thousand) placed in cell B8 does in fact reduce NPV to zero.[4] This is the critical value, below which the investment ceases to be viable. The result could have been obtained by trial-and-error. *Goal Solutions*, and similar goal-seeking packages, simply save time by conducting as many iterations as are necessary in a systematic manner without intervention by the user.

2.5 Data Regress

The previous sections of this chapter have been concerned with tabulations of data in models, where changes in certain inputs can be traced through to their consequences on the model's output. Thus, it has been possible, for instance, to show how variations in unit costs bring about changes in profit, by virtue of the logic in the formulae of the worksheet.

Rather different in character is the kind of data analysis exercise where one tabulates sets of data between which there is no proven causal connection in the sense of formal input—output relationships, but where there appears to be an association between two or more variables.

For instance, analysis of time-series data suggests that rising car ownership is accompanied by an increasing number of road casualties. Decreasing temperatures tend to be associated with increasing energy consumption. The incidence of lung cancer appears to be linked to smoking.

Whilst one can measure the strength of the association, it is not possible to prove causation, even though in examples such as those cited the implications may be fairly clear. Scientific investigations which attempt to determine cause and effect need to proceed with caution, examining the conditions under which any association occurs, before drawing inferences about the direction of the observed relationship.

Even though causation may be unproven, it is usual to refer to dependent (Y) and independent (X) variables in regression analysis. Sometimes the independent variables are called 'predictors' — i.e. they contribute to the computation of

---

4. This is not to be confused with the break-even output computed earlier, which only deals with annual operating costs and revenues, without capital recovery.

predictions for Y from the equation which is estimated. The data regress[5] command /DR is described in the *Lotus 1-2-3 Release 2 Reference Manual* (1985, p. 155) as follows:

/DR computes the coefficient values and constant for a formula that ties one or more ranges of independent variables to a range of a dependent variable. It also indicates the statistical accuracy of those values.

Table 2.6 Observations for Ultrasnaps

Resort	Y Daily Orders	X1 No. of Visitors (000's)	X2 Promotional Expenditure
1	210	9	200
2	235	10	1000
3	117	3	850
4	184	8	900
5	230	12	1100
6	403	26	900
7	298	22	850
8	314	20	1050
9	318	20	700
10	275	15	1300

In Table 2.6, data for colour film processing in ten holiday resorts is analysed by an imaginary firm called *Ultrasnaps*. In resort number 1, which accommodates 9,000 visitors during the holiday season, the firm receives 210 films for processing on a typical day throughout the season. In a larger resort, number 6, which accommodates 26,000 visitors, the number of orders recorded is 403. In general, there seems to be a positive association between numbers of visitors and orders. This can be seen in a scatter diagram (Figure 2.1) which provides a means of conducting a regression analysis. Although the line of best fit through the plot of observations was determined here by computer, a manual fit may be attempted, and the slope and intercept of the line estimated. By inspection, the intercept is approximately 100, and the slope is about 130:12, or 10.8.

Taking Y as the dependent variable and X_1 as an independent variable (implying a belief that Y, daily orders, depends on X_1, the number of visitors), these estimates yield the equation:

---

5. Only available in Release 2.0 onwards of Lotus 1-2-3.

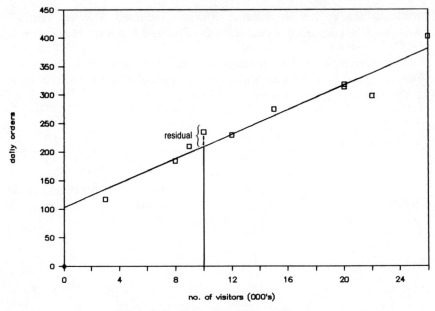

Figure 2.1 Linear Regression Scatter Diagram

$$\hat{Y} = 100 + 10.8X_1$$ (Y normally carries the character $^\wedge$ written $\hat{Y}$ to show that it is an estimate: see p. 33)

The data regress facility of Lotus 1-2-3 permits a more systematic evaluation of the association, or lack of association, between variables than is possible from inspection of a scatter diagram. It also provides greater accuracy than was attainable from inspection of the graph, and accommodates regression of a dependent variable on more than one independent variable (i.e. multiple regression). Thus, in Table 2.6 details of expenditure on a free film promotional offer conducted during the previous season are given for each resort. Multiple regression allows one to study the impact of this variable X_2 alongside X_1.

Although many other software packages are available for regression analysis, most of which offer a much more extensive analysis than is possible with Lotus 1-2-3, it is useful to be able to conduct a preliminary examination of possible relationships within this spreadsheet, even if another package is used for more detailed analysis.

2.6 The Two-Variable Linear Model

This section will describe the procedure for regression of Y on X_1 (daily orders on the number of visitors), excluding X_2 (promotional expenditure) until the next section. The task is to provide estimates *a* and b_1 in the equation:

$$\hat{Y} = a + b_1 X_1$$

To show that the results of the regression analysis are estimates based on sample data, the characters a and b_1 are used for the estimated coefficients, while A and B_1 are reserved for the intercept and slope of the true (population) relationship.[6]

The symbol $\wedge$ above the Y is there to indicate that the equation provides an *estimate* of Y, for each given value of X based on the estimated intercept and slope in the equation. Any such 'prediction' for the dependent variable should be interpreted as the mean of a distribution of possible values. The probable range will extend below and above the mean value — hence the concept of a 'prediction interval' which will be discussed in Chapter 5. Please note that in this context the $\wedge$ character has nothing to do with its use for exponentiation as a Lotus operator.

In order to use the regression facility of Lotus 1-2-3 (versions 2 and above), the following sequence is employed:

/DR (data regress)

X (mark X — range) which is C8..C17   (in Table 2.7)
[ENTER]

Y (mark Y — range) which is B8..B17
[ENTER]

(The Y range should match the X range in the number of observations)

O (set output range) which commences at cell A19 (or wherever convenient)
[ENTER]

G (go), after which command the regression output appears below the columns of data as shown in Table 2.7

NB: It is not necessary to use the 'Intercept' choice which appears after 'Output-Range' in the menu sequence, unless the user wishes to 'force' the intercept through the origin.

The regression equation is: $\hat{Y} = 102.87 + 10.73 X_1$ from the estimated 'Constant' and 'X Coefficient' estimates given in the regression output (to two decimal places). A more precise reading of the graph (Figure 2.1) would have given the same result.

---

6. *Note on the meaning of 'linear'*
   The model is linear in *parameters*. This means that transformations of the variables are permitted, for example by taking logarithms, and regressing log(Y) on log(X) etc. The equation must remain linear in terms of A and B. Thus:

   $$\log(Y) = A + B\log(X)$$

   is linear in logs and can be treated for regression purposes as a simple linear equation — see Chapter 4.

Table 2.7 Data Regress in Lotus 1-2-3

	A	B	C	D	E	F
1						
2						
3		Y	X1			
4						
5		Daily	No. of			
6	Resort	Orders	Visitors			
7			(000's)			
8	1	210	9			
9	2	235	10			
10	3	117	3			
11	4	184	8			
12	5	230	12			
13	6	403	26			
14	7	298	22			
15	8	314	20			
16	9	318	20			
17	10	275	15			
18						
19		Regression Output:				
20	Constant			102.8683		
21	Std Err of Y Est			20.4295		
22	R Squared			0.9430		
23	No. of Observations			10		
24	Degrees of Freedom			8		
25						
26	X Coefficient(s)		10.7263			
27	Std Err of Coef.		0.9320			
28						
29						
30						

By substituting values for X_1 in this equation, one may 'predict' a corresponding value for Y. Thus, for $X_1 = 10$, we predict:

$\hat{Y} = 102.87 + (10.73 \times 10)$ which is 210.17

The value actually observed was 235 and, like other comparisons between actual and predicted in this example, a difference, or residual, remains, corresponding to the vertical distance between the fitted line and the observed value (as marked in Figure 2.1). The statistical procedures *minimise* the sum of squared residuals — hence the principle of 'least-squares'.

As explained above, predictions obtained from the estimated relationship are to be regarded as mean or 'expected' values within a probability distribution, except when the equation gives an exact fit to the data, with no residuals remaining.

The regression output of Lotus 1-2-3 will now be examined in more detail:

1. The estimates *a*, intercept, and b_1, slope of the regression are in row 20 and row 26 of Table 2.7 respectively. They are described as the 'Constant' and 'X Coefficient'.

2. R Squared (coefficient of determination or the correlation coefficient squared) — row 22. This measures the proportion of the Y variance explained by the

linear influence of X_1. With R Squared equal to 0.9430, the least-squares regression of Y on X_1 accounts for 94.3% of the variance in Y.

(The percentage which remains is the residual or 'unexplained' variation of the Y values about the least-squares line.)

A perfect association between the two variables would carry an R Squared of 1, and the line of best fit would pass through every observation in the scatter diagram. The sum of squared residuals would be zero.

3. The Standard Error of Coefficient is given in row 27.

The standard error is compared with the X Coefficient in order to determine whether the slope is significant (i.e. significantly different from zero) at the 5% level. As a very crude rule-of-thumb, the Standard Error of Coefficient should be less than one-half of the Coefficient itself, ignoring any minus sign before the coefficient for this purpose.

In this regression, the standard error of coefficient, at 0.9320, is little more than one twelfth of the estimated coefficient of 10.7263.

Readers familiar with the t-distribution will be able to offer a more precise interpretation of this statistical test, and will appreciate the need to specify the 'degrees of freedom' given in row 24 of Table 2.7.

References covering the topic of significance testing are listed at the end of this chapter, and a more detailed discussion will take place in Chapter 4.

4. The 'Standard Error of Y Estimate' is given in row 21 of Table 2.7. It is a measure obtained from the residuals (vertical distances between the observations and fitted line), and will be used in developing prediction intervals in Chapter 5.

The regression output differs from the usual worksheet displays so far as instant recalculation is concerned. If any input figures for the regression are changed in the tables, we cannot obtain instant revisions for the constant or coefficients. The data regress commands have to be given again. In this regard it behaves in the same way as other 'Data' outputs from Lotus 1-2-3: for example the data tables discussed earlier in this chapter remain unchanged until the commands are repeated (although recalculation of a data table is facilitated by the presence of function key 8 which performs the necessary revision with a single keystroke).

If immediate recalculation is required, following a revision to any of the data in a regression, it is always possible to use a worksheet template such as the one given in the Appendix to this chapter (primarily included for the benefit of users of spreadsheets which do not have a built-in regression capability). Although independent software houses have produced more advanced templates for multiple regression, it is generally more convenient to use the data regress facility in Lotus 1-2-3, and forgo the luxury of instant recalculation.

2.7 Multiple Regression

Clearly, a multivariate demand function cannot be estimated by means of simple regression analysis using a scatter diagram, but the facility in Lotus 1-2-3 (release 2.0 and above) extends to multiple regression, so that in principle an increase in the number of variables need not amount to a problem in itself: the real difficulty lies in the provision of adequate data. The multiple regression technique provides 'Constant' and 'X Coefficients' in the estimated relationship:

$$\hat{Y} = a + b_1X_1 + b_2X_2 + b_3X_3 + \ldots . b_nX_n$$

With the aid of the regression output, one may examine whether the model as a whole accounts satisfactorily for the variation in the dependent variable, Y, and determine which independent variables are useful predictors.

When data is tabulated with a view to conducting multiple regression, the independent variables should be grouped together. When the X-range is requested, one should then specify the complete data range for these variables. Accordingly, in Table 2.8, the cell addresses for the first X_1 observation and the last X_2 observation denote the X-range, which is thus C8..D17.

The estimated relationship is:

$$\hat{Y} = 101.21 + 10.71X_1 + 0.0021X_2$$

However, R Squared has hardly improved at all as a result of introducing X_2, so the explanatory power of the new relationship is no better than was obtained from X_1 alone.[7]

In examining the standard errors of the X coefficients (row 27), only X_1 is significant at the 5% level. It is unnecessary to follow this up in detail here, because it can be seen immediately that the coefficient of X_2 has a standard error which actually exceeds the numerical value of the coefficient itself, while the coefficient to standard error (t-ratio) for X_1 is well above the critical value of 2. Under these circumstances, it would be usual practice to eliminate X_2 variable from the regression and re-work the estimates for the variable(s) which remain. In this case, one would simply revert to the former regression of Y on X_1.

Where the addition of independent variables, or predictors, offers an enhanced degree of overall explanation, and each variable makes a significant contribution to the relationship, variables will be added to the regression until no further improvement is achieved. At each stage, the choice of added variable rests on the degree of improvement to R squared, subject to the individual coefficients remaining significant. This approach is called 'forward regression'.

Alternatively, one may proceed through 'backward regression' by choosing

---

7. Note that R squared, the coefficient of determination, cannot fall when an additional variable is introduced. The coefficient of determination adjusted for degrees of freedom can be used for this test. In fact, by this criterion, it would be shown that the explanatory power of the regression had actually deteriorated.

Table 2.8 Multiple Regression with Lotus 1-2-3

	A	B	C	D	E	F
1						
2						
3		Y	X1	X2		
4						
5		Daily	No. of	Promotional		
6	Resort	Orders	Visitors	Expenditure		
7			(000's)			
8	1	210	9	200		
9	2	235	10	1000		
10	3	117	3	850		
11	4	184	8	900		
12	5	230	12	1100		
13	6	403	26	900		
14	7	298	22	850		
15	8	314	20	1050		
16	9	318	20	700		
17	10	275	15	1300		
18						
19		Regression Output:				
20	Constant			101.2059		
21	Std Err of Y Est			21.8293		
22	R Squared			0.9431		
23	No. of Observations			10		
24	Degrees of Freedom			7		
25						
26	X Coefficient(s)		10.7131	0.0021		
27	Std Err of Coef.		1.0085	0.0253		
28						
29						
30						

several variables in an initial regression, which are discarded one by one on the basis of significance tests, until only a subset of predictors remains.

A 'stepwise regression' facility, available in specialist statistical packages, is a popular and flexible approach. It normally proceeds in a similar manner to forward regression, but at each stage it can remove any variable which is no longer making a significant contribution to the model.

Further discussion of multiple regression in the context of demand analysis and sales forecasting will take place in Chapter 4. A useful introduction to stepwise and other procedures appears in Kvanli *et al.* (1986, pp. 535−6).

2.8 Other Data Commands

The two principal topics covered in this chapter have been Data Tables for sensitivity analysis, and Data Regress for examining data to explore possible relationships between variables. Other 'data' commands enable Lotus 1-2-3 to be used as a database, permitting the sorting of customers' accounts in alphabetical order, employees' records according to length of service, etc. These commands enhance the versatility of the spreadsheet and facilitate such tasks as invoicing and payroll administration for small businesses.

A particularly useful data command in a wide range of applications is 'Data Fill' (/**DF**). This enables a series of numbers with a common difference to be entered into a worksheet over a stated range. For instance, in column A of Table 2.8, it was possible to number the resorts 1 to 10 using this command, by stating the RANGE (A8..A17), the START value (1), and the STEP (again 1).

Of more interest in the context of decision support is the 'Data Matrix' command, which inverts and multiplies matrices. This can be used to assist optimisation in the context of simple linear programming problems, which are covered in Chapter 7. Discussion of this data command will be deferred until then.

APPENDIX: A Template for Linear Regression

The easiest way to conduct linear regression with spreadsheet software is to use Lotus 1-2-3 release 2 which features a multiple regression facility. It enables linear relationships to be established between a dependent variable (Y) and several independent variables (X_1, X_2, X_3, etc.).

A two-variable linear regression may, however, be handled using virtually any spreadsheet. Indeed, this application provides an excellent illustration of the versatility of this type of software — particularly with regard to the use of built-in functions such as average, variance, sum; and the facility to copy formulas from one part of a worksheet to another.

Once the worksheet structure has been designed, it can be saved for use with other examples, adding/deleting as many rows as are necessary, and making other minor adjustments to accommodate the required number of observations. In this way, a regression 'template' will be created.

The data for Ultrasnaps which featured in the multiple regression example will

Table 2.9 Regression with Template

	A	B	C	D	E	F
1						
2		Y	X	Y—mean	X—mean	col D
3		Daily	No. of			x col E
4	Resort	Orders	Visitors			
5			(000's)			
6	1	210	9	-48.4	-5.5	266
7	2	235	10	-23.4	-4.5	105
8	3	117	3	-141.4	-11.5	1626
9	4	184	8	-74.4	-6.5	484
10	5	230	12	-28.4	-2.5	71
11	6	403	26	144.6	11.5	1663
12	7	298	22	39.6	7.5	297
13	8	314	20	55.6	5.5	306
14	9	318	20	59.6	5.5	328
15	10	275	15	16.6	0.5	8
16						
17	MEAN value	258.4	14.5		SUM ---->	5154
18						
19		N*var(X) -->	480.5		est.slope	10.726
20					intercept	102.86

be examined in terms of just one independent variable, X, which is the number of visitors in thousands. Y, daily orders, is the dependent variable, as before. The regression will estimate a and b in the equation:

$$\hat{Y} = a + bX$$

a and b are the estimated slope and intercept of the regression line respectively.

The expressions which result from the least-squares method will be applied in the example which follows.[8]

First, obtain the estimate b by taking the ratio of two sums. The denominator is the sum of the differences (X less the mean value of X) squared, for all the X values. This is expressed in symbols:

$$\Sigma(X - \bar{X})^2$$

Since the variance of X is:

$$\Sigma(X - \bar{X})^2/N \quad (N = \text{the number of observations; Sigma} = \text{sum of})$$

we can tackle this part of the calculation by taking the variance of X (using the @VAR function of the spreadsheet) and multiplying this by the number of observations.

The numerator is rather more tedious to calculate, and involves finding the value of $(X - \bar{X})(Y - \bar{Y})$ for each observation. These values are then summed to give:

$$\Sigma(X - \bar{X})(Y - \bar{Y})$$

b is then $\quad \dfrac{\Sigma(X - \bar{X})(Y - \bar{Y})}{\Sigma(X - \bar{X})^2}$

and a is found by substituting in the equation:

$$\bar{Y} = a + b\bar{X}$$

where $\bar{Y}$ and $\bar{X}$ are the mean values of the sets of observations.

Appropriate formulae are created in the worksheet to produce these expressions. The procedure for determining the slope and intercept involves 6 main steps:

1. Find the mean values of Y and X. This is performed using the @AVG function as follows: enter in B17 the function @AVG(B6..B15); this is then copied to C17 which automatically becomes @AVG(C6..C15).

2. In cell D6 enter the formula +B6 − B$17.

---

8. An explanation of the method of least squares, the derivation of the 'normal equations' and the estimators for the slope and intercept, may be found in any standard text on econometrics — e.g. Pokorny (1987, pp. 119−20).

The latter term is a mixed cell address, being absolute in row 17 but relative in the column. This enables $Y - \overline{Y}$ to be found for every value of Y, and also $X - \overline{X}$ to be determined for every value of X, simply by copying the formula throughout the range D6..E15.

If the formula had been entered in D6 as +B6-$B$17 which uses an absolute rather than a mixed cell address, this would not have had the desired effect because the copying procedure would generate $X - \overline{Y}$ rather than $X - \overline{X}$ in column E.

3. In column F find the product of $(X - \overline{X})$ and $(Y - \overline{Y})$ for each pair of values by entering the formula +D6*E6 in cell F6. This is then copied to the range F7 to F15. The sum of these products may then be found through the function @SUM(F6..F15) which is entered in cell F17.

4. Obtain the variance of X and multiply by the number of observations. The variance of X is found with the function @VAR(C6..C15) and this is multiplied by 10.

   Thus: @VAR(C6..C15)*10 which gives 480.5 in cell C19.

5. The estimate of the slope of the regression line is now placed in cell F19 as the formula: +F17/C19

6. a is found by substituting in the equation:

   $$\overline{Y} = a + b\overline{X}$$
   i.e. $a = \overline{Y} - b\overline{X}$

   which is placed in cell F20 as the formula: +B17 - C17*F19.

This completes the estimation of the regression coefficients, indicating a relationship:

$$\hat{Y} = 102.86 + 10.73X$$

which confirms the result obtained previously.

Exercises

1. Refer back to exercise 2 at the end of Chapter 1 and retrieve your worksheet file.

   (a) Use Data Table 1 of Lotus 1-2-3 to show sales revenue (i.e. price multiplied by quantity sold), costs, and profit, for ticket sales varying between 0 and 150 at intervals of 10 tickets.

(b) Use Data Table 2 to show how the profit at full capacity (150 tickets sold) varies with changes in fixed costs ranging from £250 to £350, and a range of buffet costs: £3.00, £3.25 and £3.50.

2. Refer back to exercise 5 at the end of Chapter 1 and retrieve your worksheet file. Through trial and error, or by backward iteration (if you have this facility) find how large the initial capital sum would have to be for the IRR to be exactly 2%.

3. Use the Data Regress facility of Lotus 1-2-3 (Release 2 and above) to regress Y on X for the following observations collected by your firm over a ten-year period (alternatively, use the template set out in the Appendix to this chapter):

Year	X (advertising expenditure)	Y (sales revenue)
	(all figures in £000s)	
1	31	1520
2	15	1200
3	32	1570
4	19	1110
5	27	1290
6	23	1300
7	16	1240
8	26	1180
9	43	1700
10	36	1620

Assess the impact of advertising on the firm's sales.

4. In the 'Ultrasnaps' example (Table 2.6) data is also available for relative price in comparison with other outlets in the same resort (X3), and for annual camera sales (X4) at each Ultrasnaps shop.

Resort	X3 relative price	X4 camera sales
1	1.1	1212
2	0.9	1140
3	1.5	1835
4	1.2	810
5	1.3	2413
6	0.7	1167
7	1.5	2367
8	1.1	1419
9	0.8	543
10	1.1	986

Extend Table 2.6 which already contains observations for X1 and X2, and conduct a multiple regression of Y (daily orders) on all 4 independent variables (X1 .. X4). Comment on your result.

5. Eliminate variables X2 and X4 from the Ultrasnaps example as set out in the previous exercise, and re-work the example. Prepare a graph comparing actual daily orders with those predicted by the new regression equation.

    What would be your prediction for daily orders at a resort with 15,000 visitors and a relative price of 1.2?

References and Further Reading

Since there are few specific references, the following bibliography is mainly in the form of further reading, grouped under subject headings:

Data Tables in Lotus 1-2-3

Cain, N.W.C. and Cain, T. (1984) *Lotus 1-2-3 at Work*, Ch. 8, Part II, Reston Publishing Company, Virginia.
Jackson, M. (1985) *Creative Modelling with Lotus 1-2-3* (mainly in Ch. 4), John Wiley.

Backward Iteration

Remenyi, D. and Nugus, S. (1988) *Business Applications in Lotus 1-2-3: a Guide to Forecasting, Risk Analysis, Backward Iteration, and Simulation*, Ch. 7, McGraw-Hill.

Data Regress in Lotus 1-2-3

Cretien, P.D., Ball, S.E. and Brigham, E.F. (1987) *Financial Management with Lotus 1-2-3*, Ch. 6, The Dryden Press.
Jackson, M. (1988) *Advanced Spreadsheet Modelling with Lotus 1-2-3*, Ch. 6, Wiley.
Jorgensen, C. (1988) *Mastering 1-2-3*, 2nd edn, Ch. 12, Sybex.
Lotus Development Corporation (1985) *1-2-3 Reference Manual, Release 2*, Ch. 2, Lotus Development Corporation, Cambridge, Mass.

Financial Functions in Spreadsheets

Cretien *et al.*, op. cit., Ch. 3.

Statistical Analysis – Regression and Significance Testing
(not concerned specifically with spreadsheet techniques)

Anderson, D.R., Sweeney, D.J. and Williams, T.A. (1987) *Statistics for Business and Economics*, 3rd edn, Chs 14 and 15, West Publishing Company, St. Paul, Minnesota.

Koutsoyiannis, A. (1977) *Theory of Econometrics*, 2nd edn, Chs 4 and 5, Macmillan (repr. 1981).

Kvanli, A.H., Guynes, C.S. and Pavur, R.J. (1986) *Introduction to Business Statistics: A Computer Integrated Approach*, Chs 14 and 15, West Publishing Company, St. Paul, Minnesota.

Pokorny, M. (1987) *An Introduction to Econometrics*, Chs 2 and 3, Basil Blackwell.

———— Chapter 3 ————

INVESTMENT APPRAISAL

3.1 Characteristics of Investment

An investment, or capital expenditure, is the outlay of cash or some other resource, in anticipation of future gain. The prime characteristic of investment is the delay between the initial expenditure and the time when benefits begin to accrue. Numerous types of decision have this characteristic: for example, the installation of machinery to increase productive capacity; acquisition of modern equipment to save fuel or labour costs; purchase of a foreign currency bond in order to gain interest and capital gains. Other examples, but in the public sector, include: building a new bridge or tunnel to speed traffic flow; building new hospitals to cater for an increasing elderly population; and equipping schools and universities with computers and other teaching aids. In some instances cash proceeds may be realised — e.g. tolls from a new bridge — but in the main the benefits are non-pecuniary and the form of appraisal tends to differ from the usual analysis presented here.[1]

In all cases, whether in the private or public sector, investments are put forward on the expectation that some gain can result from the project. Some will involve speculative ventures, which run the risk of losses, although on balance the decision maker will normally *expect* to achieve a net gain. Various determinants of investment have been proposed, although all are related ultimately to the pursuit of gain. These include the *accelerator*, *substitution* and *flow of funds*.

The 'accelerator' principle is that changes in productive capacity are related to the *rate of change* in sales. Some investment will take place without sales

---

1. See Chapter 8. The reader should note that some of the benefits anticipated from projects in the private sector may not be readily quantifiable — e.g. in assessing the desirability of different plant locations. The multi-attribute techniques discussed in Chapter 8 may be appropriate for these aspects of private investment appraisal.

expansion as assets wear out and new technology is adopted, but sales growth will tend to increase the rate of capital formation as firms adjust their capacities in order to meet rising demand (either actual or anticipated).

The 'substitution' motive for investment usually refers to the adoption of capital intensive methods of production to replace those more dependent on labour. It is the saving in labour costs which is the aim, although avoidance of restrictive union practices and stoppages, and greater predictability of output, may also be involved.

The 'flow of funds' relates to *supply* rather than to the demand for capital. When opportunities for profitable investment appear, there is no guarantee that the funds will be there to finance them. Whilst a company can always exercise the option of obtaining external finance by issuing additional shares, or by borrowing, the deployment of internal funds from retained earnings is often seen as a more attractive alternative. When the latter are available the investment process is facilitated.

In providing criteria for investment appraisal, the view will be taken here that profitability is the key objective of management. Particular attention however has to be paid to the time dimension in investment, and the alternative concepts of 'present value' or 'wealth' maximisation are more theoretically sound in this context than profit maximisation. However, a rate-of-return measure of profitability is still valid if applied on a *Discounted Cash Flow* (DCF) basis.

3.2 Discounted Cash Flow

A typical investment has a profile over time as follows:

$$
\begin{array}{ccccccc}
\text{yr} & 0 & 1 & 2 & 3 & \ldots & n \\
& -C & A_1 & A_2 & A_3 & & A_n
\end{array}
$$

A capital outlay occurs at one point in time (period 0). This causes future cash receipts to change by an amount A_1 one year later, by A_2 two years later, and so on, up to the last year of the project's life which is n years. In reality, cash does not flow in and out at the year end, although most software packages, including Lotus 1-2-3, discount cash flows as if they were annual events. For greater accuracy, continuous discounting would be necessary, but in most applications the year-end discounting is adequate.

Outflows of cash are indicated with a minus sign, as is the case with the initial capital outlay. In more complex projects, other net outflows of cash arising from a prolonged gestation period, intermittent replacement expenditures, or terminal payments for restoration of property at a project's conclusion, would be similarly indicated.

In assessing any project it is necessary to ensure that the future cash flows are strictly comparable with the sum to be invested. This means that cash flow projections should be expressed at a price level prevailing in a base year. One way of tackling the problem is to set out the calculations of cost and revenue (e.g. in a worksheet) in real terms, by forecasting sales levels in physical units and applying base-year cost and price levels.

If real prices are expected to change as part of the intended pricing policy, then an appropriate adjustment may be made to future flows but, again, expectations of inflation should be omitted. Alternatively, if projections are presented to the analyst already grossed-up for inflation, this may be eliminated by using factors to deflate future flows. For instance, using the example given earlier in Table 2.4(a), the net cash flows might have been estimated on the assumption that 4% annual inflation would be experienced over the life of the project.

yr	1989	1990	1991	1992	1993	1994
flow	−680	197.60	232.87	47.23	316.04	364.82
factors of		1.04	1.04 squared	1.04 cubed	etc.	

would be applied as deflators resulting in the real flows presented in row 14, Table 2.4(a):

yr	1989	1990	1991	1992	1993	1994
flow	−680	190	215	42	270	300

Within a worksheet, the computation of the deflators, and their application to the inflated cash flows, would be entirely straightforward. Once this has been done, the obvious question to be posed is: 'Do the extra cash receipts generated by this investment $(A_1 \ldots A_n)$ offer a surplus over the original capital sum (C)?'

A traditional, but not recommended, approach is to average out the profits and express the result as a percentage return on capital. Suppose, for example, that an investment of £100,000 in additional productive capacity was expected to improve profits (net of depreciation) by an average of £15,000 over a period of four years.[2]

The average return on capital would then be 15% per annum. If the firm thought that it would cost 10% annually in interest to obtain the necessary finance, a surplus would seem to accrue to this project.

The DCF approach differs in several ways, the most important of which are: (1) cash flows rather than profits are taken as the basis of the appraisal; (2) the timing of each cash flow is critical, so that averaging large and small flows arising in different periods would invalidate the analysis. Let us now deal with these two issues.

Cash flows, rather than profits, are estimated for the anticipated life of the project. The principal difference between the two is the depreciation which is deducted year by year. It is easier to set the problem out in cash flow form, because depreciation involves an additional calculation which only complicates the issue

---

2. The cash flow, before allowing for annual depreciation of £25,000 for 4 years, would average £40,000.

by introducing the danger that capital expenditure will be double counted. That is why, in the example used in Chapter 2 (Table 2.1 and Table 2.4a), the fixed costs did not include depreciation. The net profit figure computed for each year was in fact a cash flow, rather than an accounting profit. The appraisal of the investment is then a matter of finding whether the cash flows are sufficient to justify the initial outlay and the cost of financing the investment (the cost of capital).

$$0 \quad\quad 1 \quad\quad 2 \quad\quad 3 \quad \ldots \quad n$$

$$-C \quad A_1 \quad A_2 \quad A_3 \quad\quad A_n$$

The cash flows, normally described as *net* cash flows, A_1 onwards, are net-of-tax and inflation-adjusted. The need to estimate tax liability re-introduces the complication of depreciation, since allowances for this will influence the amount of taxable profit, and thus the tax payment which will be an outflow. Delays in the collection of taxes mean that a tax liability in a particular year will be associated with the cash flow from an earlier year.

The rationale for the *discounting* of cash flows follows from the notion that money has a 'time value'. By waiting, one can normally enjoy growth in cash resources as interest accumulates. This means that any sum receivable in the future has to be larger than a cash receipt due now if it is to offer the same value to the individual. This principle stands because investment carries an opportunity cost − meaning that to justify investment in an opportunity, one has to ensure that a rate of interest is received comparable with other opportunities carrying similar risk.

Discounting is essentially the reverse of compounding. Whereas, when applying compound interest formulae, one calculates the future value (FV) of a present sum accumulating interest for a given period, in discounting one starts with a future cash sum and discounts it back to the present.

If £1.00 were invested for a year at 10% interest, it would provide £1.10. Waiting for 2 years, the proceeds would be £1.21, and so on after 3 and 4 years, as shown in Table 3.1. The general formula for compound interest is:[3]

$$FV = S(1 + r)^n$$

S is the initial sum invested, r is the interest rate expressed as a decimal, and n is the number of years. Thus £1.00 invested for 3 years at 10% interest has a future value of £1(1.1^3), or £1.331.

Alternatively, we could state that £1.331 receivable 3 years hence has a *present* value (PV) of £1.00 *discounting* at 10%. More usual, however, is the equivalent result (achieved by dividing these numbers by 1.331) that £1.00 receivable 3 years hence has a present value of £0.7513, discounting at 10%.

---

3. This expression for future value is not to be confused with the @FV function of Lotus 1-2-3, which is only used in computations for annuities.

Table 3.1 Future Values by Coumpounding

	A	B	C	D	E	F	G	H
1								
2								
3		Year -->	0	1	2	3	4	
4								
5	interest		1.00					
6	rate			1.10				
7	10.00%				1.21			
8						1.33		
9							1.46	
10								
11								
12								
13								
14								
15								
16								

Table 3.2 Present Values by Discounting

	A	B	C	D	E	F	G	H
1								
2								
3		Year -->	0	1	2	3	4	
4								
5	discount		1.0000					
6	rate			0.9091				
7	10.00%				0.8264			
8						0.7513		
9							0.6830	
10								
11								
12								
13								
14								
15								
16								

This latter figure, and the other figures in Table 3.2, are derived from the formula:[4]

$$PV = 1/(1 + r)^n$$

This can be implemented with the aid of a spreadsheet, or a special present value function built into the software may be employed. The use of this and other financial functions will be explained in the next section.

In all references to interest rates, costs of capital, rates of return, etc., **real** percentage rates (i.e. over and above the rate of inflation) are specified. Although it is preferable to determine the real cash flows in the manner explained previously, an alternative approach is to set out the cash flows at price levels expected in

---

4. This expression for present value is not to be confused with the @PV function of Lotus 1-2-3, which is only used in computations for annuities.

the future, and then choose a higher discount rate which incorporates an inflation premium. Thus a 15% discount rate applied to money cash flows affected by a 5% inflation rate would give *approximately* the same results as a real discount rate of 10% applied to real (adjusted for inflation) cash flows.[5]

3.3 DCF Methods of Appraisal

It is through the process of discounting and the calculation of present values that provision is made for the opportunity cost of capital in investment appraisal. Although manual calculations can be performed with the assistance of tables, it is assumed here that a microcomputer spreadsheet will be used for modelling purposes, and that the present value function normally built in to such software will obtain the desired results.

For purposes of exposition some simplifying assumptions will be made initially. In the first instance, the projects under consideration will be independent, and without far-reaching repercussions on the micro-economy. Additionally, three assumptions which will be relaxed at an early stage are that: knowledge is perfect; projects are not mutually exclusive; there are no budgetary constraints.

Net Present Value

It has been demonstrated in section 3.2 that the essence of DCF is to ensure that all cash inflows and outflows are accounted for *at the time they occur*. An important implication of this is that capital expenditures are identified as outflows of cash principally at the beginning of a project's life, rather than as year-by-year consumption according to a depreciation formula. Indeed any deductions for depreciation would involve double counting, and should be avoided except as a means of calculating the tax liability which has to be assessed on the accounting profit generated, rather than on the cash flows.

The net present value (NPV) of a project is determined firstly by discounting the stream of cash flows at the appropriate discount rate, to measure its (gross) present value. Secondly, the immediate outflow (at time period 0) is deducted to give the project's **net** present value. When using a spreadsheet, it is important to note that the appropriate range of flows to be discounted usually excludes the initial outflow. This means that the Lotus function @NPV really determines the gross, rather than the net, present value.

If the full range of flows from period 0 were subject to the @NPV function, the year 0 figure would be treated as if it were 1 year in the future, and all future flows would similarly be displaced by one time period.

Provision for the initial flow, therefore, should be made separately. Another

---

5. The effective discount rate achieved by this method would be slightly smaller at 9.52%.

point to note is that the range of flows should not include any blank entries even if there is no cash flow anticipated in a particular year — the correct procedure is to enter zero in the appropriate cell of the worksheet. As a simple illustration of NPV consider Table 3.3. Here we have an initial outlay of £1,000 followed at yearly intervals by two net cash inflows of £685. If the cost of capital is 10%, then these two flows will be discounted at this rate, and the initial capital outflow deducted to give the NPV for the whole project.

Table 3.3 Discounting the Cash Flows

	A	B	C	D	E F	G	H	I
1	..							
2								
3	Year		0	1	2			
4								
5	OUTLAY (£)	1000						
6	INFLOW (£)		685	685				
7	=================================							
8	NET FLOW	-1000	685	685				
9	=================================							
10	NET PRESENT VALUE at			10% ------> £189				
11					====			
12								

The range of flows to be discounted at a rate 0.1 (10%) in Table 3.3 is C8 to D8, giving a present value of £1,189. The figure of £189 which appears in cell F10, is, however, a true NPV which is net of the initial outflow of £1,000. The latter does not need to be discounted, since it is already expressed as a present value.

The NPV in cell F10 is found, then, from the formula: @NPV(C10,C8..D8)+B8, in which we discount the range C8 to D8 at a rate specified in cell C10, and finally add in any year-0 flows undiscounted. The manual calculation proceeds as shown below.

The present value of the cash flows is:

$$\frac{685}{(1+0.1)} + \frac{685}{(1+0.1)^2}$$

which gives the above result of £1,189 for the gross PV, and £189 for the NPV.

Alternatively, the separate factors of 0.909 (i.e. 1/1.1) and 0.826 (i.e. $1/1.1^2$) could have been obtained from tables or, since a constant figure (annuity) is involved, the cumulative figure of 1.736 (i.e. 0.909 + 0.826) could have been multiplied by £685 to give the same answer.

The fact that a positive NPV emerges demonstrates that the project is worth-while. Given that the two cash flows of £685 together have a present value of £1,189, the firm could justify an outlay of this magnitude, on which it would be able to pay precisely 10% interest per annum (on capital outstanding), and also to recover the full capital sum. Since only £1,000 has to be spent in order to enjoy benefits worth £1,189 in present terms, there is clearly a surplus of £189 (having allowed, too, for the 10% cost of capital).

Internal Rate of Return

In the above application of NPV a known discount rate of 10% was assumed. Since the project generated a surplus at that rate, it can be appreciated that it is in fact yielding a rate of return in excess of 10%. A trial-and-error approach for determining the rate generated by the project is illustrated in Table 3.4. The result is called *internal* rate of return (IRR) because it is determined without reference to an external interest rate or cost of capital, unlike NPV.

Table 3.4 IRR by Trial and Error

	A	B	C	D	E	F	G	H
1								
2			discount rate					
3		FLOW (£)	22.0%	24.0%	23.8%			
4								
5	year 1	685	561.48	552.42	553.21	←	+$B5/(1+E$3)	
6	year 2	685	460.23	445.50	446.78	←	+$B6/(1+E$3)^2	
7	==							
8	TOTAL PV		1021.70	997.92	1000.00	←	+E5+E6	
9	==							
10								
11			try 1	try 2	success			
12					●			

Even if no IRR function is incorporated in the spreadsheet, it is easy enough to home in on the answer, given the speed of recalculation permitted within the standard NPV function. The aim by this route is to arrive as close as possible to zero NPV − in other words, one is finding the discount rate which results in the project breaking even, with the total PV equal to the outlay.

Some spreadsheets (including Lotus 1-2-3) do include an IRR function (@IRR). In this instance the specified range includes the initial (negative) cash flow; and a lower limit or 'guess' is also inserted in the function to speed up computation time (also to avoid misleading solutions − see section 3.4). In this example, having found in Table 3.3 that a discount rate of 0.1 (10%) left a surplus, this rate could be used as the guess for the derivation of IRR. A cell for IRR (not shown) in Table 3.3 would take the function @IRR(0.1,B8..D8). The resulting IRR of just under 24% gives the maximum rate which could be paid on (borrowed) capital outstanding given the cash flows which arise from the project.

Three new projects appear in Table 3.5. For the moment, let us assume that we are only concerned with the acceptability of each project in its own right. Issues connected with ranking are not to be raised at this juncture. Since each project gives a positive NPV at the appropriate discount rate, set here at 7%,

Table 3.5 Appraisal Using both NPV and IRR

	A	B	C	D	E	F	G	H	I	J
1										
2	Year	0	1	2	3	4		NPV (7%)		IRR
3	==							========		======
4										
5	project A	-1000	375	375	375	375		270		18.5%
6	project B	-1000	250	325	425	500		246		16.2%
7	project C	-1000	500	425	325	250		295		21.2%
8										
9										
10										

all three projects would be regarded as acceptable. If the IRR were applied as the criterion, the same conclusion would be drawn, since each project gives a return in excess of 7%.

If a negative NPV had appeared, this would have indicated unacceptability, as would any IRR less than the cut-off rate of 7%. In fact, both criteria should normally give the same answer for accept or reject appraisals, with IRR equalling the discount rate when NPV = 0 which would indicate a break-even position.

To summarise the use of functions in the spreadsheet, taking Project A in Table 3.5 for purposes of illustration:

NPV at 7% is shown in cell H5 as $@NPV(0.07, C5..F5) + B5$

IRR is shown in cell J5 as $@IRR(0.1, B5..F5)$

where 0.1 (or 10%) is the 'guessed' rate and B5..F5 encompasses the full range of cash flows, including the capital outlay, unlike the NPV function which requires a separate term for the year 0 flow.

Although IRR gives a ranking in Table 3.5 which is consistent with that of NPV, this is not always the case. Indeed, inverse rankings are possible, as we shall see.

3.4 Choice of Appraisal Method

Surveys of practice suggest that investments are frequently tested by an informal appraisal to filter out less viable projects before they are subject to any formal analysis whether this be through DCF, or the traditional methods such as payback or average return. (The traditional methods are explained in section 3.8.)

In a comparative survey by Scapens, Sale and Tikkas (1982), it was found that only 54% of UK companies used DCF, at some stage at least, as against 84% of US companies. This is symptomatic of the failure of many British companies to treat investment in a rigorous manner.

Surveys have shown that companies generally use more than one technique for investment appraisal. In a study by Pike (1983) the order of popularity for the 'primary' method used was: internal rate of return (IRR); then about equal were payback and average rate of return (ARR); last was net present value (NPV). However, only 26% of firms used a single method, and 79% of firms used payback at some stage, which was a higher rating than any other investment appraisal technique.

Paradoxically, NPV, which is seen as most sound and versatile in the standard texts on investment appraisal, is viewed with least favour by management.   Even where companies have adopted NPV as a formal policy for investment appraisal, it is frequently used alongside one or more of the other techniques, and the results of appraisal are often presented in several dimensions. One of the reasons put forward for this behaviour pattern has been the relative complexity of calculation for the two DCF methods, coupled with a lack of familiarity with the precise meaning of NPV in particular.

These obstacles to the more widespread use of NPV can, and should, be removed now that spreadsheet packages containing financial functions are available. Once the financial data has been prepared, it is no more difficult to analyse in terms of NPV than in any other form. In fact, NPV is almost universally available as a spreadsheet function. IRR is available in Lotus 1-2-3 and several, but not all, packages.

The traditional techniques of payback and average rate of return may still be applied, but specific functions have not been provided in the major spreadsheets and appropriate formulae have to be built up, or templates acquired, to perform the necessary operations.

Cretien *et al.* (1987, Chapter 13) present a capital budgeting model for use with Lotus 1-2-3. It analyses capital projects in terms of five criteria: normal payback; payback with discounted flows; NPV; IRR; and profitability index (PI). (The latter will be discussed in the context of capital rationing.) A sixth criterion, ARR, could easily be added to Cretien's model if desired.

There remains the task of persuading management of the relevance and validity of the widely available spreadsheet DCF functions. Familiarity with the traditional methods means that one should, perhaps, continue to offer NPV and IRR alongside payback and ARR, together with any other criteria, such as those offered by Cretien.

One advantage of IRR over NPV in persuading managers to use DCF is that they are more likely to respond favourably to a profitability measure which can be expressed as a percentage return on capital outstanding (IRR) than to one which gives a measure of discounted surplus above the initial sum invested. Although this is an issue mainly concerned with presentation rather than technical merit, IRR does have the additional virtue that it contains a built-in test for sensitivity to the cost of capital. For instance, having estimated that project C's internal rate of return is 21.2% (in Table 3.5), as against a cost of financing it of 7%, the project is seen to be viable, and will remain so, even if that cost rises to 15% or, indeed, right up to 21.2% at which rate the project breaks even.

Figure 3.1 shows how the viability of project C changes as the discount rate

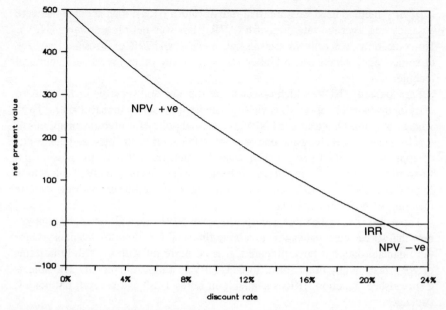

Figure 3.1 NPV and IRR for Project C

is varied. At 0% NPV is £500 − the undiscounted sum of the inflows less outflow. At 7% the NPV is £295 (as computed in Table 3.5). At 21.2% NPV is zero, thus locating the project's IRR, and above this discount rate NPV becomes negative.

Although IRR is usually calculated as a single value peculiar to (or internal to) a given project, in exceptional circumstances multiple rates may arise in different ranges of discount rates. For this reason an approximation (indicated by the 'guess') when applied to a series of cash flows must be specified. In most cases, the complication will not arise, and it is suggested in the reference manual that a guess between 0 and 1 (0% and 100%) will provide the correct result for most projects, which means that the discount rate applied in the NPV computation could be used as the guess.

An inappropriate guess may, however, bring misleading results even when there is only one meaningful positive solution. For example, both series of flows (A) and (B) in Table 3.6 clearly yield returns in excess of 70% − both have NPVs greater than zero when discounting at this rate, yet project B's IRR is shown as minus 100%! The problem here is that a guess of 10% (i.e. 0.1) is too low for convergence to the correct solution of 78.28%, and the procedure iterates from 10% in the opposite direction.

In general, it is better to err on the high side in 'guessing' the internal rate of return. A Figure of 50% is suitable for most applications (although in most of the examples used in this chapter a guess of 10% has been perfectly adequate).

Table 3.6 Problems with the 'Guess' When Using IRR

	A	B	C	D	E	F	G	H	I	J
1										
2	Year		0	1	2	3	4		NPV (70%)	IRR
3	==								=======	========
4										
5	project A		-30	0	0	0	300		6	77.8%
6	project B		-30	0	0	170	0		5	-100.0%
7										
8										
9									guess at 10%	
10										
11										
12	project A		-30	0	0	0	300		6	77.8%
13	project B		-30	0	0	170	0		5	78.3%
14										
15									guess at 50%	
16										

This can be lowered for less favourable projects or for pessimistic sensitivity analyses. In the main, few problems will be encountered in practice, and the IRR is a useful adjunct to NPV in the presentation of results from a DCF analysis, particularly when the decision is simply to accept or reject.

3.5 Special Cases with IRR

There are two main problem areas with internal rate of return, one of which relates to the possibility of multiple solutions (which affects the choice of the 'guess' in Lotus 1-2-3), while the other is concerned with ranking.

1. Multiple Solutions

This problem usually occurs when substantial commitments arise at the end of a project's life — typically an obligation to restore property to its original condition following mineral exploitation, or excavation to lay pipelines.

In the example set out in Table 3.7, a company whose cost of capital is 18% finds that a project with a terminal outflow has an NPV of 413 (all units in £000). It has two internal rates of return, one of which is 5.4% and the other 42.7%. The latter is obtained by applying a higher guess of 50% as compared with the usual 10%. There is a major difficulty in interpretation — for example, if the IRR is only 5.4%, should we not reject the investment at a discount rate of 18%? If so, why does the NPV show a positive value at this discount rate?

If we take the higher IRR figure of 42.7%, does this mean that the project will be acceptable at all discount rates up to that figure, and if not, why not? The position is clarified considerably by plotting a graph of NPV against the discount

Table 3.7 Project with Multiple Solutions for IRR

	A	B	C	D	E	F	G	H	I	J	K	L
1												
2	Year	0	1	2	3	4		NPV (18%)		IRR		
3		===						========		======		
4		-5500	4000	9000	2000	-10000		413		5.4%	guess 10%	
5												
6		-5500	4000	9000	2000	-10000		413		42.7%	guess 50%	
7												
8												
9												
10												

rate, as in Figure 3.2. In this particular case, we can see that the project is acceptable at discount rates *between* the two solutions for IRR. Unacceptable results emerge when the discount rate is lower than 5.4%, or higher than 42.7%.

The most puzzling feature of the curve's behaviour is the rising portion from 0 to 20%. Normally one expects the NPV curve to behave as in Figure 3.1, showing a gradual decline, and a single intercept on the discount rate axis. The difference here is that the terminal outflow presents a financing opportunity which necessitates an extension of the meaning of discount rate to cover both lending and borrowing aspects of financing.

If, in raising the discount from 0 to 20%, we assume that surplus funds may be re-invested more profitably, the liability at the end of the project will become

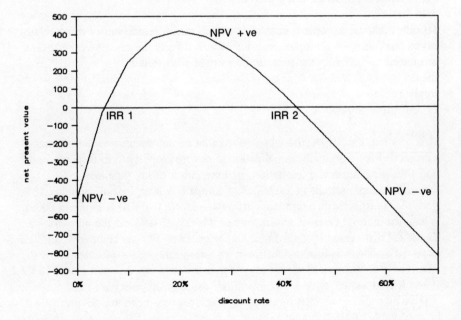

Figure 3.2 Multiple Solutions for IRR

less of a burden, since it may be financed out of a smaller 'sinking fund' – i.e. the surpluses generated by the penultimate year. As we raise the discount rate beyond 20%, however, the (present) value of those surpluses falls faster than does the financing requirement, and the NPV starts to fall.

In this type of case, the dual IRR does have a meaning, but it can only be safely interpreted by appealing to the behaviour of NPV.[6] The IRR may be modified to remove the ambiguity, through a variation known as 'extended yield'. This concept will not be discussed further here, since it is likely to confuse decision makers rather than to persuade them of the merits of DCF. The interested reader may learn more of this variation from one of the traditional investment appraisal texts, namely, Merrett and Sykes (1963).

What should be stressed is that once the NPV concept is understood and accepted, it provides the key to virtually all types of investment appraisal, and avoids most of the complications associated with IRR. This is particularly true of the second special case to which we now turn.

2. Ranking of Projects

This problem applies when dealing with *mutually exclusive* projects – i.e. choices between various options, only one of which is to be selected, usually on account of duplication of function. In such instances, one needs a criterion to demonstrate which option generates the biggest surplus.

In Table 3.8, the projected cash flows from three word-processing systems are set out. Although system X entails a smaller outlay than either of the others, it offers facilities which would meet a large proportion of the department's medium-term needs, and there would be no point in acquiring either system Y or Z, once the decision had been taken to adopt X. Similarly, the selection of Y or Z would imply rejection of system X.

Table 3.8 Ranking Using NPV and IRR

	A	B	C	D	E	F	G	H	I	J
1										
2	Year	0	1	2	3	4		NPV (5%)		IRR
3	===							=========		=======
4										
5	project X	-1000	200	400	450	450		312		16.3%
6	project Y	-1500	600	550	460	460		346		15.1%
7	project Z	-1500	200	600	900	450		382		14.3%
8										

6. In some cases more than two solutions for IRR may emerge, and it is impossible to judge which ranges denote viability, and which indicate unacceptability, without first tabulating or graphing NPV.

The NPV computations show that project Z offers the biggest surplus, yet the IRR column reverses the ranking and places Z at the bottom of the list. It is not immediately apparent which criterion should predominate, but the 'mutually exclusive' clause points to the adoption of NPV.

By choosing the project with the largest NPV, we are creating the largest possible surplus from the available options. Admittedly, if we were also able to invest in the higher IRR options, larger benefits per pound invested would accrue, but project Z offers a larger total investment, at a slightly lower return, resulting in the biggest net surplus.

This is obvious in comparing system X with system Z. The initial investment in Z is greater, and despite a smaller percentage rate the total proceeds of Z are superior. Less obvious is the comparison between Y and Z, since both systems require the same initial outlay. However, by year 1, project Y has less capital outstanding than project Z, and the same kind of result emerges − i.e. larger surplus on account of the capital invested, despite a slightly smaller percentage rate.

Even if the reader remains convinced that system X is the one to choose, it is easy to demonstrate that Z is even better. From the worksheet set out in Table 3.8, perform the following operations:

a. in cell A9, place a label Z − X
b. in cell B9, use the formula +B7−B5
c. copy this formula from B9 to the range C9..F9
d. copy the NPV and IRR functions from H7..J7 to H9..J9

The result should demonstrate beyond doubt that the extra investment of £500 offers a surplus (NPV = £70). Moreover, the IRR of this additional investment is 10.3% (usually called the 'incremental yield'), which is higher than the 5% cost of capital. So anyone convinced of the merits of system X should be prepared to spend an additional £500 to enjoy the benefits offered by system Z.

This result only applies if there are unlimited funds available at the specified cost of capital. If there were capital rationing enforced because of borrowing restrictions, or limits imposed by a parent company (see section 3.11(b) below), it would no longer be sufficient just to show that extra investment resulted in additional NPV. Efficient use of the scarce funds would also have to be demonstrated.

3.6   Rent or Buy?

The choice between renting or buying is offered in many aspects of business − e.g. office equipment for typing, printing, photocopying, etc.; company vehicles; excavating equipment; and so on. The problem is a special case of ranking mutually exclusive projects, which was tackled in the previous section. The patterns of cash flows are markedly different between renting and buying, as illustrated in Table 3.9.

Table 3.9(a)   Rent-or-Buy Decisions

	A	B	C	D	E	F	G	H	I	J	K
1											incremental
2	Year	0	1	2	3	4		NPV (10%)			yield
3	===							========			==============
4											
5	RENT	-290	-270	-252	-235	-220		-1071			
6	BUY	-800	-20	-19	-18	-17		-859			
7											
8	BUY-RENT	-510	250	233	217	203		212		28.8%	
9											
10											

Table 3.9(b)   Rent-or-Buy Decisions

	A	B	C	D	E	F	G	H	I	J	K
1											incremental
2	Year	0	1	2	3	4		NPV (30%)			yield
3	===							========			=============
4											
5	RENT	-290	-270	-252	-235	-220		-831			
6	BUY	-800	-20	-19	-18	-17		-841			
7											
8	BUY-RENT	-510	250	233	217	203		-10		28.8%	
9											
10											

With rental, the annual commitments are relatively even. Outright purchase involves a heavy initial outlay, but it offers savings in subsequent years. To make comparisons strictly valid, however, some allowance for extended warranty or maintenance costs should be made. Let us assume that such adjustments have been made and that the flows are 'real' — i.e. expressed in year 0 prices. Moreover, to avoid tax complications[7] we shall imagine that the choice relates to a *consumer* durable such as a TV/Video package, rather than to a commercial investment.

The NPV of renting in this example when the discount rate is 10% (Table 3.9(a)) is −£1,071, compared with −£859 for buying the equipment. A better way of expressing this result is to omit the minus signs, and call the values 'present costs'. Thus buying has a lower present cost than renting, at the discount rate of 10% specified in this example. This result, however, will be reversed at a higher discount rate — e.g. at 30%, as shown in Table 3.9(b), where renting has a present cost of only £831 compared with £841 for buying. The switch-over occurs at 28.8% which is the incremental yield — i.e. the IRR on the extra money invested in outright purchase.

For most individuals, with costs of capital less than 28.8%, the purchase in this example would be more attractive than rental. If, however, one had to resort to some of the more expensive forms of credit to finance the purchase (where

---

7. In practice, companies are often confronted with options to lease, rather than to rent. The tax implications of a leasing arrangement are an essential part of the appraisal:- see Pike and Dobbins (1986, Chapter 13).

real costs in excess of 30% are not unknown), rental could be a viable proposition.

The economic meaning of the *present cost* of an option is the lump sum which would have to be set aside at t = 0 at the specified real interest (discount) rate, in order to finance all the outflows associated with a project. An associated concept is 'annual equivalent cost' which will now be discussed alongside other concepts and issues which arise with DCF.

3.7 Variations on the Basic Discounting Approaches

a. Annual Equivalent Cost (AEC)

If an investment is appraised in terms of its costs, as in the previous example where the benefits of the two alternatives were judged to be equal, the result may be presented as a present cost (or negative NPV), which is a value at year 0.

Sometimes, especially where competing projects have differing expected lives, decision makers prefer to receive the results of analysis in terms of the average yearly commitment over the life of each project — formally defined as the annual equivalent cost (AEC). Although this approach is most frequently adopted in the public sector (for example, in the NHS, where an 'option appraisal' methodology is employed, as described in Chapter 8), there is no reason why the domestic TV rental example just considered should not be handled in the same way.

At a discount rate of 10%, it was found that the present cost of rental was £1,071. This is equivalent to four annual payments, starting a year hence, of £338. This is found in Table 3.9(c) by using the Lotus function @PMT in column J of the worksheet. The function takes the form: @PMT(principal, interest rate, term). In cell J6 we type @PMT(H6,0.1,4) which may be copied to cell J7 to provide the annual equivalent cost of buying, which is £271.

This 'payment' function is also useful for calculating mortgage or instalment credit repayments. One may calculate the annual repayments — for example, of a £30,000 loan over 25 years, say, at a 12% interest rate. The function would

Table 3.9(c) Annual Equivalent Cost

	A	B	C	D	E	F	G	H	I	J	K
1								present		annual	
2	Year		0	1	2	3	4	cost		equivalent	
3										cost	
4	==							========		============	
5											
6	RENT	−290	−270	−252	−235	−220		1071		338	
7	BUY	−800	−20	−19	−18	−17		859		271	
8											
9											
10											

contain: @PMT(30000,0.12,25) or the cell addresses holding those magnitudes. The answer is £3,825.

b. Annuities

In many series of cash flows, a fairly constant annual inflow is projected over the life of the investment, although in some instances this may just be an approximation to the underlying reality. One can find the present value of such an 'annuity' by using another financial function in Lotus 1-2-3, namely the @PV function, which appears as @PV(payment, interest rate, term). So to find the present value of an annuity lasting 40 years of, say, £8,000, discounting at 15%, one requires a cell containing: @PV(8000,0.15,40). The reader may check that this gives an answer of £53,134. If an initial outlay of £25,000 were needed to generate such an annuity, the net present value would be: £53,134 − £25,000 = £28,134. A full worksheet could of course be used to perform all the necessary calculations.

c. Perpetuities

A special case of an annuity is a 'perpetuity' which is literally a perpetual annuity but, in practice, is a constant stream of cash, or other benefits, stretching into the very distant future. Principles of share valuation rest on the assumption that companies expect to survive for many years to come, and as a first approximation to valuation a company's income may be discounted by treating it as a perpetuity.

The longer the expected life of an annuity, the closer it is to the perpetuity value. The latter may be found very quickly without recourse to spreadsheet functions or other computational aids by taking the formula: PV (perpetuity) = A/r, where A is the annual flow, and r is the discount rate.

So the present value of a perpetuity of £1,000 at a discount rate of 10% is £1,000/0.1 = £10,000. Any year 0 expenditure to set the project in motion would then be deducted to give the NPV. In Table 3.10, this perpetuity is compared with a similar annuity lasting for 10, 20, 30, 40, and 50 years using the @PV function.

The perpetuity in cell I8 is the formula +B6/G2
The annuity in cell I10 is the function @PV($B$6,$G$2,10)
This annuity is copied to the range I11..I14, inserting the appropriate number of years (20, 30, 40, and 50).

It can be seen that the 50-year annuity may be approximated satisfactorily by the perpetuity − true PV = £9,915 as compared with £10,000. Even with a 40-year period, the error is relatively small.

Table 3.10   Annuity Compared with Perpetuity

	A	B	C	D	E	F	G	H	I	J
1										
2					discount	rate	10.0%			
3									present	
4	Years duration		10	20	30	40	50	value		
5	== ======									
6	annual flow	1000								
7										
8	perpetuity								10000	
9										
10	annuity		1000						6145	
11				1000					8514	
12					1000				9427	
13						1000			9779	
14							1000		9915	
15										
16										
17										
18										
19										
20										

Table 3.11   Traditional Approaches Compared with DCF

	A	B	C	D	E	F	G	H	I	J	K	L
1												
2					discount	rate	10.0%					
3												
4	Year		0	1	2	3	4		NPV	IRR	ARR	payback
5	== ===== ===== ===== =======											
6	project A	−1000	200	300	400	600		140	15.3%	12.5%		
7	cumulative flow		−800	−500	−100	500						
8	years in deficit		1	1	1	0						4
9												
10	project B	−1000	600	400	300	200		238	23.1%	12.5%		
11	cumulative flow		−400	0	300	500						
12	years in deficit		1	0	0	0						2
13												
14	project C	−2000	500	1500	200	200		−19	9.5%	5.0%		
15	cumulative flow		−1500	0	200	400						
16	years in deficit		1	0	0	0						2
17												
18												
19												
20												

+ C6 + D6   @IF(D7<0,1,0)   @SUM(C6..G6)/4/ − C6   @SUM(D8..G8) + 1

3.8   Traditional Methods of Appraisal

a.   Average Rate of Return

The average rate of return, sometimes called accounting rate of return (ARR), expresses the average profit of an investment as a percentage of the original capital sum invested. For example, in Table 3.11, project A requires an initial capital outlay of £1,000. This is depreciated over 4 years on a 'straight line' basis (these calculations are not shown in Table 3.11) at £250 per annum, giving accounting profits from years 1 to 4 of: minus £50, plus £50, £150 and £350. The average profit is £125, which is 12.5% of the original sum invested.

In the worksheet, this figure is given in cell K6, although it is computed more directly than in the process just described. The formula used is: @SUM(C6..G6)/4/ − C6. Column K is in percentage format to give the required result. The formula may then be copied to K10 and K14 to compute the ARR for projects B and C respectively. The ARR for a project would be compared with a target rate of return, or a cost of borrowing, to determine its acceptability (or merit rating in ranking projects).

b. Payback

The payback period is the simplest concept of all in investment appraisal. It only involves finding out how many years' cash flows will be needed to recover the initial investment. In its basic form, which we use here, no allowance for interest on capital outstanding is made, but some companies use a more sophisticated form which is adjusted for interest.

Taking project A in Table 3.11, it can be found by inspection that the project still has not recovered the initial outlay by period 3. It is only during the fourth year that the investment has been fully paid back. Although a worksheet is not really required to compute the payback period if this is all that a company requests for its appraisals, for purposes of comparison with the other main criteria it is useful to display all results simultaneously, so provision has been made in Table 3.11 for the computation of payback (unadjusted for interest).

In row 7, the cumulative cash flow is shown year by year. Once the year 1 figure has been computed (− 800 in cell D7 for which the formula is +C6+D6), successive running totals comprise the previous figure plus the current year's cash flow. Thus, E7 contains the formula +D7+E6. This can be copied to the range F7..G7, and the whole series of cumulative flows can then be copied to the ranges: D11..G11 and D15..G15.

The years in deficit are determined using the @IF logical function of Lotus 1-2-3. This is presented in general as:

@IF(condition,x,y)

which outputs x if the condition is TRUE and y if the condition is FALSE. Starting with cell D8, the function is:

@IF(D7<0,1,0)

So a value 1 appears as output in cell D8 to show that the cumulative cash flow is still negative after year 1. This function is then copied to the range E8..G8, and the whole row can be copied to rows 12 and 16 to serve projects B and C.

A final element in these rows is the actual payback figure, which is the number of years in deficit plus one. The formula @SUM(D8..G8)+1 is keyed into cell L8, to give a 4-year payback period for project A (i.e. the payback is achieved *during* the fourth year). Greater precision to provide fractional parts of a year is possible, but this would complicate the worksheet unnecessarily. The computed payback period is then compared with a policy target, so if the company set a three-year payback period it would reject project A.

A much easier task would be to include interest due on capital outstanding, which would simply require an enhancement of the deficits in the cumulative flows. For example, instead of £800 being the deficit for project A after 1 year, 10% interest on the capital of £1,000 would also be due, making £900 in total. By year 2 interest on this deficit of £900 would be due, and so on. The reader will find it a useful exercise to modify the worksheet to accommodate this refinement.

c. Payback and ARR Compared with DCF

Let us first consider the output of the appraisals for projects A and B in Table 3.11. Both have the same average rate of return because, over their four-year lives, the same *average* profits are anticipated. In fact, the positive cash flows are the same in total, but reversed over time.

The implication of this ARR result is that one should be indifferent between project A and project B, but the DCF principle that *timing* is crucial clearly points to a different conclusion. Project B offers its more substantial cash flows in the early years which puts it at an advantage compared to project A. The DCF criteria demonstrate this superiority with NPV and IRR of £238 and 23.1% for B, compared with 140 and 15.3% for A.

The payback approach to appraisal does favour projects with large early flows but, when adhered to slavishly, neglects the cash flows occurring beyond the payback period. Project C performs badly on account of its small cash flows in years 3 and 4 by all criteria other than payback, but recovers the initial outlay in only two years.

It is often suggested that the main purpose of payback is to avoid risk, and the adoption of rapid payback ventures certainly minimises the likelihood that problems involving liquidity will arise. Although payback does offer a safeguard in this respect, it should not be used as a defence against preparing a long-term investment strategy, or against the planning of future financing needs.

At one time, it could be argued that ARR served a useful purpose in providing appraisals which were rapidly performed in comparison with DCF. No tables were required, and in many cases mental arithmetic sufficed. In those cases where the ARR provides a good approximation to the IRR, there is still some merit in having a rough-and-ready screening device.

Project A, for example, has an ARR which is reasonably close to its IRR and, if the pattern of flows exhibits a build-up towards the end of the project's life, the approximation will generally be a good one. An exaggeration of the pattern in project A — starting with a smaller flow and ending with a larger one — could give an ARR equal to the IRR. For example

$$-1000 \quad 60 \quad 120 \quad 360 \quad 960$$
gives ARR = IRR = 12.5%

Against this, projects with high initial benefits are under-valued by ARR, and there is no computational advantage if the full project appraisal is conducted through the medium of the spreadsheet. Consequently, given the ease of applying the DCF criteria through the spreadsheet's financial functions, and their technical superiority, these will be the mainstay of the remaining appraisals used as examples in this chapter.

Now that the principles of discounting have been discussed, and a comparison has been made with the traditional appraisal methods, it is time to consider some of the practical issues which complicate investment appraisal and which exploit the capabilities of the spreadsheet to the full.

3.9 Writing-Down Allowances and Taxation

So far, the reader has been urged not to make deductions for depreciation in the DCF analysis, even though they do feature in the traditional ARR computation. In DCF one incorporates all capital expenditures displayed at the time of their occurrence, so that any further deduction for capital consumption would involve double counting.

However, it is important that the projections measure the true improvement in a company's cash flow following the commencement of the project in question. Associated with a profitable project will be a tax liability, so that the net improvement to a company's wellbeing will be the *net* (of tax) cash flows, and it is these which should feature in the appraisal. Whilst ensuring that double counting does not take place, it becomes necessary in the appraisal to calculate the tax liability according to the depreciation formula required by the authorities.

In Table 3.12, the corporation tax rate and income tax rate are set out at the top left of the worksheet. The latter is needed to compute the rate of advance corporation tax (ACT) which is due when dividends are paid, whereas the mainstream corporation tax payment will be due at a later date (assumed to be one year in arrears here).[8]

If dividends of £10,000 are paid to shareholders when the standard rate of income tax is 25%, they are treated as net of tax, with the company paying one-third of £10,000 in tax on behalf of the shareholders. In effect, the dividends are 'grossed up' to £13,333, and 25% tax is levied on the latter to leave £10,000.

---

8. For a discussion of the impact of taxation on investments, see Hirst (1988, Chapter 4). In practice, dividend policy would seldom be re-appraised in connection with a capital project, although this example illustrates the impact of a £10,000 increase in dividends.

Table 3.12 Depreciation, Taxation and Residual Values

	A	B	C	D	E	F	G	H	I	J	K	L	M	N	O
3	Corporation Tax Rate		0.35												
4	Income Tax Rate		0.25												
5	Advance Corporation Tax		0.33	+D4/(1-D4)											
6	Annual Depreciation		0.25	(writing down allowance)											

	A	B	C	D	E	F	G	H	I	J	K	L	M	N	O
8	Year	Sales	Material	Wages	Maintce	Capital	Book	Deprec	Residual	Tax'bl	Tax	Divis	ACT	Tax-ACT	Net
9		revenue		& sals	& other		value		value	profit	on t-1		due on t-1	on t-1	Flow
11	1989	0	0	0	0	(100,000)	100,000	25,000	0	(25,000)	0	0	0	0	(100,000)
12	1990	90,000	22,000	25,000	3,000	0	75,000	18,750	0	21,250	(8,750)	10,000	3,333	(8,750)	45,417
13	1991	110,000	28,000	28,000	6,000	0	56,250	14,063	0	33,938	7,437	10,000	3,333	4,104	40,563
14	1992	100,000	24,000	26,000	10,000	0	42,188	10,547	0	29,453	11,878	10,000	3,333	8,545	28,122
15	1993	95,000	24,000	25,000	15,000	0	31,641	(1,359)	33,000	32,359	10,309	10,000	3,333	6,975	53,691
16	1994	0	0	0	0	0	0	0	0	0	11,326	0	0	7,992	(7,992)
18	TOTALS	395,000	98,000	104,000	34,000			67,000		92,000	32,200				59,800

Cell formula annotations:

- H: +G11*$D$6
- H15: +G15-I15
- J: +B11-C11-D11-E11-H11
- K: +$D$3*J11
- M: +L12*$D$5
- N: +K14-M13
- O: +B11-C11-D11-E11+F11-N11+I11

NPV @10%	27,648
IRR	22.7%

Notes:

1. Dividends will be increased by £10,000 if the project is accepted. ACT of £3,333 will be payable in each of 4 years. The dividends thus affect the phasing of the tax burden, but the dividends themselves are benefits to shareholders, and are not deducted as costs.

2. Residual (scrap) value is £33,000 in 1993, as compared with a written down value of £31,641. The excess is entered as a negative depreciation value for 1993. If the scrap value had been less than the written down value, the remaining allowance would have continued to attract relief even after disposal. Here, the discrepancy has little effect on future tax reliefs.

3. Tax is paid during the year following the profit. In period t a net tax payment is made, based on the liability in respect of profits for $t-1$ less ACT paid in period $t-1$. For example, a net tax payment of £8,545 will be payable in 1992 − comprising 35% corporation tax on £33,938 (1991), i.e. £11,878, less ACT of £3,333 paid in 1991.

The income tax rate of 0.25 is displayed in cell D4, the ACT rate of 0.33 is computed in D5 [formula: $+D4(1-D4)$], and the tax payment of £3,333 is computed at cell address M12, and below for subsequent years. The corporation tax rate is taken to be 35%, as shown in cell D3.

Throughout, it is assumed that the tax due on company profits will be paid one year later, apart from the advance payment associated with the enhanced dividends.

The assumed rate at which assets depreciate for corporation tax assessment is taken to be 25%. Thus capital expenditure on machinery amounting to £100,000 would attract a 'writing down allowance' of £25,000 during the tax year of its acquisition. Even if the new asset does not generate any cash until the following year, the allowance may be taken out of existing profits to reduce the tax liability on current profits, if this is advantageous for the company.

Thus in 1989 when the machinery is purchased, the net cash flow is $-£100,000$ (as shown in cell O11), but the taxable profit of the company in that year will fall by £25,000 (cell J11), and the tax due in 1990 will be reduced by 35% of this figure (i.e. by £8,750), computed in cell K12 as the formula: $+\$D\$3*J11$ and copied as far as cell K16.

The net flow for 1990 (cell O12) is enhanced by this tax saving, the formula for that cell being:

$$
\begin{array}{llllll}
+B12 & -C12 & -D12 & -E12 & -M12 & -N12 \\
\text{sales} & \text{material} & \text{wages} & \text{maintenance} & \text{ACT} & \text{mainstream} \\
\text{rev.} & & & & & \text{corp. tax}
\end{array}
\left[
\begin{array}{ll}
+F12 & +I12 \\
\text{capital} & -\text{ve} \\
\text{residual} & +\text{ve}
\end{array}
\right]
$$

This is sales revenue less all the costs (apart from depreciation), less ACT and corporation tax (liability here negative), plus asset values realised. The latter will be zero until the machinery is sold off in 1993 when the project is expected to terminate, but it is included in the formula for copying purposes.

Dividends are benefits to shareholders, and so are not deducted in the cash flow computation. They are only here to demonstrate their influence on the phasing of the tax burden.

The 1991 cash flow is computed, in row 13, from the relationships established in row 12. The corporation tax liability is now positive (£4,104) as shown in cell N13 (computed as $+K13-M12$). This comprises £7,437 due as 35% of the profit for 1990 less ACT of £3,333 paid in 1990.

K13 is the output of the formula: $+\$D\$3*J12$ where J12 (1991 profit) is $+B12-C12-D12-E12-H12$ (i.e. revenue less costs *including* depreciation)

and M12 is the output of the formula: $+L12*\$D\$5$

All other values in column N are obtained from related formulae.

The only item which requires special treatment is the residual value at the end of the project. By 1993, the written-down value of the machinery will be £31,641 (cell G15). This is the 1992 value less 25% depreciation, which is, in turn, the 1991 value less depreciation, and so on. If the residual value exceeds the written-down value, the surplus will be taxable, and a 'balancing charge' becomes payable.

The treatment of this surplus in the worksheet has been to enter it as a negative depreciation in cell H15, based on the formula: +G15−I15 which differs from the formulae used elsewhere in column H. The taxable profit for 1993, appearing in cell J15, is enhanced by this item.

As a cross-check on all the computations, column totals are given in row 18. It can be seen that sales revenue less the costs of materials, wages and maintenance, less capital consumption (depreciation), results in aggregate profits of £92,000. Total tax liability over the period is £32,200, leaving net flows totalling £59,800.

The NPV (discounting at 10%) of £27,648 and the IRR of 21.7% summarise the appraisal based on the cash flow projections given in Table 3.12. Either way, the project is seen to be acceptable.

The estimation of revenues and costs is the subject matter of subsequent chapters in this book, but it should be apparent that these magnitudes are not known with certainty, neither are future tax rates and depreciation allowances. One way of handling uncertainty is to conduct sensitivity analysis (other considerations relating to imperfect knowledge will be discussed in the final section of this chapter).

3.10 Sensitivity Analysis

Sensitivity analysis, asking 'what if?' questions, may be pursued item by item, just changing cells in which estimates are uncertain, critical, or of particular interest. One may also use the backward iteration facility available in some spreadsheets in order to find, for example, how far sales revenue in 1993 would have to fall in order to result in zero NPV.[9]

The answer to this question is that sales revenue of £35,630, instead of the £95,000 projected, would render the project unacceptable at the 10% discount rate (assuming that the same cost levels would be experienced). The reader can confirm this result by replacing the contents of cell B15 with this computed value. A wider ranging sensitivity analysis may be conducted with the aid of the Lotus data table facility.

1. Data Table 1

A convenient portion of the worksheet containing the appraisal should be set aside for the data table. Table 3.13 would be held within the worksheet holding Table 3.12 − in fact, directly below it.

---

9. Lotus 1-2-3 requires the 'Goal Solutions' add-on; alternatively, the result may be obtained by trial-and-error.

Table 3.13 Data Tables for Sensitivity Analysis

	A	B	C	D	E	F	G	H	I	J	K	L	M	N	O
38															
39	DATA TABLE 1					DATA TABLE 2									
40															
41	corp.														
42	tax														
43	rate	NPV	IRR							residual	value				
44		+021	+022			NPV -->	+021	20000	25000	30000	35000	40000			
45	0.25	33702	24.7%				0.25	26841	29480	32119	34758	37397			
46	0.27	32492	24.3%				0.27	25792	28369	30946	33522	36099			
47	0.29	31281	23.9%				0.29	24742	27257	29772	32287	34801			
48	0.31	30070	23.5%			corp.	0.31	23693	26146	28598	31051	33504			
49	0.33	28859	23.1%			tax	0.33	22644	25034	27425	29815	32206			
50	0.35	27648	22.7%			rate	0.35	21594	23923	26251	28580	30908			
51	0.37	26437	22.3%				0.37	20545	22811	25078	27344	29610			
52	0.39	25227	21.8%				0.39	19495	21700	23904	26108	28313			
53	0.41	24016	21.4%				0.41	18446	20588	22730	24873	27015			
54	0.43	22805	21.0%				0.43	17397	19477	21557	23637	25717			
55	0.45	21594	20.5%				0.45	16347	18365	20383	22401	24419			
56															
57															

Suppose we wish to investigate the impact of changing a single variable (e.g. the corporation tax rate) on two or more outputs — both NPV and IRR, in this instance. The two cells along the top row hold the formulae +O21 (the NPV cell address in Table 3.12) and +O22 (the IRR cell address). To the left of these is a blank cell, and below this a series of corporation tax rates. The rectangular area of the worksheet: A44..C55, is the range specified here for the data table. At this stage it is blank apart from the various corporation tax figures and the single NPV and IRR values.

The command sequence starts with: **/DT1**
after which the user is prompted for the table range A44..C55

When the input cell 1 is requested, the cell address for corporation tax is entered, which is D3 in Table 3.12. Thereafter one waits for a few seconds if the computer has a maths co-processor fitted, rather longer if not, and the array of figures appears as in the left portion of Table 3.13. The analysis shows that neither NPV nor IRR are unduly sensitive to changes in the corporation tax rate, and that even a rate of 45% could be tolerated.

2. Data Table 2

This alternative form of data table obtains variations of a *single* output in response to changes in *two* inputs. In this example, we examine how NPV responds to changes in the corporation tax rate and the residual value.

The range here is G44..L55. The top left corner cell is *not* left empty as in Data Table 1, but holds the initial NPV output — i.e. its formula here is +O21. Apart from the top row and left column, the data table is blank at this stage.[10]

The command sequence is: **/DT2**

after which one is prompted for the range: G44..L55

and then the addresses of both inputs (1, which is the tax rate — cell D3, and 2, which is the residual value — cell I15). The final result is the rectangular array on the right of Table 3.13.

This shows that a low residual value, coupled with an unfavourable tax rate, could erode the NPV quite substantially, although neither input on its own has a large impact. The project remains viable over the ranges of input values considered here.

---

10. For cells B44, C44 and G44 the format chosen is 'TEXT' which means that formulae rather than their values will be displayed. This enables the cells to stand out from the numerical array which subsequently appears. To format a range in this way, one uses the command sequence **/RFT** after which one is prompted for the range to which this format will apply.

3.11 Advanced Topics

a. Economic Life

Machines start to deteriorate from the moment of their commissioning, and their operating costs will rise. The optimal life will depend on how far this deterioration is offset by lower capital costs per annum as an asset is kept in service. This optimal, or economic, life will usually differ from the physical working life that could be extracted from a machine.

Let us now attempt to find the period over which a machine will offer the most favourable combination of capital and operating costs. To explain how the worksheet is set up, we shall examine years 1, 2 and 3 (rows 8, 9 and 10) in Table 3.14.

Table 3.14 Economic Life of Equipment

	A	B	C	D	E	F	G	H	I
1					capital				
2					7500				
3		operating							
4	year	cost	disc	AEC	AEC	perc.	PV	AEC	
5		increase	rate	cost	capital	recov	recov	recov	TOTAL
6		1000	6.0%						
7									
8	1	0	0	0	7950	0%	0	0	7950
9	2	1000	890	485	4091	0%	0	0	4576
10	3	2000	2569	961	2806	0%	0	0	3767
11	4	3000	4946	1427	2164	0%	0	0	3592
12	5	4000	7935	1884	1780	0%	0	0	3664
13	6	5000	11459	2330	1525	0%	0	0	3856
14	7	6000	15450	2768	1344	0%	0	0	4111
15									
16			cumulative						
17			discounted					min AEC	3592
18									

@NPV($C$6,$B$8..B14) @PMT(C14,$C$6,A14) @PMT($E$2,$C$6,A14)

If a machine is kept for one year, it will be at peak operating efficiency, so operating costs will be at their minimum. If, however, it is kept in service for a second year, deterioration will cause operating costs to increase. Here it is assumed (cell B6) that there is a linear deterioration of £1,000 each year, and the annual operating cost excess over year 1 is shown alongside each year in column B.

The discounted (to year 0) value of the operating costs is given in column C at a discount rate of 6% as specified at the head of that column (cell C6). For a machine in service 2 years, operating costs (excess over year 1) are 0 in the first year and £1,000 in the second, which are discounted to give £890 (cell C9). This year 0 value has an annual equivalent cost over 2 years of £485.

The AEC is a valuable DCF criterion in the context of options with different expected lives. In this problem, the optimal life is the central issue, and a straightforward comparison of NPVs (or present costs) would be inappropriate when each option has a different life. By year 3 the operating cost excess will be:

year	1	2	3
cost	0	£1,000	£2,000

This series has a present value at 6% of £2,569, with an AEC over 3 years of £961. The formulae which apply are:

column C (discounted costs)   for cell C9 we have
                                     @NPV($C$6,$C$8..C9)

this keeps the discount rate and year 1 flow fixed as the formula is copied down the column, but expands the range of flows year by year.

column D (AEC of operating costs)   for cell D9 we have
                                     @PMT(C9,$C$6,A9)

which is copied down column D as far as the final year.

In column E, the year 0 capital expenditure on the machinery is converted to annual equivalent costs over periods ranging from 1 to 7 years (note that £7,500 spent now is equivalent to £7,950 by the end of year 1, at a 6% discount rate).

We shall ignore columns F, G and H for the moment and focus on the two series we have created in columns D and E. What we are left with is operating costs, which rise for every year of service, in column D. Working in the opposite direction, in column E, we have annual (equivalent) capital costs which decline the longer the asset is kept in service. These opposing effects are illustrated in Figure 3.3.

This combination of operating and capital costs gives a U-shaped total cost curve which has its minimum value of £3,592 here at 4 years. Column I of the worksheet is used to give the totals for each year.

There are various complications which might be explored: for instance, *obsolescence*, as well as deterioration, places machinery of older vintages at an operating cost disadvantage. This is due to the technical superiority of innovations which enable production costs to be lowered. The incorporation of obsolescence will tend to shorten the economic life of machinery, provided that replacement costs do not absorb the advantage.

A feature of the analysis so far is the omission of resale values, which may be entirely justified if there is no second-hand market for the equipment, or if technological change is so rapid that values of old equipment plummet. In some instances, for example vehicles, the resale value has an important part to play in determining the economic life.

Obviously, the net capital cost is somewhat diminished if a certain proportion is recovered when the asset is retired from service. This can be seen in Table 3.15, where 60% of the original cost is recovered after one year, reducing the

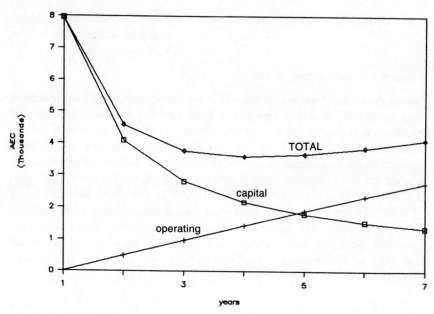

Figure 3.3 Economic Life

one-year AEC by £4,500 to £3,450. To create column F, it is assumed that an additional 20% of value is lost in each of the following years, so that each figure in the column, beyond cell F8, is 80% of the preceding figure.

To obtain column G, starting with G8, we take the formula:

$$+F8*\$E\$2/(1+\$C\$6)^{\wedge}A8$$

Table 3.15 Economic Life of Equipment with Resale Values

	A	B	C	D	E	F	G	H	I
1					capital				
2					7500				
3		operating							
4	year	cost	disc	AEC	AEC	perc.	PV	AEC	
5		increase	rate	cost	capital	recov	recov	recov	TOTAL
6		1000	6.0%						
7									
8	1	0	0	0	7950	60%	4245	4500	3450
9	2	1000	890	485	4091	48%	3204	1748	2829
10	3	2000	2569	961	2806	38%	2418	905	2862
11	4	3000	4946	1427	2164	31%	1825	527	3065
12	5	4000	7935	1884	1780	25%	1377	327	3337
13	6	5000	11459	2330	1525	20%	1040	211	3644
14	7	6000	15450	2768	1344	16%	785	141	3971
15									
16			cumulative						
17			discounted					min AEC	2829
18									

$$+F8*\$E\$2/(1+\$C\$6)^{\wedge}A8 \qquad @PMT(G8,\$C\$6,A8)$$

that is, present value of the resale value = percentage recovered
$\times$ capital outlay/
$(1 + \text{discount rate})^n$

where n is the number of years

Each of the present values in column G is converted into an AEC in column H using the @PMT function, and this is deducted from the sum of capital and operating costs to give lower total cost figures than before in column I.

Previously (Table 3.14), it was the short-life options which were most heavily penalised by the assumption that all the asset's value would be lost on retirement from service. Now that this penalty is partially removed, we find that the minimum AEC is achieved at a shorter life (£2,829 for a 2-year life in Table 3.15).

Further elaboration of the analysis would entail incorporation of depreciation allowances against tax, and reference to the obsolescence factor mentioned previously. Such ramifications are clearly within the capabilities of the spreadsheet but, for the moment, their implications will be left to the reader's imagination.

b. Capital Rationing

Capital rationing occurs when desirable projects are available for financing, but funds are insufficient for all of them to be started. This may happen if a firm has a borrowing limit imposed on it by its creditors, or the time is inauspicious for raising new equity finance. Perhaps a company headquarters will enforce limits on capital spending in order to exercise tight control over the decisions of its operating companies. However, in some unsuccessful companies, limits are imposed as:

permanent panic measures born out of the constant shortage of cash.
(Goldsmith and Clutterbuck 1985, p. 147)

Whatever the source of the restriction, managers should try to deploy the available funds so as to obtain the largest surplus. The problem differs from the ranking of mutually exclusive projects in that all the projects could, in principle, be adopted. It is the shortage of funds, rather than any duplication or incompatibility, that is the source of the problem.

As we have seen, the measure of surplus advocated for investment decisions is NPV, so presumably the solution to the problem is to rank the competing projects in terms of NPV. This, however, is not the whole story, and the correct approach will depend upon the extent of the rationing problem — whether it is over just one year, or over a period of several years.

Suppose that the only restriction applies to the present — i.e. year 0, in which investment is restricted to £225 (thousand). To finance all six projects (A to F) would require £300 (thousand), so we need a mechanism to choose between them.

Table 3.16 Capital Rationing — Single Period

Year		A	B	C	D	E	F	FINANCE AVAILABLE
				Project				
Year	0	-75	-75	-30	-15	-75	-30	225
	1	-75	-105	-150	-30	0	-75	(£ thousand)
	2	-40	150	-45	75	300	-150	
	3	300	225	450	-150	150	450	
	4	150	75	375	150	150	150	
	5	150	0	0	150	0	150	
ARR		43%	38%	67%	18%	175%	39%	
payback		3	3	3	4	2	3	
NPV @10%		244.7	173.8	390.7	102.6	388.1	311.5	
IRR		48%	51%	71%	54%	129%	66%	
profit index for yr 0		3.3	2.3	13.0	6.8	5.2	10.4	
								************ TOTAL NPV: 1437.6 ************
Quantity Adopted		1.0	0.0	1.0	1.0	1.0	1.0	
								TOTAL FINANCE 225
Finance Used		75	0	30	15	75	30	************

All the flows and the various criteria are tabulated in a worksheet, within which lies Table 3.16. The payback period has been entered directly — it was determined by inspection rather than any worksheet computation. NPV and IRR rely on the usual Lotus functions, while ARR uses a formula built up from first principles.

The usual DCF criteria, and the traditional ARR and payback, offer rather different rankings. Without taking the comparison any further, let us just note that project B, whilst not impressive in comparison with its competitors, at least does not come bottom of the list by any of the usual criteria. Yet, at the end of the day, this is the project which will be rejected, as indicated by comparison of the *profitability index* for each project.

The reason for appealing to this index, which is computed as the NPV per pound invested in year 0, is that the initial scarcity of funds acts as a limiting factor. Optimisation is achieved by ranking in terms of benefit (NPV) per unit of limiting factor, and this is what the profitability index achieves. The rank order is then: C, F, D, E, A, and B. The first five fully absorb the available finance, and are recommended, but B has to be rejected because of insufficient finance, despite offering a surplus at the given discount rate of 10%.

The 'Quantity Adopted' row is prepared manually here, having noted the results of the ranking, and the worksheet then computes the total NPV generated, and provides a check on the finance used. The reader should now be able to create formulae to facilitate this process.

If whole projects cannot be financed in line with their rank order, it may be possible under some circumstances to adopt fractional parts in order to absorb the finance up to its limit. Otherwise, it may be to the firm's advantage to accept a project with an unfavourable profitability index, rather than leave any funds unused.

A complicating factor which has not been explored here is that a company's usual discount rate, applicable in the absence of capital rationing, does not adequately reflect the true cut-off rate, which is effectively raised under capital rationing. This topic is treated at some length by Bromwich (1976, Chapter 10).

The problems of both fractional solutions and modified discount rates are also encountered in the multi-period capital rationing case, but the main consideration becomes the allocation of scarce resources subject to several constraints. Linear programming provides a solution, as will be explained in Chapter 7.

3.12 Risk and Uncertainty in Investment Appraisal

In Table 3.17, Project A comprises an initial outflow of £1,000 followed by two cash inflows of £900. Unlike previous examples used in this chapter, the inflows are not single-valued assumptions, but based on a probability distribution, with outcomes of £700 or £1,100, probability 0.5 for each, whose mean, or 'expected value' is £900.

The expected value is found by taking:

$$EV = (0.5 \times 700) + (0.5 \times 1,100) = 900$$

A change in the probabilities, or the constituent money values, will require recalculation of the expected value. The same kind of calculation can be extended to as many outcomes/money values as are included in the distribution, each weighted by its probability of occurrence.

Another attribute of the probability distribution which will command attention is a measure of dispersion, such as the variance. If each of the possible values in the distribution has the same probability, the @VAR function of Lotus 1-2-3 may be used to determine variance (or @STD to determine the standard deviation, which is the square root of the variance).

The word 'risk' will be used to convey an imperfect, but probabilistic, knowledge of outcomes. 'Uncertainty' normally refers to situations of imperfect knowledge where probabilities are not available. However, under uncertainty the decision maker can usually impute probabilities by judgement to a range of outcomes, even if such probabilities are 'subjective', and not of the same 'objective' quality as those obtained from analysis of frequencies or prevalence (as calculated by insurance companies in their analyses of risks).

Hertz and Thomas (1984, p. 7) suggest that the distinctions between risk and uncertainty

> have limited value in the practical process of risk assessment and analysis.

Consequently, they propose a definition of risk which is broadened to encompass elements of what would traditionally have been called 'uncertainty'.

Table 3.17 Risk in Investment Appraisal

	A	B	C	D	E	F	G	H	I	J	K
1											
2											NPV
3						NPV	NPV	NPV			cert.
4						mean	var	loaded			equiv.
5						(@ 5%)					
6											
7	year-->			0	1	2					
8	Project	A		-1000	900	900	673				
9									(+5%)		
10		range	from-->	700	700			69,189	562		
11			to	1100	1100						
12			(probabilities = 0.5)								
13											
14		cert. equiv		840	840	(c.e. coeff. =		0.93)			562
15											
16	***
17	year-->			0	1	2					
18	Project	B		-1000	900	900	673				
19									(+10%)		
20		range	from-->	600	600			155,676	463		
21			to	1200	1200						
22			(probabilities = 0.5)								
23											
24		cert. equiv		787	787	(c.e. coeff. =		0.87)			463
25											
26	***
27	year-->			0	1	2					
28	Project	C		-1200	1050	1050	752				
29									(+20%)		
30		range	from-->	600	600			350,271	312		
31			to	1500	1500						
32			(probabilities = 0.5)								
33											
34		cert. equiv		813	813	(c.e. coeff. =		0.77)			312
35											
36	***
37											
38											
39											
40											

$$@VAR(D10..D11)/(1.05)^2 + @VAR(E10..E11)/(1.05)^4$$

In selecting between options, the most widely advocated procedure[11] in the project analysis literature is mean—variance (M/V) analysis.

Use of the M/V approach implies risk aversion in the form of preference for a smaller variance of payoffs — all other things being equal. Thus, if a decision maker were confronted with two risky choices, X and Y, both with expected payoffs of £5 million, but with variances of £1 million and £2 million respectively, the optimal choice would be X, assuming a risk averse decision maker.

A corollary of this proposition is that confronted by two projects carrying equal risk, as measured by the variance of money values, a decision maker would prefer the one with the higher expected value.

Apart from the M/V approach, other ways of handling the problem of risk include the loading of the discount rate to include a risk premium, and the application of 'certainty equivalents'.

---

11. Attributed to Markowitz (1952).

The mean−variance rule, when used in conjunction with NPV, is not entirely straightforward. Difficulty is not apparent in the computation of the mean, for the expected values of the cash flows are discounted in the usual way, but the variance of the NPV is based on the variances of each of the cash flows discounted at the *square* of the usual discount factors.

These discounted variances are summed to give the variance of NPV. There is also a complication in making comparisons where there is a large difference in the magnitude of returns from the projects. In such cases, it may be desirable to take the 'coefficient of variation' in order to introduce a scaling factor. This coefficient takes the standard deviation divided by the expected value as the measure of risk.

Loading the discount rate involves taking the expected values of the cash flows in the usual manner but, when discounting takes place, the cost of capital plus a risk premium is used. The larger the level of risk present, the larger will be the premium. The variance of the payoffs serves as a proxy for the level of risk.

Certainty equivalents are based on the premise that a risk-averse decision maker would be indifferent, at some point, between a risky (expected) sum of money and a *certain* sum of money of lower value. In effect, the risky variable cash flows are replaced by constant cash flows offering equivalent utility to the decision maker. The amount by which the expected value of each cash flow is 'deflated' to yield its certainty equivalent will again be related to the variance as an indicator of the amount of risk attached to each cash flow.

If the allowances for risk are made consistently for a stream of cash flows which exhibits the same mean and variance throughout, the adjustments *via* either certainty equivalent or loading the discount rate should achieve broadly the same effect.

Returning now to Table 3.17, three projects, *A,B,C*, are appraised. In each case the NPV at a (riskless) discount rate of 5% is found, based on the expected value of the cash flows. The variance of the NPV is then computed in the manner described above.

For example, the variance for the NPV of project A is calculated in cell G10 as:

@VAR(D10..D11)/1.05^2+@VAR(E10..E11)/1.05^4

This formula may be copied to cell addresses G20 and G30.

If the M/V rule were now applied, project *A* would be preferred to *B* (same expected NPV, but lower risk). It would be less easy to choose between *A* and *C*, because although *C* offers a higher expected value, it is also considerably more risky.

Whilst no claims to precision are to be made here, the alternative ways of allowing for risk do at least permit a ranking of sorts to be achieved. Let us suppose that the variance in NPV for project *A* (subjectively) appears to warrant a risk premium of 5%, meaning a total discount rate of 10%. For **B** a 10% premium is added, and 20% for project **C**.

The revised NPVs are computed in column H headed 'NPV loaded', and the order of preference is seen to be **A,B,C**. We would have more confidence in this ranking if the certainty equivalent method gave the same result. Figures have been deliberately chosen in this example so that *exactly* the same result emerges.

The figures necessary to achieve this correspondence are: 840 for each flow from project **A**; 787 for each flow from project **B**; and 813 for each flow from project **C**.[12]

It is highly unlikely, of course, that precisely the same results would have emerged from the two methods in practice, but reasonable care in applying these risk-adjustment procedures should at least result in similar rankings. With the figures taken here, for instance, an NPV variance in the range 50,000 to 100,000 called for a loading of 5% to the discount rate (as with project A). Loadings of 10% were applied for variances in the range 100,000 to 200,000 (for project B), and 20% for variances in the range 200,000 to 400,000 (for project C).

Setting the certainty equivalents consistently required a reduction factor (sometimes called the certainty-equivalent coefficient) of 0.93 (from 900 to 840) for project **A**, 0.87 (from 900 to 787) for project **B**, and 0.77 (from 1050 to 813) for project **C**. These coefficients are shown in cells H14, H24 and H34. Whilst these coefficients are not directly linked to the discount rate loadings, the rankings would not have been affected if we had taken, for convenience, coefficients of 0.95, 0.90, and 0.80 for the certainty equivalents of projects **A**, **B**, and **C**, respectively which do have an obvious connection with the loadings.

In presenting the results of an appraisal where risk adjustments have been incorporated, it is important that the analyst states precisely how the allowance for risk has been made, and the scale of such adjustments, whether these be by loading the discount rate or by reducing risky cash flows to certainty equivalents. Indeed, in allowing for risk, the analyst should have consulted management to ascertain the degree of aversion exhibited by those taking the decisions.[13]

Internal rate of return (IRR) is not calculated in Table 3.17 where comparisons are being made between projects. It may be used, however, as a test of acceptability for *individual* investments. A higher cutoff rate may be applied to allow for risk, with IRR calculated from the expected cash flows, unadjusted. Alternatively, the usual rate may be retained, but the IRR would then be computed from the certainty equivalents of the project's cash flows.

---

12. In fact, backward iteration using *Goal Solutions* was employed to obtain these figures, but trial-and-error would have produced the same results eventually.
13. Methods for assessing risk aversion through utility functions are discussed in Hertz and Thomas (1984, Chapter 5).

APPENDIX: A Note on Portfolio Theory[14]

The underlying principle of portfolio theory is that the combining of assets (either financial or physical) into a diversified portfolio can permit a reduction of risk as measured by the variance of returns. The amount by which the variance will be reduced depends on the correlation between the individual assets' returns.

For example, if the income streams from two securities were perfectly correlated, no risk reduction would be enjoyed by combining them in a portfolio, since returns would peak at the same time and enter their troughs at the same time. However, if the returns are statistically independent, ups and downs may be offset to a degree, and diversification can lower the overall risk. In practice, it is likely that part of the risk can be reduced through diversification, particularly if the investments cater for different markets which have their own distinctive behaviour patterns, although there remains a general tendency for the fortunes of most sectors to be influenced by the business cycle, which means that some positive correlation between profits is likely to remain.

In portfolio theory, risk is treated as two separate components: the diversifiable component, which is described as 'unsystematic', and the undiversifiable component (associated with economic activity in general), which is described as 'systematic'. It is this latter portion which is regarded as relevant in applying a risk premium, or other adjustment, when cash flows are being discounted.

This decomposition of risk into the two components is a feature of the so-called 'capital asset pricing model' (CAPM). The appropriate discount rate is identified for a project by taking the riskless interest rate plus a premium which depends on the estimate of the responsiveness of the project's returns to changes in returns on assets in the economy generally. The degree of responsiveness is stated as β (Beta).[15]

In Figure 3.4, the Beta for a particular company is found by plotting the percentage return on its shares over time, against the percentage return on a diversified market portfolio, period by period. The slope of the fitted line is Beta, which is found to be 1.56 in this example (from a Lotus 1-2-3 regression output). Large companies can obtain estimates of Beta from the London Business School's quarterly, *Risk Measurement Service*, which also supplies this statistic for broad industrial sectors.

With Beta at 1.56 in this illustration, let us suppose that the real risk-free interest rate is 5%, and the expected return on a market portfolio exceeds this by 9% (see Hirst 1988, p. 71 for a justification of this latter figure which is called the 'risk premium on the market'). The expected return on the company's equity will then be:

---

14. See the list of further reading at the end of this chapter: Sharpe (1964), Lintner (1965), and Myers and Turnbull (1977).
15. A useful reference for this topic is Hirst (1988) and Levy and Sarnat (1986, Chapter 13).

risk-free rate + (company's Beta × risk premium on the market)

= 5%   + (1.56   ×   9%)

= 19%

This would be the opportunity cost of capital to the company if financed entirely by equity. It effectively includes a risk premium of 14% (= Beta × risk premium on the market).

A *project's* Beta, and thus the appropriate risk premium to apply in appraisal, will tend to differ from the company's Beta, but the computations require more information than is likely to be available in practice. To simplify the procedure, Hirst (op. cit., p. 73) proposes a schedule of adjustment factors for different classes of project which, he claims, 'has proved workable in practice.'

The implications of the CAPM for risk adjustment in investment appraisal are that any major project[16] which is likely to change the overall risk structure of the company needs to be analysed with an appropriate risk premium built into the discount rate, reflecting the systematic risk associated with it (project Beta value).

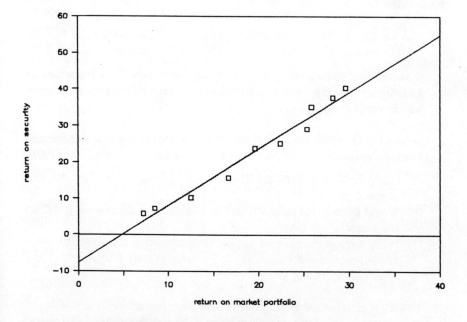

Figure 3.4 Capital Asset Pricing Model: Estimation of Beta

---

16. In the extreme case, a 'project' could be the takeover of a complete company operating in entire-ly different markets.

On the other hand, if the investment appraisal is concerned with relatively small projects, whose individual characteristics are not expected to make much of an impact on the total risks facing the company, it is justifiable to apply a single risk-adjusted discount rate to all such projects, reflecting the systematic risk which characterises the company's operations as a whole. These implications of the CAPM cast some doubt on a simplistic treatment of risk through loaded discount rates.

Finally, in relating risk to the question of sensitivity analysis, it is of immediate interest to management whether risk is likely to lead to failure — i.e. to attainment of a negative NPV. Whether or not adjustments are made to the expected cash flows, or to the company's usual discount rate, a consideration of the circumstances in which a project would return a negative NPV, or an inferior NPV to rival projects, is vital.

Thus risk analysis should not be seen as a substitute for sensitivity analysis. The two can work hand-in-hand, with risk analysis summarising the characteristics of the distribution of cash flows, and sensitivity analysis determining the set of values under which a recommendation can be maintained.

Exercises

1. Use the annuity present value function @PV, of Lotus 1-2-3, to find the present value of £5,000 received annually for 30 years discounting at 20%.

    If the 30-year annuity were used as an approximation for a perpetuity of £5,000 (i.e. £5,000 per annum anticipated for ever), find the percentage error which would result.

2. In Table 3.11, reduce the initial capital outlay for project C to £1,000, and reverse the cash flows for years 1 to 4 (i.e. £200, £200, £1,500, £500).

    (a) Compute NPV at 10%, the IRR, the ARR (average rate of return), and payback period.
    (b) Would the original project B still be preferable to the new project C on any count?
    (c) If the three projects (with project C as revised in this exercise) were mutually exclusive, what would be your overall assessment of the opportunities facing you?

3. You have been invited to a timeshare apartment presentation, at which you are quoted £6,500 for a one-week share. The contract lasts for 80 years, after which there is no residual value from the initial expenditure of £6,500.

    Your annual charges, which may change over time, would be £120 plus VAT (currently at 15%) for maintenance, and a club membership fee of £40 (inclusive of VAT).

    (a) Calculate the total Annual Equivalent Cost of the proposal if your cost of capital is 4% (use the Lotus 1-2-3 function @PMT to transform the capital outlay into its annual equivalent).

    (b) If a week's apartment rental in a comparable location currently costs £400, evaluate this rental against the timeshare arrangement.

4.   In Table 3.16, the year-3 cash inflow forecast for project B is raised from 225 to 425 (£000s). How would you now allocate the available finance, and how much larger would be the overall NPV of the selected investments?

5.   Change the corporation tax rate to 50% for the example which features in Table 3.12. Also, raise the initial capital outlay to £130,000, and appraise the project again using both NPV and IRR criteria.

References and Further Reading

Cretien, P.D., Ball, S.E. and Brigham, E.R. (1987) *Financial Management with Lotus 1-2-3*, The Dryden Press.
(This book is specifically geared to the needs of the Lotus user, and utilises a wide range of facilities available in Release 2 of Lotus 1-2-3.)

Bromwich, M. (1976) *The Economics of Capital Budgeting*, Penguin Books.
Goldsmith, W. and Clutterbuck, D. (1985) *The Winning Streak*, Penguin Books (repr. 1988).
Hertz, D.B. and Thomas, H. (1983) *Risk Analysis and its Applications*, John Wiley (repr. 1984).
Hirst, I.R.C. (1988) *Business Investment Decisions*, Philip Allan.
Levy, H. and Sarnat, M. (1986) *Capital Investment and Financial Decisions*, 3rd edn, Prentice-Hall.
Lumby, S. (1984) *Investment Appraisal*, 2nd edn, Van Nostrand Reinhold.
Markowitz, H.M. (1952) 'Portfolio selection', *Journal of Finance*, pp. 77–91.
Merrett, J. and Sykes, A. (1966) *The Finance and Analysis of Capital Projects*, 3rd edn, Longman.
Pike, R. (1983) 'A review of recent trends in formal capital budgeting processes', *Accounting and Business Research*, Summer, pp. 201–8.
Pike, R. and Dobbins, R. (1986) *Investment Decisions and Financial Strategy*, Philip Allan.
(Pike and Dobbins include program listings in BASIC for capital budgeting – Chapter 18.)

Scapens, R.W., Sale, T.J. and Tikkas, P.A. (1982) *Financial Control of Divisional Capital Investment*, Institute of Cost and Management Accountants, London.

For an introductory treatment of Investment Appraisal, see:

Mott, G. (1987) *Investment Appraisal: A Guide to Profit Planning* (revised edition), Pan Books.

(This text does not involve spreadsheet work, although a microcomputer program written in BASIC is listed in its Appendix 4.)

Further Reading on the Theory of Investment and Finance

Brealey, R. and Myers, S. (1984) *Principles of Corporate Finance*, 2nd edn, McGraw-Hill.
Franks, J.R. and Scholefield, H.H. (1977) *Corporate Financial Management*, 2nd edn, Gower Press.
Freear, J. (1980) *The Management of Business Finance*, Pitman.
Hertz, D.B. (1964) 'Risk analysis in capital investment', *Harvard Business Review*, January–February, pp. 95–106.
Lintner, J. (1965) 'The valuation of risky assets and the selection of risky investments in stock portfolios and capital budgets', *Review of Economics and Statistics*, pp. 13–37.
Myers, S.C. and Turnbull, S.M. (1977) 'Capital budgeting and the capital asset pricing model: good news and bad news', *Journal of Finance*, pp. 321–36.
Sharpe, W.F. (1964) 'Capital asset prices: a theory of market equilibrium under conditions of risk', *Journal of Finance*, pp. 10–18.

Chapter 4

DEMAND ANALYSIS AND ESTIMATION

Introduction

In Chapter 2, the data regress facility of Lotus 1-2-3 (release 2 and above) was introduced. This has the potential for estimating demand functions from time-series and cross-section data, and from the results of experiments. The spreadsheet also provides a vehicle for forecasting through the investigation of trends in time-series data, with or without regression. For some purposes, however, specialist statistical packages enable a more detailed analysis to be undertaken, and reference will be made to these at appropriate junctures. The subject of forecasting receives more extensive treatment in Chapter 5.

4.1 Determinants of Demand

Before examining the contribution of the microcomputer to the estimation of demand relationships, it is useful to consider which variables might influence demand. Those which are likely to feature in many relationships include: the price of the product itself and the price of substitutes; the income of households; and the advertising and other promotions undertaken by companies. The demand for durable goods will probably be affected by credit conditions, including availability of loans and interest rates, particularly for expensive items such as houses and cars.

Sales of producers' goods, i.e. plant and machinery, are not only influenced by monetary conditions, but also by wider economic policy considerations — e.g. tax changes and investment incentives. Moreover, the demand for such goods is a derived demand, which means that firms tend to add to their productive capacity if there is an expectation of growth in sales of products which will utilise the capacity.

The microeconomic theory of demand places emphasis on the price—quantity

85

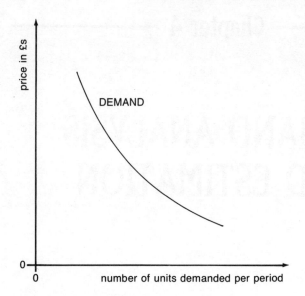

Figure 4.1 Downward-Sloping Demand Curve

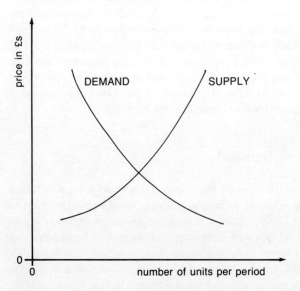

Figure 4.2 Intersection of Supply and Demand

relationship. Whilst it is assumed that in most cases the law of downward-sloping demand will apply taking the market as a whole (see Figure 4.1), the extent to which price variations may be exploited by management to influence demand is limited by the market structure in which the product is being sold. If the firm's output of a product is small relative to the demand in total, it will tend to be a price taker or follower and regard the prevailing price as given by the market.

In the theory of perfect competition, the price is determined impersonally by the interaction of supply and demand. Sales revenue to the firm is then quantity sold multiplied by a *given* price, the latter occurring at the intersection point of the market supply and demand curves.

Under monopoly conditions, the firm has discretion over price, and its sales revenue is then quantity sold multiplied by the price which it chooses. The firm must observe the inverse price—quantity relationship, where it applies, in the sense that attempts to sell more output will necessitate price reductions, and vice versa. Although few firms are strict monopolists, it has long been recognised in economic theory (Robinson 1933 and Chamberlain 1933) that some market power may be gained by firms in more competitive environments through the act of product differentiation, in the form of branding or packaging.

4.2 Marketing Concepts

The brand concept lies at the heart of demand analysis in marketing treatments of the subject. A brand may be defined as:

> an identifiable version of a product which a consumer could perceive as being distinctive in some way from other versions of the product.   (Watkins 1986, p. 3)

Thus Coca Cola and Pepsi Cola are rival brands of a soft drink; Heineken and Carlsberg are competing brands of lager.

In explaining choices between brands, increasing emphasis is being placed at both theoretical and practical levels on product characteristics. A leading influence in this direction has been Lancaster (1971). Whereas traditional microeconomics examined the choices between *commodities* in the pursuit of utility maximisation, the commodities in Lancaster's approach to consumer theory are no longer the immediate source of utility. Instead, consumers receive utility from *characteristics*, and it is the delivery of these by goods, or brands of goods, which shapes consumers' preferences.

In communicating the distinctive nature of the brand to consumers, characteristics such as the quality, shape, size, colour, package, name, after-sales service, reputation for reliability, promotions involving gifts or vouchers, are all emphasised by the marketing function of a business.

A fundamental marketing principle is that the 'marketing mix' — comprising product policy, promotional policy, pricing policy, and distribution policy — needs to be viewed as an integrated strategy, rather than as separate decision areas.

Different marketing-mix strategies tend to be conceived for different market segments classified, for example, on the basis of socio-economic group, or some other dimension such as business/leisure use. Segmentation is a phenomenon which appears in the economist's theory of price and is apparent in price discrimination activities of business — for example in airlines charging different fares for the business and tourist markets.

Devising the appropriate marketing mix for each segment is an important element of strategic planning. In developing a 'positioning strategy' a firm will aim for a market segment in which it can gain a differential advantage over its rivals, not just through the medium of price, but by any of the other elements in the marketing mix — e.g. better quality or design, more effective advertising, whatever research reveals are those attributes of the brand which are valued by the consumer and command his attention.

4.3   Multivariate Demand Functions and Elasticity

A demand function may be written in the form:

$$Q = f(X_1, X_2, X_3, X_4, X_5, X_6, \ldots)$$

For instance, the quantity (Q) consumed of a chocolate bar (per month) might depend on price (X_1), advertising expenditure (X_2), the weight of each chocolate bar (X_3), the value of holiday competition prizes (X_4), personal disposable income (X_5), and the price of rival brands (X_6).

The variables which are included will depend on whether Q (the quantity demanded per period of time) refers to the entire market for a product, or to the product (brand) of an individual firm. In the latter case, the price of rival brands will be particularly important, as will the advertising strategies of competitors.

The purpose of demand estimation is to find out which variables $X_1 \ldots X_n$ influence demand, to determine the strength of each influence, and to find an appropriate functional form — whether it be linear, something like:

$$Q = 2157.79 + 1.23A - 61.53P + 4.29D$$

A = advertising
P = real price
D = distribution coverage

(Croome and Horsfall 1982, *Demand for Kellogg's Super Noodles*)

— or exponential, for instance:

$$q = 29.36p^{-0.939}n^{0.910}g^{0.363}$$

p = average retail price of beer
n = average price index of other commodities
g = an index of the strength of beer

(Stone 1945, *Demand for Beer*)[1]

---

1.   Strictly speaking, the quantities Q and q in these regression equations are predicted quantities, and the usual notation would be $\hat{Q}$ and $\hat{q}$ (see Chapter 2).

Even if the demand function is not linear in variables, it may still be estimated using the regression facility of Lotus (or using any other linear multiple regression package) if the function is linear in **parameters**. For instance, Stone's estimated demand function may be written in logarithmic form:

log q = log 29.36 − 0.939 log p + 0.910 log n + 0.363 log g

which is linear in logs.

Another example of an equation which is linear in parameters, but not linear in variables, is a cubic or some other polynomial:

$$Q = A + B_1 X + B_2 X^2 + B_3 X^3$$

This equation, too, may be estimated with the aid of the usual packages, by regressing Q on the variable X itself, the square of X, and the cube of X.

Although decision analysis may warrant a full exploration of potential changes in several of the independent variables in a demand function, for many purposes a consideration of the impact of changes in just *one* variable is what is required. The concept of elasticity may then be of value.

The *elasticity* of a simple demand function, Q = f(P), relating quantity demanded to price, is the percentage change in the dependent variable Q brought about by a unit percentage change in the independent variable P. In a multivariate demand function:

$$Q = f(X_1, X_2, X_3, X_4, X_5, X_6, \ldots)$$

elasticity may be determined for each independent variable

$$\text{elasticity} = \frac{\%\ \text{change in Q}}{\%\ \text{change in X}} \quad \text{or} \quad \frac{\dfrac{\Delta Q}{Q}}{\dfrac{\Delta X}{X}} \quad \text{or} \quad \frac{\Delta Q}{\Delta X} \times \frac{X}{Q}$$

− where Q and X represent actual (for a *point* measure of elasticity) or average values (for an *arc* measure of elasticity) of Q and X, and ΔQ is the change in variable Q brought about by a change (ΔX) in variable X, while all other variables are held constant. If the variable X is price, elasticity will usually be negative − given the tendency for quantity and price to be inversely related.

It may be possible to measure the arc elasticity (average value of elasticity over a range) for an independent variable in the demand function without a full knowledge of that function. By making observations at two points in time and checking that all other influences have remained unchanged, an elasticity estimate may be obtained.

For instance, it was argued in the *Sunday Times* of 15 May 1988 that a price increase of 5 pence the previous February had forced down sales of the 'quality' dailies. Collectively, *The Times*, *The Daily Telegraph* and *The Independent* showed lost sales over a month of 38,200 from an average circulation of 1,952,000 −

i.e. 1.957%. The price increase of 5 pence from 25p to 30p represents an increase (on the average price in this range) of 18.182%. The price elasticity of demand is therefore $-1.975/18.182 = 0.108$. Strictly speaking, this should be written as -0.108 to show that a 1% *increase* in price brings about a *decrease* of 0.108% in quantity demanded.

This result indicates that demand is price inelastic (value less than unity), although all three newspapers raised their prices almost simultaneously, and an individual paper's attempt to raise price might meet with a more elastic response if its rivals were less obliging. Interestingly, the quality daily whose circulation fell most during that month was the *Guardian* which had not raised price, but whose layout had been completely revamped.

If the demand function is linear in variables and parameters:

$$Q = a + b_1 X_1 + b_2 X_2 + b_3 X_3 + \ldots b_n X_n$$

— the coefficient b_i of the demand determinant X_i, is its partial differential, and the point elasticity may be computed as $b_i . X_i'/Q'$.

For instance, in explaining the influence of advertising, price, and distribution coverage for monthly periods 14–27 after the launch of Kellogg's Super Noodles (see above), the following regression was obtained from time-series data:

$$\hat{Q} = 2157.79 + 1.23A - 61.53P + 4.29D$$

A = advertising — a cumulative measure with an assumed decay
    rate
P = real price
D = distribution coverage

If a point is taken (i.e. one set of values for the variables in this equation), at which price elasticity is to be measured, the calculation proceeds as follows:

If A is 125 units, P = 30 pence, and D is 65 (%), substitution in the estimated equation gives:

$$\hat{Q} = 2157.79 + 1.23(125) - 61.53(30) + 4.29(65)$$

$$= 744.49$$

This should lie fairly close to the observed value of Q (thousand units sold in the month) if the equation is to have good predictive power.

Price elasticity is now computed as

$$-61.53 \ P'/Q'$$
or $-61.53 \times 30/744.49$
$$= -2.48$$

Advertising elasticity works out as:

$$1.23 \times 125/744.49$$
$$= \underline{+0.20}$$

The investigators (Croome and Horsfall 1982) concluded that Super Noodles was 'advertising responsive' since, at the average level, the increase in sales generated by a 1% increase in advertising would comfortably exceed the cost of the latter. It was also seen as 'price sensitive', suggesting that a price cut could generate additional sales volume.

Although the elasticity measures in this study were computed from a statistical analysis of time series observations, some of the accompanying 'Advertising Case Histories', in the volume compiled by Broadbent (1984), illustrate how cross-sectional data from experimentation can monitor the effectiveness of advertising. For example, one commercial television region can be maintained as a control area, and the impact of advertising variations may be examined in the others. The same principle of direct market experimentation may be applied to price and other components of the marketing mix.

For forecasting purposes, it is often more convenient for the results in demand estimation to be presented as elasticities, particularly when the consequences of changes in a single variable are being assessed. Although elasticities sometimes change from point to point, as they would with the Super Noodles linear equation, there are special cases where elasticity remains constant, so long as the particular mathematical form holds good.

4.4 Elasticity and Logarithmic Functions

Although the choice of functional form is a complex matter, and it is tempting, therefore, to commence analysis with a simple linear regression, statisticians frequently find that a good fit to observed consumption data can be obtained using exponential or logarithmic functions. The example of the demand for beer in the UK in the inter-war period cited above (Stone 1945) provides such an illustration:

$$\hat{q} = 29.36p^{-0.939}n^{0.910}g^{0.363}$$

where $\hat{q}$ = predicted demand for beer (in bulk barrels)
          p = average retail price of beer
          n = average price index of other commodities
          g = an index of the strength of beer
(Y = national income was included in some of the relationships)

The equation may also be presented as a function which is linear in logs:

$$\log \hat{q} = \log 29.36 - 0.939 \log p + 0.910 \log n + 0.363 \log g$$

Despite its apparent complexity, the function indicates elasticity with respect to any of the independent variables without any further computation at all. Taking the equation in its exponential form, all we need do is read off the power to which each variable is raised in order to determine the relevant elasticity magnitude.

Thus the estimated price elasticity of demand is -0.939, a value which remains constant throughout the full range of prices for which this equation is valid. Alternatively, taking the logarithmic form and inspecting the coefficient of log p, the same answer is returned.

In fact, Stone conducted several different regressions on the time-series data, and obtained varying estimates for price elasticity, depending on which variables were included. In some equations, income was included, but its influence was negligible in explaining observed variations in consumption, and the income elasticity 'never far from zero'.

To show how regressions in logarithmic form may be conducted, more recent data for beer consumption in the UK (1970 to 1985) will be analysed using Lotus 1-2-3. Three stages are involved:

1. Transformation of the original data into natural logarithms using the built-in mathematical function @LN.
2. Regression of the logarithm of the dependent variable on the logarithms of the independent variables.
3. Prediction using the estimated regression coefficients (elasticities), and conversion back to the units in which quantity was originally expressed using the @EXP function.[2]

The relative price of beer (*relpr*) is based on retail price data for beer deflated by changes in the general retail price index. An index (1980 = 100) is used for this variable. All figures for consumption (*cons*) are in thousands of hectolitres. The income measure is personal disposable income (*PDI*) at 1980 prices in millions of pounds.

The data sets appear in columns B, D, and E of Table 4.1. These are transformed into natural logarithms using the function @LN. The first transformation appears in cell C5 into which the functional entry @LN(B5) is made. This may then be copied down column C. Similar operations produce columns F and G to give LOGPDI and LOGREL.

The data regress /DR command is given with the following ranges specified when prompted:

X-Range   F5..G20
Y-Range   C5..C20
Output-Range D25 (i.e. the output will lie beyond this cell)

---

2. Any result expressed in natural logarithms ($\log_e$) can be transformed back using @EXP. That is why this base was used, rather than base 10 in stage 1. The latter, if required may be obtained by using the Lotus function @LOG.

Table 4.1   Regression with Variables in Logarithmic Form

	A	B	C	D	E	F	G	H	I
1									
2				1980 prices					
3	YEAR	cons	LOGCONS	PDI	relpr	LOGPDI	LOGREL	LOGPRED	PRED
4									
5	1970	56366	10.93962	122554	105.03	11.7163	4.65424	10.95185	57060
6	71	58562	10.97784	124117	103.58	11.7289	4.64031	10.96596	57870
7	72	59975	11.00168	134559	101.94	11.8097	4.62440	11.01251	60628
8	73	62637	11.04511	143186	96.25	11.8718	4.56695	11.07522	64552
9	74	63988	11.06645	142105	93.03	11.8643	4.53295	11.09195	65641
10	75	65627	11.09174	142832	92.73	11.8694	4.52966	11.09625	65924
11	76	66531	11.10542	142744	94.99	11.8688	4.55379	11.08162	64966
12	77	65891	11.09575	139549	97.01	11.8461	4.57480	11.05873	63496
13	78	67802	11.12434	149654	97.22	11.9160	4.57699	11.08954	65483
14	79	68248	11.13090	158031	95.57	11.9705	4.55982	11.12476	67830
15	80	65490	11.08965	160297	100.00	11.9847	4.60517	11.10434	66459
16	81	62317	11.03998	158110	106.31	11.9710	4.66639	11.06163	63680
17	82	60921	11.01733	157726	110.38	11.9686	4.70392	11.03819	62206
18	83	62232	11.03862	161301	114.50	11.9910	4.74061	11.02668	61493
19	84	62082	11.03621	165671	117.66	12.0177	4.76780	11.02279	61254
20	85	61507	11.02690	170124	119.55	12.0442	4.78372	11.02550	61421
21									
22									
23									
24									
25					Regression Output:				
26				Constant			8.3380		
27				Std Err of Y Est			0.0226		
28				R Squared			0.8445		
29				No. of Observations			16		
30				Degrees of Freedom			13		
31									
32				X Coefficient(s)	0.4593	−0.5946			
33				Std Err of Coef.	0.0673	0.0793			
34									
35									

Sources: CSO; Department of Employment.

The intercept option is not used, unless one wishes to force the regression through the origin. So the next menu choice is **G** for Go, and the regression output then appears as shown. The X-Coefficients for the transformed variables (0.4593 and −0.5946) are the estimates for income and price elasticity, respectively.

Initial impressions are that both income and price elasticities are significant, when one compares the X-Coefficients with their standard errors. Both coefficients (ignoring the minus sign for the transformed price variable) exceed twice the standard error by a comfortable margin, so that it is unnecessary to compare with the precise *t*-statistic. R squared is 0.8445, which means that the transformed income and price variables together account for nearly 85% of the variation in the (logarithm) of beer consumption.

Note on the Use of the *t* Distribution

The regression coefficients that are computed will vary from one data sample to the next. Each coefficient will be distributed as *t*, with the number of degrees of freedom and standard error shown in the regression output. A 95% confidence interval for estimating the (true) value of each parameter is provided by $b \pm t_{0.025} \times$ SE (standard error of the coefficient). Thus the true value of the price elasticity of beer, ignoring the minus sign, will lie in the range:

$$0.5946 \pm (2.160 \times 0.0793)$$
i.e. 0.5946 ± 0.1713
with a probability of 0.95

The statistic $t_{0.025}$ for 13 degrees of freedom is 2.160 as shown in this calculation, thus refining the approximate factor of 2 mentioned above.

There are two types of related significance test using the t distribution, which may be conducted on the regression coefficients. One may test the hypothesis that the parameter is significantly different from zero, which requires a two-tail test.[3] Otherwise, one may test the hypothesis that the parameter is greater than (or less than) zero, using a one-tail test.

Using the t-statistic, one may test that the elasticities which have been estimated in the above exercise are significantly **different** from zero with a two-tail test. The figures for the coefficient/standard error ratios are 6.8247 for income and $(-)7.4981$ for price. The required t value is 2.160 and, since both ratios exceed this figure, the estimates of both elasticities are significant at the 5% level (i.e. two-tail test using $t_{0.025}$).

For a one-tail test, the required statistic is $t_{0.050}$ for 13 degrees of freedom, using a significance level of 5%. Tables provide a figure for $t = 1.771$ for this level. Although the two-tail test is more common in regression analysis, it is sometimes argued that the one-tail test is more appropriate when evaluating price and income elasticities, since the negative and positive signs are expected to arise as a matter of course for many products.

(A useful summary of hypothesis testing on the regression coefficients is given in Kvanli *et al.* (1986, p. 465) and in Koutsoyiannis (1981, Chapter 5) — the latter explaining the rationale for the one-tail test when the regression involves economic variables.)

Interpretation of the Elasticities

Both coefficients have a numerical value which is less than one, which indicates that beer is both price and income inelastic. Although the example is only illustrative, being restricted to just two predictors, the result for price elasticity is not out of line with other recent studies — e.g. Reekie and Blight (1982) — who estimated price elasticity from a linear regression to be -0.423. The study used monthly UK data for the period 1974–1978. As those authors point out, it is

---

3. In hypothesis testing, the analyst considers the pair of hypotheses for a two-tail test: Null hypothesis *Ho:* $B = 0$ [i.e. true (population) coefficient is zero — independent variable has no influence.] Alternative hypothesis *Ha:* $B \neq 0$. *Ho* is rejected if the computed t ratio exceeds the required t value (from tables).

only the generic product beer which can be regarded as price insensitive. *Individual* brewers cannot expect to raise prices without suffering a fall in volume, unless their rivals can be persuaded to follow suit.

Reekie's income elasticity is much lower than the one computed here: 0.065 as against 0.459. The latter figure is almost certainly an over-estimate of the influence of income, and has emerged because other significant variables have been omitted from the regression. In addition to the two predictors used in the above example, the Reekie study included advertising expenditure, temperature, trend and seasonal variables, and prices of other alcoholic drinks.

Predicted and Actual Consumption

The regression shown in Table 4.1 can be used to predict given values of relative price and income. The prediction will be in terms of the log of consumption as computed from the equation:

predicted LOGCONS = 8.3380 + 0.4593 LOGPDI − 0.5946 LOGREL (LOGPRED)

For the observations already present in Table 4.1, predictions of logcons (labelled LOGPRED in column H of the worksheet) can be made by substituting in this equation, using the appropriate cell addresses to create a spreadsheet formula. Thus, for 1970, the formula:

+ $G$26 + $F$32*F5 + $G$32*G5

is entered in cell H5 of the worksheet. This can be converted to a prediction with the logarithmic transformation reversed by entering @EXP(H5) in cell I5. Copying H5 and I5 to other locations in their respective columns enables predicted consumption to be computed for all of the original observations.

The comparison of predicted and observed (the difference being 'the residual') is naturally important in order to test how well the demand model fits the data. Despite the significant contribution of each variable, and the overall explanatory power of the relationship (R squared almost 85%), further tests on the residuals are desirable, as will be seen when the phenomenon of 'autocorrelation' is explored.

If the user is satisfied with the performance of the historical 'predictions', the model can be used to forecast, by substituting new values for price and income, and computing the predicted consumption. Having established formulae within the worksheet in columns H and I for prediction, it is a simple matter to extend their application to new values in an appropriate location of the worksheet.

Alternatively, having obtained elasticity estimates, one may provide forecasts which relate to a change in a *single* variable − e.g. a price rise of 1% in the price of beer, relative to the retail price index, would cause consumption to decline by 0.5946 of 1%, according to the computed coefficient. To the extent that the brewing industry can exercise some control over the price of beer, the forecast is conditional on decisions being taken, and it thus provides a test as to whether proposed options are desirable. Income is a rather different matter, not in any sense being a controllable variable but one, nevertheless, which is seen as an influence in most forecasts.

4.5 Extensions to the Elasticity Concept

Competitive and Complementary Relationships

In practice, the sales of one product cannot be predicted satisfactorily without a consideration of related products. Demand is said to be *competitive*, if the products are substitutes, when *raising* the price of one of the products causes an *increase* in the consumption of the other product, the price of the latter remaining unchanged.

Demand is described as *complementary* if an increase in the consumption of a product causes an increase in the consumption of the associated product. A price *reduction* for product X (causing consumption of X to increase) thus *increases* the quantity purchased of product Y, if X and Y are complements.

In a study by Rea and Lage (1978) the demand for international telephone services, in one of the regressions for the period 1969–73, was estimated as:

$$\log TP = 6.609 + 0.062 \log TRADE - 1.718 \log PTP + 0.353 \log PTX$$
$$\qquad\qquad\qquad\qquad\qquad\qquad\qquad\text{(price)}\qquad\text{(price telex)}$$

$$- 1.425 \log PTG + 2.656 \log DISINC$$
$$\text{(price telegrams)}\qquad\text{(real household income)}$$

(Each independent variable is measured in real terms, using a price index as a deflator.)

As well as yielding estimates for the price elasticity (elastic at -1.718) and income elasticity (elastic at 2.656), estimates for the cross-price elasticities with both telex and telegrams are given in the coefficients of their respective logs. Thus, cross-elasticity between telephone calls and the price of telegrams is -1.425. This is elastic, and the negative sign is indicative of a complementary interrelationship. The cross-price elasticity between telephone calls and telex is positive (inelastic at $+0.353$), and suggestive of a competitive interrelationship. The authors were unable, however, to regard the latter interrelationship as being firmly established at the usual significance levels.

Relationships between Price and Advertising

Firms use a variety of methods to determine advertising expenditure, including a simple rule of thumb that advertising should be set at a predetermined percentage of sales revenue (past, present, or expected). Other considerations include 'affordability' and 'matching competitors' (see Piercy 1985, 1986, 1987).

The Dorfman—Steiner (1954) theorem shows that a firm wishing to maximise profits in the short run will set advertising and price in such a way that the advertising-to-sales ratio is equal to the advertising elasticity/price elasticity ratio.

$$A/PQ = E_A/E_P$$

where A is advertising expenditure and PQ is the sales revenue (price × quantity) and E_A, E_P are the elasticities, with the minus sign for price elasticity removed.

Suppose that a firm sells a breakfast cereal, and estimates the demand function with the aid of a spreadsheet package. It uses a linear-in-logs regression which gives a significant estimate of price elasticity of 2.0, and advertising elasticity of 0.16. These figures would imply an advertising-to-sales ratio of 0.16/2.0, which is 8%.

Although the Dorfman—Steiner theorem appears to give a precise result for firms wishing to use a percentage of sales formula to set their advertising budgets, it requires that the firm is able to determine a marketing mix (including a product quality variable) which is optimal as a complete package. The sales revenue to which the percentage is applied must also be optimal in terms of consistency with profit maximisation.

In addition to the problem of achieving overall optimisation, there is the difficulty of accommodating dynamic effects such as high initial advertising judged to be necessary to penetrate the market, or price promotions to boost demand in anticipation of future benefits.[4] Another problem is interdependence between firms, which means that the result has to be interpreted either on an assumption of no response from rivals, or on the basis of an optimal policy for the whole market, assuming collusion.

Nevertheless, for a mature market where the struggle for market shares may be less urgent, and interdependence and dynamic considerations may be less important, the rule does offer a guide for the determination of the advertising budget, provided that the elasticities are relatively stable.

As an application of the Dorfman—Steiner theorem, Cowling (1972) used estimates of price and advertising elasticities (from 'loglinear' relationships) for the following UK markets: cars, tractors, margarine, coffee and toothpaste. The results which conformed most closely to the theorem's predicted ratios were for margarine and toothpaste:

margarine elasticity ratio 0.138   adv/sales ratio 0.098
toothpaste elasticity ratio 0.120   adv/sales ratio 0.153

The advertising/sales ratios for the durable goods markets were, however, much lower than their computed elasticity ratios, suggesting either non-optimal behaviour

---

4. There is a dynamic analogue to the Dorfman—Steiner theorem, but this only tackles advertising.

in those markets, or peculiarities of the demand for durable goods (see Cowling 1972, pp. 102−3) which render them less suitable for the Dorfman−Steiner treatment.

4.6 Problems of Econometrics

The regression facilities available in Lotus 1-2-3 and other software packages may be employed in a variety of applications, in scientific and medical enquiries as well as the business and economic issues confronted in this text. Although much of the discussion here has been of relevance to all such uses, the application of regression analysis to the economic and business areas − the subject of 'econometrics' − has to tackle a number of problems which relate to the idiosyncracies of data analysis in this setting.

The multiple regression technique estimates parameters for the function:

$$Y = a + b_1X_1 + b_2X_2 + b_3X_3 + \ldots b_nX_n$$

Although the computer can perform such regressions as have been described very quickly, it is advisable to discuss the results with a competent statistician or econometrician before taking any important decisions based on such analysis. The issues which an expert might consider in the context of demand estimation would typically include: the identification problem, multicollinearity, autocorrelation and heteroscedasticity.

The *identification problem* arises because the data which is analysed in demand studies is the quantity purchased, rather than the quantity demanded. The difference in meaning becomes clearer if one goes back to the market supply and demand curves (Figure 4.2). The point of intersection in that diagram, apart from indicating the equilibrium price, shows the corresponding quantity. This is both the quantity demanded and the quantity supplied. The intersection point is in effect the solution to a pair of simultaneous equations, rather than an isolated point on a demand curve.

In Figure 4.3 there are four such intersection points, which result from changes in supply conditions over time. If demand conditions have remained fairly stable over the same period, the four intersection points will give rise to a scatter which starts to mark out the underlying demand function. Remember that the observer does not yet know what the underlying curves are: all he sees is a time series of quantity−price combinations which he may subject to regression analysis in an attempt to identify a demand curve.

However, suppose that, instead of the curves shown in Figure 4.3, we have a single supply curve, and several movements in the original demand curve. A scatter of points will result, but now the fitted line will have an upward slope, and will correspond more to the underlying supply function.

In order to isolate the simultaneous relationships, it is necessary to include the variables which have caused the shifts in either set of curves. This reinforces

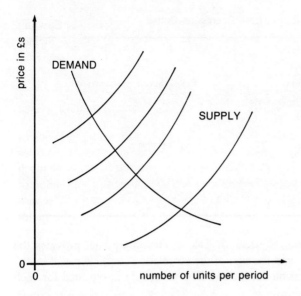

Figure 4.3 The Identification Problem

the need to obtain more than just quantity—price data, and to use multiple rather than simple regression techniques. A large division of the subject matter of econometrics is concerned with simultaneous equation estimation methods, but these are beyond the scope of this book.

Multicollinearity is a problem often encountered when using time-series data in multiple regression. For a regression to be able to account for variations in the dependent variable, it is necessary for the separate influences of the independent variables to be detected. If these explanatory variables are highly correlated, the estimates of the coefficients will be unreliable, and their standard errors will become large.

Removal of all but one set of the intercorrelated variables is sometimes attempted in order to produce more reliable estimates. This procedure not only requires statistical expertise, but a sound understanding of the nature of the model under investigation. Thus, while the elimination of a variable, say household income, may improve a regression in terms of alleviating the multicollinearity problem, it may not be justifiable on theoretical grounds if there is good reason to believe that the variable does have an influence.

Another way of approaching the problem is to obtain separate estimates from cross-section studies to facilitate the separation of parameters.

The presence of multicollinearity may be detected by intercorrelating the independent variables of the regression. The regression facility in Lotus 1-2-3 permits a rather tedious computation, indicated in Table 4.2, conducted by taking variables in pairs, and running data regress. The correlation coefficient is R, but

Table 4.2 Correlation Coefficient from Regression Output

```
          D       E       F       G       H       I       J       K
34
35              (LOGPDI on LOGREL)
36
37            Regression Output:              Correlation coefficient:
38  Constant              9.3788
39  Std Err of Y Est      0.0896
40  R Squared             0.2140                    0.4626   <---- @SQRT(G40)
41  No. of Observations       16
42  Degrees of Freedom        14
43
44  X Coefficient(s)  0.5451        <----- sign is positive
45  Std Err of Coef.  0.2792
46
47
48
49
50
```

the regression output yields R squared. Taking the square root provides the required numerical value, and the sign of the correlation coefficient will be the same as that of the regression coefficient. The procedure is repeated for each pair of independent variables.

Most statistical packages, such as **Minitab**TM, will produce a 'correlation matrix' to supplement the regression output if required. This produces a complete set of correlation coefficients in one operation, and facilitates considerably the examination of intercorrelation between variables when several independent variables feature in the regression. The correlation matrix for the demand-for-beer regression in Table 4.3 shows R = 0.463 between predictors, which is below the level of 0.7 often regarded as critical.

Heteroscedasticity may appear in the form of increased errors arising (deviations of the scatter about the regression line) as the size of the explanatory variable(s) increases. It is often encountered in cross-section data — for example, in conducting a household expenditure survey we may find that the high-income groups exhibit a greater variation of spending on restaurant meals than is displayed by poorer groups, simply because there is more scope for behaviour differences.

The problem may be apparent from inspection of a scatter diagram in a two-variable regression, or from an examination of the size of the residuals in relation to each independent variable in a multiple regression. At that stage it may be possible to eliminate the problem by taking the *fraction* of income spent on meals, in the case just cited, rather than the *absolute* expenditure of each household.

Table 4.3 Correlation Matrix

```
              LOGCONS    LOGPDI
LOGPDI         0.414
LOGREL        -0.536     0.463
```

If this, or any of the other problems discussed here, persists, the model's reliability for prediction purposes will be lessened. If heteroscedasticity is not accommodated, predictions to levels at the upper end of the data range will be subject to increasing error.

Autocorrelation is a problem associated with regressions which utilise time-series data. The least-squares regression model requires that there should not be a regular pattern to the residuals about the fitted line. If, however, the deviations for successive observations exhibit a systematic pattern, then auto-correlation is present.

Positive autocorrelation means that observations above the line tend to be followed by observations in the same region. Then a shift below the line may occur with successive observations again being associated. (For an illustration of positive autocorrelation, see the Appendix to this chapter, in particular Figure 4.4(a).) Negative autocorrelation means that an observation above the line of best fit will be followed by one below the line, then above, then below, and so on. The problem may result from trends and cycles which are present in economic variables, or from the omission of explanatory variables from the regression. The fitting of an inappropriate function to the data may also cause autocorrelation, and logarithmic forms may be attempted if autocorrelation appears in the standard linear regression.

A test for autocorrelation is the Durbin–Watson *d* statistic (see Kvanli *et al*. 1986, p. 681). It may be computed from the Lotus spreadsheet with the aid of an add-on program, *Spreadsheet Regression*^{TM}, which will provide a range of diagnostic statistics.[5]

Alternatively, a specialist package for statistical analysis may be preferred to the spreadsheet, once this level of complexity is reached. Because most statistical packages will compute the Durbin–Watson statistic, it is useful to demonstrate how that facility may be employed in the context of the example already developed. In Table 4.4, the original 1970–85 demand-for-beer regression is re-worked using Minitab.[6]

The range of possible values for the Durbin–Watson statistic is from 0 to 4, with an 'ideal' value of 2. When the latter prevails, the errors are uncorrelated. As the statistic approaches zero, increasing positive autocorrelation is experienced, and at 0.82 (highlighted at the bottom of Table 4.4) it appears to be present in this regression. Between 2 and 4, increasing negative autocorrelation is indicated. (A table of critical values for the Durbin–Watson statistic is given in Kvanli *et al*. (1986, p. 833), with instructions for use on p. 682.)

---

5. Registered trademark of The Background Development Company. This product enables users of Lotus 1A and Symphony to enjoy a full regression facility.
6. Use of this package will be described more fully in Chapter 5. The subcommand 'DW' can be used in conjunction with 'REGRESS' in Minitab. Other packages deliver the Durbin–Watson statistic as part of their standard regression output, including one called *Polaris* (developed by GOODE SOFTWARE of Cardiff). This inexpensive package also offers correlation matrices, and provides a wide range of statistical tests and mathematical utilities.

Table 4.4   Minitab Regression Output with DW Statistic

```
The regression equation is
LOGCONS = 8.34 + 0.459 LOGPDI - 0.595 LOGREL

Predictor         Coef         Stdev       t-ratio          p
Constant        8.3380        0.7100         11.74      0.000
LOGPDI          0.45929       0.06728         6.83      0.000
LOGREL         -0.59458       0.07927        -7.50      0.000

s = 0.02256      R-sq = 84.4%      R-sq(adj) = 82.1%

Analysis of Variance

SOURCE           DF           SS            MS           F          p
Regression        2      0.035929      0.017964      35.30     0.000
Error            13      0.006616      0.000509
Total            15      0.042545

SOURCE           DF        SEQ SS
LOGPDI            1      0.007298
LOGREL            1      0.028631

Durbin-Watson statistic = 0.82
```

Remedies for autocorrelation are given in most statistical and econometrics texts. Kvanli *et al.* list some of these (op. cit. pp. 683–4). A detailed treatment of the subject is given in Koutsoyiannis (1981, Chapter 10), in which various systematic procedures for correcting autocorrelated errors are described.

The predictive power of a model is impaired by the presence of autocorrelation, and one would have reservations about using the demand-for-beer model as estimated in this chapter as a basis for preparing forecasts. The prime test for autocorrelation is the Durbin–Watson statistic, and a template for computing this is a highly desirable accessory when using Lotus 1-2-3.

Alternatively, when the user has conducted preliminary regressions within Lotus 1-2-3, he may prefer to transfer the data to a specialist statistical package when more detailed analysis is required. Most specialist packages recognise the advantages conferred by spreadsheet analysis and permit the transfer of data to and from Lotus 1-2-3.

APPENDIX: Illustration of Autocorrelation and its Correction

In the demand-for-beer model developed in this chapter, autocorrelation was not only a problem in the regression for the period 1970–85, but also for the period

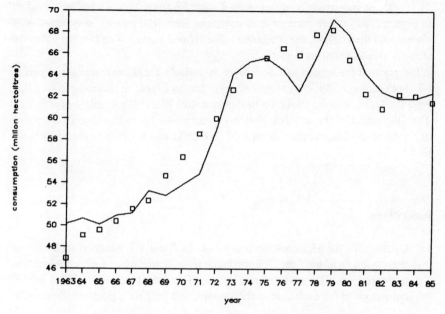

Figure 4.4(a)   Actual and Predicted Beer Consumption

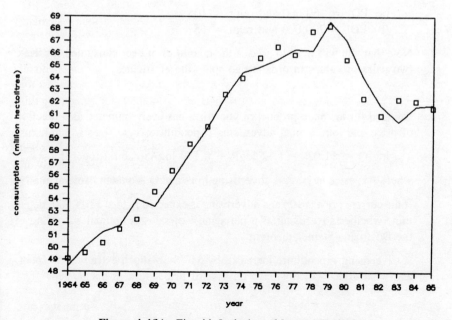

Figure 4.4(b)   Fit with Inclusion of Lagged Variables

1963−85, as shown overleaf in Figure 4.4(a). Positive autocorrelation is evident in Figure 4.4(a) where successive observations (scatter of points) lie systematically above, and then below, the predicted values (fitted curve). The Durbin−Watson statistic is computed as 0.69.

Inclusion of the lagged variables *price in period t-1* and *consumption in period t-1* (both as logarithmic transformations), for each year in the sample (starting with 1964), yielded the fit shown in Figure 4.4(b) (the PDI variable was omitted). The alleviation of the autocorrelation is confirmed by an increase in the value of the Durbin−Watson statistic to 1.72, which is much closer to the ideal value of 2.

Exercises

1. Use the data for beer consumption set out in Table 4.1, but conduct the linear regression *without* the logarithmic transformations: i.e. consumption regressed on PDI and relative price. Tabulate predicted against actual consumption for each year in the sample, and prepare a graph of the results.

2. From the X Coefficients shown in the regression output of your solution to exercise 1, find the income and price elasticities at the points:

    (a) PDI = 160,000 and relpr = 105
    (b) PDI = 200,000 and relpr = 65

    Note that you will need to predict the quantities of beer consumed for these two pairs of values in order to compute the elasticities.

3. Demand for the main product of your firm has been estimated as a function of price and total annual advertising expenditure:

    $\log Q = 11.02 - 1.12 \log P + 0.179 \log A$ (natural logarithms)

    where P is price in £s. A is advertising in £s and Q is quantity sold annually.

    If the current price is 10p and advertising is expected to total £105,000, determine whether advertising as a percentage of sales is optimal according to the Dorfman−Steiner theorem.

    If advertising expenditure increases by 5%, how much extra will be spent, and what effect will this have on sales if prices remain unchanged?

4. In a sample of 10 leading companies in Europe, the turnover and profit figures are as follows:

Company	Turnover (£m)	Profit (£m)
1	60,210	6,220
2	35,800	3,340
3	22,730	1,750
4	20,610	180
5	18,320	530
6	17,460	890
7	15,240	1,130
8	15,070	1,310
9	14,820	580
10	14,410	1,380

Calculate the average ratio of profits to turnover in this sample, express profit as a function of turnover, and determine the correlation coefficient.

References and Further Reading

Broadbent, S. (ed.) (1984) *Twenty Advertising Case Histories*, Holt, Rinehart and Winston. This collection includes the following study cited in the text: Croome, P. and Horsfall, J.
— 'Advertising: key to the success of Kellogg's Super Noodles'.

Chamberlin, E.H. (1948) *The Theory of Monopolistic Competition*, 6th edn, Harvard University Press.

Cowling, K. (ed.) (1972) *Market Structure and Corporate Behaviour: Theory and Empirical Analysis of the Firm*, Gray-Mills, London. This includes Cowling's own study, 'Optimality in firms' advertising policies: an empirical analysis'.

Dorfman, R. and Steiner, P.O. (1954) 'Optimal advertising and optimal quality', *American Economic Review*, pp. 826–36.

Dorward, N. (1987) *The Pricing Decision: Economic Theory and Business Practice*, Harper and Row. (Chapter 6 of Dorward's book provides a useful summary of demand analysis and estimation, including examples of both linear and exponential demand functions.)

Koutsoyiannis, A. (1977) *Theory of Econometrics*, 2nd edn, Macmillan (repr. 1981).

Kvanli, A.H., Guynes, C.S. and Pavur, R.J. (1986) *Introduction to Business Statistics: A Computer Integrated Approach*, West Publishing Company, St. Paul, Minnesota.

Lancaster, K.J. (1971) *Consumer Demand: A New Approach*, Columbia University Press.

MacArthur, B. (1988) 'Boosted prices force sales down', *Sunday Times*, 15th May, p. C6.

Piercy, N. (1985) 'What *really* determines advertising and marketing budgets?', *ADMAP*, December, pp. 612–18.

Piercy, N. (1986) 'The politics of setting an advertising budget', *International Journal of Advertising*, pp. 281–305.

Piercy, N. (1987) 'The marketing budgeting process: marketing management implications', *Journal of Marketing*, October, pp. 45–59.

Pokorny, M. (1987) *An Introduction to Econometrics*, Basil Blackwell.

Rea, J.D. and Lage, G.M. (1978) 'Estimates of demand elasticities for international telecommunications services', *Journal of Industrial Economics*, pp. 363–81.

Reekie, W.D. and Blight, C. (1982) 'An analysis of the demand for beer in the United Kingdom', *Journal of Industrial Affairs*, pp. 45–9.

Robinson, J. (1933) *The Economics of Imperfect Competition*, Macmillan.

Stone, R. (1945) 'The analysis of market demand', *Journal of the Royal Statistical Society*, pp. 286–391.

Watkins, T. (1986) *The Economics of the Brand: A Marketing Analysis*, McGraw-Hill.

Chapter 5

DEMAND FORECASTING

5.1 Prediction Using Statistical Methods

The main purpose in obtaining estimates of regression coefficients and/or elasticities is to be able to predict or forecast. Although one tends to think of prediction and forecasting as virtually synonymous, there are subtle differences in meaning.

For one thing, a prediction need not be concerned about the future. It is often used in the sense of 'confirmation' — such as when one inserts previously observed values of the independent variables, as they occurred in the past, into a regression equation. The predictive power of any model may be judged in these terms and, if satisfactory, it might then be employed for forecasting purposes — i.e. projection into the future.

Whatever the nature of the prediction, be it confirmation of the past or a forecast of the future, it is unsatisfactory to quote a point estimate. A regression does not, in general, yield a precise relationship, and part of the variation in the dependent variable remains unexplained (revealed by the presence of residuals). Predictions need to include a confidence interval or prediction interval, to allow for the unexplained variation in the model.

In the next section, predictions for a multivariate example will be obtained, but in the remainder of this section, predictions and their intervals will be developed for the 'Ultrasnaps' two-variable regression which appeared in Chapter 2.

Using Lotus 1-2-3 for Prediction

In Table 5.1 data for colour film processing in 10 holiday resorts is analysed by *Ultrasnaps* using Lotus 1-2-3.

Having examined the regression output, Ultrasnaps is satisfied to use the equation:

106

Table 5.1 Prediction with Lotus 1-2-3

```
        A           B              C            D          E          F
1
2                   Y              X1
3                   Daily          No. of                  Predicted
4       Resort      Orders         Visitors                Orders
5                                  (000's)
6       1           210            9                        199
7       2           235            10                       210
8       3           117            3                        135
9       4           184            8                        189
10      5           230            12                       232
11      6           403            26                       382
12      7           298            22                       339
13      8           314            20                       317
14      9           318            20                       317
15      10          275            15                       264
16
17                  MEAN OF X      14.5
18                  N*var -->      480.5
19
20                  Regression Output:
21      Constant                                102.87
22      Std Err of Y Est                         20.43
23      R Squared                                 0.943
24      No. of Observations                      10
25      Degrees of Freedom                        8
26
27      X Coefficient(s)           10.73
28      Std Err of Coef.            0.93
29
30      PREDICTED MEAN Yo          285.22  +/-             15.84
31      FOR Xo =                           lower           269.38
32          17                             upper           301.05
33
34      PREDICTED INDIV. Yo        285.22  +/-             49.70
35      FOR Xo =                           lower           235.51
36          17                             upper           334.92
37
38                       t.025 is 2.306   for 8 degrees of freedom
39
40
29-Oct-88  06:57 PM
```

mean (cell E30)

*** $2.306 * \$D\$22 * @SQRT(1/\$D\$24 + (A32 - \$C\$17)^2/\$C\$18)$

individual (cell E34)

***** $2.306 * \$D\$22 * @SQRT(1 + 1/\$D\$24 + (A36 - \$C\$17)^2/\$C\$18)$

$$\hat{Y} = 102.87 + 10.73 X$$

for prediction purposes

In particular, the firm intends to install processing facilities in another resort which accommodates 17,000 visitors. In order to plan capacity, an estimate of daily orders is required.

All this requires is substitution of $X = 17$ in the above equation, so that:

predicted orders $(\hat{Y})$ = 102.87 + (10.73 × 17) = 285. Cell C30 contains a spreadsheet formula which provides this result.

Beyond this cell, predictions are given in a more elaborate form. They now appear as two *ranges* of values, rather than as a point estimate of 285.22 orders. Both ranges comprise this estimate ± a particular figure, with the second range (labelled Predicted Individual value) being substantially larger than the first (labelled Predicted Mean value).

The interval for the predicted mean value provides an answer to the question: 'What *average* daily sales would emerge from processing units in a sample of resorts which have 17,000 visitors?' However, the question which Ultrasnaps is asking is rather different: 'How many orders will a processing service in an *individual* resort with 17,000 visitors expect to handle?' In answering the former question, a smaller interval can be cited because an average is more predictable than an individual value.

It is usual to quote a 95% confidence interval − i.e. a range within which the actual value has a 0.95 probability of resting. The first step in constructing either type of interval is to take the t distribution and find $t_{0.025}$ from statistical tables for 8 degrees of freedom (the latter indicated in the regression output).[1] The appropriate t value for 95% confidence is 2.306 and it is used as indicated in the formulae displayed at the bottom of Table 5.1 for cells E30 and E34.

It is not the intention here to explain the derivation of the relationships which lie behind this display, but the source of some of the terms will be clarified. Take, first of all, the interval for the predicted mean in cell E30. After the 2.306, from the t distribution, we have the cell address $D22. This is the standard error of Y estimate from the regression output. In fact it is the only part of the Lotus regression output which has not yet been used directly.

Moving on, inside the @SQRT bracket, is the cell address $D$24 which is simply the number of observations. Further on is A32 which is the cell used to hold X_0 − the particular value of the independent variable for the prediction (i.e. 17 here). $C$17 is a cell used to compute the mean value of X, and $C$18 holds the variance of X (using the @VAR function), multiplied by the number of observations (N).

The interval in which we are really interested (cell E34) is similarly constructed but contains a one plus (1+) the previous contents of the @SQRT bracket, thus enlarging the interval. This is the only point to note in comparing the formula for cell E34 with that for cell E30. The interval which this formula yields for an individual X_0 is ±49.70. This gives a prediction in the range 235.51 to 334.92 at the 95% confidence level.

The two types of prediction interval are illustrated in Figure 5.1. The central line is the original regression line of best fit which we use to obtain point predictions. Prediction of a mean value creates an interval bounded by the two sets of symbols, and an individual predicted value lies in the wider band delineated by the two outer curves. The interval (of either type) is at its narrowest around

---

1. For a 90% confidence interval, one would take $t_{0.05}$.

Table 5.2(b)   Minitab Regression Output with Predictions

```
MTB > REGRESS C1 ON 1 PREDICTOR IN C2;
SUBC> PREDICT FOR C2;
SUBC> PREDICT 17.

The regression equation is
ORDERS = 103 + 10.7 VISITORS

Predictor        Coef        Stdev     t-ratio        p
Constant        102.87        14.98       6.87      0.000
VISITORS       10.7263       0.9320      11.51      0.000

s = 20.43       R-sq = 94.3%        R-sq(adj) = 93.6%

Analysis of Variance

SOURCE          DF           SS           MS         F         p
Regression       1         55283        55283     132.46    0.000
Error            8          3339          417
Total            9         58622

Unusual Observations
Obs.VISITORS      ORDERS        Fit Stdev.Fit   Residual   St.Resid
  7     22.0      298.00     338.85      9.52     -40.85      -2.26R

R denotes an obs. with a large st. resid.

     Fit   Stdev.Fit         95% C.I.            95% P.I.
  199.41      8.25    ( 180.38, 218.43)   ( 148.59, 250.22)
  210.13      7.70    ( 192.37, 227.90)   ( 159.77, 260.49)
  135.05     12.51    ( 106.18, 163.91)   (  79.79, 190.31)
  188.68      8.86    ( 168.25, 209.11)   ( 137.32, 240.04)
  231.58      6.87    ( 215.74, 247.43)   ( 181.87, 281.30)
  381.75     12.51    ( 352.89, 410.62)   ( 326.49, 437.01)
  338.85      9.52    ( 316.89, 360.80)   ( 286.86, 390.83)
  317.39      8.25    ( 298.37, 336.42)   ( 266.58, 368.21)
  317.39      8.25    ( 298.37, 336.42)   ( 266.58, 368.21)
  263.76      6.48    ( 248.82, 278.70)   ( 214.33, 313.20)

  285.22      6.87    ( 269.37, 301.06)   ( 235.50, 334.93)


MTB > STOP
```

rather than by transfer from Lotus) for the Ultrasnaps example, the user types in READ C1 C2, so that the data for 'Orders' and 'No. of Visitors' will be placed in the first two columns of the worksheet.

The data is typed in when the prompt DATA> appears, thus:

DATA> 210 9 and then ENTER   (leave one space between the two numbers)
DATA> 235 10
etc. as shown in Table 5.2(a)

When all 10 rows of data have been entered, the DATA prompt appears again, but this time the command END is used to terminate data entry. After pressing the ENTER key, the words 10 ROWS READ appear on the screen.

When the MTB> prompt appears, it is useful to continue input with a NAME for each column, as shown in Table 5.2(a). To display the columns, the command PRINT C1 C2 is used, and the data appears with the titles and the row numbers. If corrections are necessary, these may be effected using the command LET. Thus, if an error had been made in column 1, row 10, this could be corrected by using: LET C1(10) = 275.

DELETE ERASE and INSERT are also useful commands for modifying the contents of the worksheet. The reader is advised to learn more about these from a Minitab handbook such as Ryan *et al.* (1985), or Miller (1988).

Once the data has been checked, the file may be saved under a suitable name – e.g. 'ULTRA' which should be enclosed by single quotes as shown in Table 5.2(a)

Table 5.2(b) sets out the regression procedure in the first 3 lines, followed by the output. Various forms of wording are acceptable for the REGRESS command, but it must be clear as to which variable is being regressed (dependent variable) on which predictor(s) (independent variables). The command as shown:

REGRESS C1 ON 1 PREDICTOR IN C2
satisfies this requirement

Because predictions are required using the PREDICT subcommand of REGRESS, a semi-colon is typed after the above command (before pressing ENTER). Minitab then replies with the prompt SUBC>.

As there is only one predictor (VISITORS in C2), there is no confusion in identifying the appropriate value, or range of values, for prediction. Thus the subcommand PREDICT 17 will give predicted orders for a resort with 17 (thousand) visitors.

One may type PREDICT FOR C2 to give predictions for all of the *original* values. In the example this option was chosen, together with the prediction for 17,000 visitors. (See lines 2 and 3 of Table 5.2(b).) A semi-colon is placed at the end of each subcommand until all requirements have been specified. A full stop is then placed after the final subcommand. Had it been required, the Durbin–Watson statistic could have been requested using the subcommand DW. However, the observations are cross-sectional, and not sequential as a time series. Auto-correlation, then, is not on the agenda for this example.

Once the final subcommand has been given, the data is processed, and the regression output begins to appear on the screen. The parts of the output common to the Lotus 1-2-3 regression output have been highlighted in Table 5.2(b) for the reader's convenience.

The tabulation within Table 5.2(b) of 'Analysis of Variance' (called the ANOVA table) will not be discussed here. Its use is described in Kvanli (1986) p. 505. Moving on to the final part of the table, the point predictions are displayed in the column headed 'Fit', first of all for the 10 original observations, then for 17 (thousand) visitors, which stands apart at the bottom of the table.

The column which tabulates the standard deviation of the fitted values is followed by the two columns which are of greatest interest here, namely the 95% C.I. (confidence interval for predicted mean) and 95% P.I. (prediction interval for individual values) of the predictor. Both intervals correspond almost precisely to those obtained from the Lotus worksheet (Table 5.1).

Minitab is one of the most effective packages when it comes to prediction from regression, and the procedure for deriving confidence and prediction intervals from *multiple* regressions is straightforward. However, the incorporation of suitable formulae into the Lotus worksheet for this purpose is not practicable without a supplementary package or a more sophisticated template than the one constructed in Table 5.1.

On the other hand, a virtue of the spreadsheet medium in this context is that the predictions may be subject to sensitivity analysis more easily − e.g. with the aid of the data table facility of Lotus 1-2-3 − so that even if the regression is undertaken through another package, it may be worthwhile transferring back to the spreadsheet for this reason alone.

5.2 Multiple Regression in Forecasting Using Minitab

In this section, the Minitab/Lotus 1-2-3 interface will be employed to transfer data from spreadsheet to statistical software for more detailed analysis.

Let us assume now that a regression is to be carried out with a view to forecasting the quantity which will be sold for a set of future values of several independent variables.

The example which appears in this section utilises time-series data. This is typical of many regression analyses conducted for forecasting purposes, although the projection into future time periods does not preclude the use of cross-sectional data from experiments or surveys, which may be a valuable alternative source for the computation of some elasticity estimates.

The final display which will feature regression through Minitab (Table 5.2(c)) starts with time-series data tabulated in a Lotus 1-2-3 worksheet file, named FORECAST.WK1, which is subsequently converted to a Minitab file FORECAST.MTW. In general, the name chosen for the Lotus file will be retained, unless the user prefers otherwise. The file extension is changed from WK1 to MTW during conversion.

The example here refers to a software company whose main product is an accounting package, called SOFTY 999, which is to be the subject of a sales forecasting exercise. Sales data have been compiled in the familiar spreadsheet form. Although not shown here, an initial regression has already been conducted which suggests that all the variables selected − computer sales, business profits, and

Table 5.2(c)   Minitab Interface to Lotus 1-2-3

```
F1:  (H)  'Table 5.2 (c) Minitab interface to Lotus 1-2-3
```

	A	B	C	D	E	F	G
1	PERIOD	SFTsales	CMPsales	BUSprof	PRICE		
2	1	141	205	107	120		
3	2	162	268	115	118		
4	3	182	285	131	110		
5	4	157	249	112	113		
6	5	167	294	110	121		
7	6	195	305	137	125		
8	7	203	295	136	109		
9	8	173	273	128	121		
10	9	179	275	125	117		
11	10	180	280	128	130		
12	11	189	290	130	115		
13	12	191	288	132	118		
14	13	202	298	131	109		
15	14	208	312	137	108		
16	15	209	310	138	105		
17	16	205	308	135	110		
18	17	197	275	129	91		
19	18	194	275	129	96		
20	19	205	293	134	92		

```
C>MTB123


        *** MINITAB Interface to Lotus 1-2-3 (R)    Release  2.2 ***
               Copyright 1988 by MINITAB, Inc.


CTRL-C to quit.
_INPUT FILE: FORECAST
 Converting Lotus123 v2 or Symphony v1.1 to MINITAB

           LOTUS file: FORECAST.WK1
           MINITAB file: FORECAST.MTW

No matching ranges; using default conversion.


 Conversion complete.

C>MINITAB




MINITAB Release 6.1.1 *** COPYRIGHT - Minitab, Inc. 1987
Standard Version *** Storage Available: 16179
OCT. 29, 1988

MTB > RETRIEVE 'FORECAST'
 WORKSHEET SAVED  7/ 2/1988
```

```
Worksheet retrieved from file: FORECAST.MTW
MTB >


MTB > PRINT C1-C5

 ROW   PERIOD   SFTsales   CMPsales   BUSprof   PRICE

   1       1       141        205       107      120
   2       2       162        268       115      118
   3       3       182        285       131      110
   4       4       157        249       112      113
   5       5       167        294       110      121
   6       6       195        305       137      125
   7       7       203        295       136      109
   8       8       173        273       128      121
   9       9       179        275       125      117
  10      10       180        280       128      130
  11      11       189        290       130      115
  12      12       191        288       132      118
  13      13       202        298       131      109
  14      14       208        312       137      108
  15      15       209        310       138      105
  16      16       205        308       135      110
  17      17       197        275       129       91
  18      18       194        275       129       96
  19      19       205        293       134       92
MTB > ERASE C1
MTB > REGRESS C2 ON 3 PREDICTORS IN C3-C5;
SUBC> DW;
SUBC> PREDICT 313,127,104.


The regression equation is
SFTsales = 22.9 + 0.300 CMPsales + 1.06 BUSprof - 0.510 PRICE

Predictor       Coef        Stdev      t-ratio          p
Constant       22.93        19.19        1.19        0.251
CMPsales      0.30006      0.05973       5.02        0.000
BUSprof        1.0622       0.1620       6.56        0.000
PRICE        -0.50999      0.09332      -5.46        0.000

s = 3.909      R-sq = 96.6%      R-sq(adj) = 95.9%

Analysis of Variance

SOURCE        DF          SS          MS          F         p
Regression     3        6422.5      2140.8      140.09     0.000
Error         15         229.2        15.3
Total         18        6651.7


SOURCE        DF        SEQ SS
CMPsales       1        4798.9
BUSprof        1        1167.2
PRICE          1         456.3

Unusual Observations
Obs.CMPsales   SFTsales          Fit  Stdev.Fit   Residual   St.Resid
   3     285   182.000      191.501      1.000     -9.501      -2.51R
   5     294   167.000      166.285      3.357      0.715       0.36 X

R denotes an obs. with a large st. resid.
```

Table 5.2(c)   *Continued*

```
X denotes an obs. whose X value gives it large influence.

Durbin-Watson statistic = 1.66

      Fit   Stdev.Fit        95% C.I.            95% P.I.
  198.714        2.291   (193.830,203.598)   (189.054,208.374)


MTB > CORRELATE C2-C5

           SFTsales  CMPsales   BUSprof
CMPsales    0.849
BUSprof     0.924      0.779
PRICE      -0.526     -0.178    -0.334
```

the product's price — are useful predictors. These independent variables are labelled CMPsales; BUSprof and PRICE.

However, since time-series data has been employed — possibly subject to auto-correlation — and because a prediction interval is required from the multiple regression, the data is transferred to Minitab for further analysis.

Note that the initial Lotus worksheet display has been set out so that the column headings are all in row 1, with the observations following immediately from row 2 onwards. The conversion process will treat the first row from the spreadsheet as the column names, and the subsequent entries as the data for each variable column by column.

To effect conversion, the user enters the subdirectory containing the Minitab system (normally \MINITAB when installed on a hard disk), and keys in the command:

  MTB123   [ENTER]

Assuming that the file for transfer has a WK1 file extension (i.e. Lotus 1-2-3 version 2), and that it has been saved/copied to the MINITAB subdirectory, the user need only enter the filename (e.g. FORECAST, as in this example) when prompted. (Note: Lotus 1-2-3 and Symphony files with WKS, WR1 or WRK extensions may be converted to Minitab, and conversion in the reverse direction can also take place, but the procedures are slightly different.)

If no range names were designated in the original file, the default conversion will apply, and the user will be advised when conversion is complete, exactly as shown in Table 5.2(c). The use of range names during spreadsheet analysis would facilitate conversion if only a restricted set of columns were required for transfer. In such an instance, the range names COL1, COL2, etc., would be used to designate those spreadsheet columns which were to become columns C1, C2, etc., of the Minitab worksheet. Redundant spreadsheet areas would remain without range names. (Note that if regression has already been conducted using the Lotus

Data Regress facility, the results should be eliminated, or be set apart from the named ranges, before transfer to Minitab.) However, in this example, the default conversion without named ranges was employed and a new file, FORECAST.MTW, has been created.

The statistical procedures of Minitab are accessed by typing the command:

MINITAB [ENTER after each command/subcommand]

and the newly created file is retrieved with the command:

RETRIEVE 'FORECAST' (or whatever filename has been used)

The worksheet columns may be displayed by typing:

PRINT C1-C5

If we now look at the presentation of data at this stage, as set out in Table 5.2(c), it may be desirable to make some changes before analysis takes place. The layout of this example, in which the time periods are identified by numbers starting with period 1, effectively duplicates the Minitab row numbering.

ERASE C1

will remove the data from the 'PERIOD' column, although a blank column C1 remains. Accordingly, the appropriate regress command remains:

REGRESS C2 ON 3 PREDICTORS IN C3-C5;

The semi-colon is placed at the end of this command to allow subcommands to be entered for the Durbin–Watson statistic, and for prediction (choosing as an example CMPsales = 313; BUSprof 127; and PRICE = 104).
Thus:

DW;

followed by

PREDICT 313,127,104. [full stop after 104]

The outputs from these subcommands appear at the end of the usual regression output. The Durbin–Watson statistic is 1.66 and the prediction is:

198.714 (189.054,208.374)

Autocorrelation is not revealed as a problem (doubt would arise below 1.55 according to the DW tables).

Finally, the correlation matrix is obtained in Table 5.2(c). As one might expect, business profits are correlated with computer sales, but the problems associated with multicollinearity are not apparent, given the significant contribution of each variable.

(Note: unlike other examples used in this book, the Constant term is not significant at usual levels. The t-ratio is 1.19, which only satisfies a 25% significance level — this is the meaning of the p value shown as 0.251. One might question, therefore, whether the estimated intercept is significantly different from zero. However, this result does not lead us to doubt the contribution made by the independent variables, each of which performs well in terms of the t-ratio.)

The regression equation is:

$$\text{SFTsales} = 22.9 + 0.300 \text{ CMPsales} + 1.06 \text{ BUSprof} - 0.510 \text{ PRICE}$$

If only point forecasts are required, appropriate values for the independent variables may be substituted to provide further forecasts, and it would be quite adequate to revert to the spreadsheet medium for this purpose. However, if prediction intervals are required, it is preferable to stay with Minitab.

To some extent the choice of medium will depend on the nature of the forecasts required, and it is useful here to distinguish between type I and type II forecasts. In type I, the values of all the independent variables are either treated as given, or are known with certainty. They are 'plugged in' to the regression, and a prediction, with interval, is obtained.

In type II forecasts, where there is uncertainty surrounding the future values of the independent variables, it is much more difficult to calculate the consequent error. The prediction interval, as normally computed, only relates to the imperfect fit of the regression and does not allow for uncertainty in the independent variables. In this case, the ability to generate data tables in a spreadsheet to provide *conditional* forecasts is invaluable, particularly where external forecasts (e.g. of national income — see section 5.5) provide an input to the firm's own forecasts.

Even where there is no uncertainty in the type II sense, the decision maker may still wish to derive conditional forecasts by manipulating any *controllable* variables such as price and advertising which feature in the regression. In this instance, the prediction interval concept is perfectly valid, but sensitivity analysis would provide another useful dimension in the search for an optimal set of decision variables. Again, there is merit in reverting to the spreadsheet medium for this purpose.

5.3   Moving Averages in Time-Series Analysis

In practice, time-series data is used extensively in regressions conducted for forecasting purposes, and the principles follow those outlined in the previous section, with predictions being based on responses to the independent variables. Regression may also be used to fit a trend line to observations in time sequence, without attempting to measure the influence of independent variables.

Many forecasting exercises, however, do not rely on regression analysis, or any other sophisticated measurement techniques. The simplest type of forecast is based on the assumption that future sales per period of time will be the same as current sales, or that the present growth rate will be maintained. In some cases, the assumption will be that the present share of the market can be maintained, or that some percentage increase/decrease can be anticipated.

A complication which rapidly becomes apparent is that, while sales may have a tendency to rise or fall over the years, there may be fluctuations between the months or seasons within a year. This means that sales may not exhibit a steady rise or fall, but a trend can usually be isolated from the seasonal variations through a process known as time-series decomposition. This can be conducted as a spread-sheet exercise without regression.

Table 5.3 displays the quarterly domestic gas consumption (millions of therms) for the UK and, as one might expect, there is a distinct seasonal pattern to the data. A regression conducted by the author, but not shown here, shows that it is temperature which accounts for over 90% of the variation in consumption. Since temperature is an uncontrollable and unpredictable variable, it is difficult to prepare short-term forecasts from models which include a temperature variable. Whilst econometric procedures are useful for measuring the longer-term influences on consumption,[3] the seasonal variations can be captured quite effectively through the moving averages technique.

Table 5.3 is constructed from a Lotus 1-2-3 worksheet which shows domestic gas consumption over 39 time periods in column D. The figure for the last quarter of 1987 is not available at the time of this study, so @NA is entered in cell D44, to prevent any misleading aggregate or average results for this and later periods being computed. In fact, the NA as an *output* will appear in cell E42 when the moving averages are computed.[4]

If a quarterly figure is replaced by the average over 4 quarters when this kind of seasonal pattern appears, the fluctuations will be largely smoothed out. Moving from one period to the next, the difference between the old and the new average will give an indication of the prevailing trend. When the 'moving averages' are plotted for all the data in this example, a trend line emerges as shown in Figure 5.2.

The problem with averaging quarterly data is in choosing which quarter should be lined up with the computed average. For instance, the average of the first 4 quarters (not shown in the worksheet) is 1815. Strictly, this should be placed exactly mid-year, rather than alongside either period 2 or period 3. Similarly, the average for the 4 quarters covering periods 2,3,4, and the first quarter of the second year, works out as 1978, and this could be placed alongside either period 3 or period 4. The usual solution is to 'centre' the moving averages, which

---

3. See, for example, Wigley and Vernon (1983).
4. This is a safeguard advocated by Jackson (1985) in the preparation of a worksheet for moving averages. A more detailed spreadsheet-based time-series decomposition may be found in Kyd (1986).

120   MANAGERIAL DECISIONS WITH THE MICROCOMPUTER

Table 5.3 Moving Averages

	A	B C	D	E	F	G	H	I	J	K
1					(@SUM(D5..D8)+@SUM(D6..D9))/8					
2	year and	DOM cons				@AVG(F9,F13,F17,F21,F25,F29,F33,F37)				
3	quarter	mill therms								
4				moving AVG				FORECAST		
5	1978	1	2808		DOM/AVG					
6		2	1393			seasonal				
7		3	866	1897	0.4566	ratios		period	season	trend
8		4	2194	1995	1.0996			1987 4	3117	2608
9	1979	1	3458	2014	1.7168	1.6558		1988 1	4356	2631
10		2	1533	2036	0.7529	0.7320		2	1942	2653
11		3	878	2051	0.4281	0.4097		3	1096	2676
12		4	2356	2027	1.1622	1.1949		4	3224	2698
13	1980	1	3414	2015	1.6944					
14		2	1389	2065	0.6726					
15		3	923	2104	0.4386					
16		4	2713	2122	1.2784			+E41+E46*3		
17	1981	1	3371	2135	1.5792			+K8+$E$46		
18		2	1574	2158	0.7295					
19		3	838	2212	0.3788					
20		4	2981	2218	1.3439					
21	1982	1	3542	2213	1.6003					
22		2	1450	2202	0.6585					
23		3	923	2168	0.4257					
24		4	2804	2200	1.2746					
25	1983	1	3451	2232	1.5462					
26		2	1793	2219	0.8079					
27		3	836	2251	0.3714					
28		4	2790	2267	1.2306					
29	1984	1	3719	2258	1.6469					
30		2	1655	2250	0.7357					
31		3	902	2277	0.3961					
32		4	2655	2337	1.1360					
33	1985	1	4074	2362	1.7250					
34		2	1781	2396	0.7435					
35		3	972	2467	0.3940					
36		4	2855	2533	1.1271					
37	1986	1	4447	2559	1.7376					
38		2	1936	2563	0.7553					
39		3	1026	2578	0.3980					
40		4	2833	2572	1.1015					
41	1987	1	4588	2541	1.8055					
42		2	1745	NA	NA					
43		3	971							
44		4	NA							
45				trend over 2 years						
46				22.42	◄——— (E41−E33)/8					
47										
48										
49										
50										

Sources: CSO: *Economic Trends; Monthly Digest of Statistics.*

means that period 3 takes the average of the first and second of these calculated values: i.e. (1815+1978)/2 = 1897 (rounding up the 0.5).

This 'centred' moving average of 1897 is the first figure to appear in column E of Table 5.3, and it is computed as:

(@SUM(D5..D8)+@SUM(D6..D9))/8

This formula may be copied down column E as far as row 42, at which point no further averages may be computed. All cell addresses in the formula are relative, with the effect that one new cell enters the average, and one (the earliest) drops out, at each forward step.

Since column E exhibits a fairly steady upward trend, with only minor downward movements, the assumption that the cycle is over 4 quarters seems to be confirmed. If, for some reason, the period of the cycle were 5 quarters, fluctuations would remain, and the moving averages would have to be set for 5 rather than for 4 quarters.

The isolation of the trend is the first stage of the 'decomposition' procedure. To determine the seasonal movement in the next stage, column F of the worksheet is used to compute consumption as a ratio of the moving average. A *ratio*, rather than a *difference*, is chosen here on the grounds that the magnitude of the fluctuations in Figure 5.2 seems to increase as the trend line rises.[5]

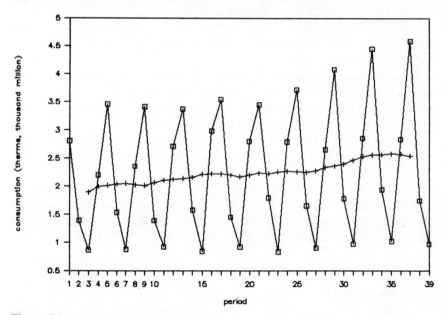

Figure 5.2   Domestic Gas Consumption

Starting with cell F7, in Table 5.3, the ratio of 0.4566 is computed as +D7/E7. This formula is copied down column F, to give a ratio up to and including cell F41. The figures computed in column G are based on these ratios. For the first quarter of 1979, the seasonal to the trend ratio is 1.7168. On average, though, the first quarter ratio in later years is smaller than this. Overall, the first quarter ratio is 1.6558, which is found from the function:

---

5.   This means that one is assuming 'multiplicative' seasonality rather than 'additive' seasonality.

@AVG(F9,F13,F17,F21,F25,F29,F33,F37)

The remaining entries in column G are obtained by averaging the appropriate cells for quarter 2, then quarter 3, and finally quarter 4.

To prepare a forecast, it is assumed that the trend will continue into the immediate future. Over the final 8 quarters for which moving averages are available, the series has grown at a rate of 22.42 per quarter. This is obtained from the formula (E41 − E33)/8 placed in cell E46. In this example the rate of growth in consumption does vary over time, and that is why the trend has been taken over a relatively short period.(If the trend line were more or less linear over the whole time series, an alternative approach would be to regress consumption against time, and obtain the slope as a measure of the trend.)

The last moving average appears in 1987, quarter 1 (cell E41). In order to forecast the trend to the fourth quarter of that year (cell K8), it is necessary to add 3 times the trend of 22.42 to the final moving average.

Thus in cell K8 we have: +E41+E46*3, which works out as 2608. In cell K9, we have: +K8+$E$46 which is copied to K10, K11, and as far as the period for which the trend is plausible.

Here, the forecast is just for 5 quarters. It would be unwise to rely on this approach for more than about two years ahead, given that one is merely projecting an observed trend without seeking an explanation for it. The underlying causal factors might well change and render the forecast invalid.

The seasonal pattern is introduced into the forecast by noting that the first forecast is for the fourth quarter of 1987, so that the appropriate seasonal factor is found in cell G12. Thus cell J8 contains: +K8*G12. Similarly, J9 contains K9*G9, the latter being the cell address used for the first quarter seasonal factor.

Similar formulae are used in cells J10, J11, and J12 to provide forecasts for the remainder of the year ahead. So for 1988 the full forecast for domestic consumption, quarter by quarter, is: 4356, 1942, 1096, and 3224 (million therms).

5.4   Error Measurement in Forecasting, and Exponential Smoothing

(a)   Error Measurement

Suppose that the model based on moving averages is to be compared with an econometric model for forecasting gas consumption. If one model consistently produced smaller discrepancies than the other, it would be judged as more reliable. Various measures of forecast error have been proposed to enable different forecasting procedures to be compared. The most popular of these is the mean squared error (MSE), as calculated in Tables 5.4(a) and (b) which will be considered shortly.

An alternative measure of forecast error is the 'Theil Inequality Coefficient' (Theil 1966 is discussed in Koutsoyiannis 1981, pp. 492−5). This, too, is

Table 5.4(a)   Theil's Inequality Coefficient

	A	B	C	D	E	F	G	H
1								
2				X	Y	Y−X	$(Y-X)^2$	X^2
3								
4	observed	forecast	diff sq	actual	forecast	change	change	
5				change	change	error	error sq	
6	4860	4790	4900					
7	2135	2139	16	−2725	−2721	4	16	7425625
8	1167	1209	1764	−968	−926	42	1764	937024
9	3466	3333	17689	2299	2166	−133	17689	5285401
10	4902	4985	6889	1436	1519	83	6889	2062096
11	2211	2225	196	−2691	−2677	14	196	7241481
12	1299	1257	1764	−912	−954	−42	1764	831744
13	3680	3702	484	2381	2403	22	484	5669161
14								
15			sum				sum	sum
16			33702				28802	29452532
17								
18					U =	0.0313 ◄— @SQRT(G16/H16)		
19								
20					MSE =	4213 ◄—+C16/8		

Table 5.4(b)   'No Change' Forecast

	A	B	C	D	E	F	G	H
1								
2				X	Y	Y−X	$(Y-X)^2$	X^2
3								
4	observed	forecast	diff sq	actual	forecast	change	change	
5				change	change	error	error sq	
6	4860	4790	4900					
7	2135	4860	7425625	−2725	0	2725	7425625	7425625
8	1167	2135	937024	−968	0	968	937024	937024
9	3466	1167	5285401	2299	0	−2299	5285401	5285401
10	4902	3466	2062096	1436	0	−1436	2062096	2062096
11	2211	4902	7241481	−2691	0	2691	7241481	7241481
12	1299	2211	831744	−912	0	912	831744	831744
13	3680	1299	5669161	2381	0	−2381	5669161	5669161
14								
15			sum				sum	sum
16			29457432				29452532	29452532
17								
18					U =	1.0000		
19								
20					MSE =	3682179		

calculated in Tables 5.4(a) and (b) where it is given its usual designation, *U*.

Taking the worksheet as set out in Table 5.4(a), columns A and B are used to record the observed values and forecast values respectively. Let us imagine that, at some date in the future, forecasts of gas consumption have been made with the aid of the moving averages model and these are compared, in due course, with the actual consumption. (The figures shown here are purely speculative.) Proceeding down the columns, successive figures are quarterly observations and forecasts in time sequence.

The MSE approach to measuring the forecast error is shown in column C, where the difference between observed and actual is squared for each forecast. The column sum in C16 is divided by the number of observations to give the mean squared error which is computed in cell F20. (Alternatively, the @AVG function could be applied to the range C6..C13.) This can then be compared with the MSE which results from other forecasting models over the same period.

Theil's inequality coefficient is based on an analysis of the *changes* which are forecast by the model. These are shown in column E of Table 5.4(a). Starting with an observed consumption of 4,860 (cell A6), and a next period forecast of 2,139 (cell B7), the implication is that consumption is going to fall by 2,721 (cell E7). So the formula for E7 is $+B7-A6$, which is copied to E8..E13.

The actual change is then subtracted from the forecast change (column F). The result in each case is squared (column G), and the column sum is placed in cell G16. The actual changes of column D are squared in column H, and the column sum is placed in cell H16.

Theil's inequality coefficient is computed in cell F18 as:

$$U = @SQRT(G16/H16)$$

In terms of the symbols used in the worksheet of Table 5.4(a), the coefficient squared is:

$$U^2 = \frac{\text{sum of } (Y - X)^2}{\text{sum of } X^2}$$

The coefficient has a value of zero if the changes from period to period are forecast perfectly. Its value will be unity if the forecaster predicts that no change will take place from period to period.

This latter result is exhibited in Table 5.4(b) where each 'forecast' is simply the actual figure for the previous period. It can be seen that U is now 1.0000, compared with 0.0313 computed in Table 5.4(a). The MSE has also deteriorated considerably as compared with Table 5.4(a).

The advantage in computing U is that a comparison can be made with the naive 'no change' forecast. If U is greater than 1.0, it means that the forecasting model in use is inferior to a forecast which requires no model at all. If, however, the model produces a coefficient approaching zero, it is capable of forecasting changes accurately. The coefficient of 0.0313 obtained above is clearly superior to a naive forecast, but it is possible that an alternative model could do even better (U closer to zero).

The purpose of both Theil's coefficient and the MSE is to facilitate comparison between models. In the technique of exponential smoothing, a comparison is made between alternative 'smoothing constants', and the minimisation of MSE is an appropriate basis for the choice of constant.

(b) Exponential Smoothing

Forecasting by moving averages can be modified through exponential weighting which permits more recent data to have a greater influence on the forecast. The most recent data receives the largest weighting, while the data furthest back in time receives the smallest weighting. The change is geometric so that successive weights differ by a constant ratio. The final average includes all past sales figures, but the influence of the most distant data will be negligibly small.

The technique is employed in preference to conventional moving averages when the purpose is not so much to eliminate seasonal variations as movements of a less predictable nature, such as are illustrated in Table 5.5, from which a boat-building firm is going to prepare a forecast of orders for the year ahead. In Figure 5.3 the pronounced zig-zag (accentuated by the scale on the Y-axis) relates to the original data and the smoother trend line is the forecast which we are going to derive shortly.

Although the incorporation of differential weights results in an expression in exponential form which might appear to complicate matters, this smoothing technique enables a forecast to be obtained from just two items of data: namely the most recent observation and the previous forecast.

The forecast for period $t+1$ is the smoothed value for period t. This smoothed value (S_t) is found from the relationship:

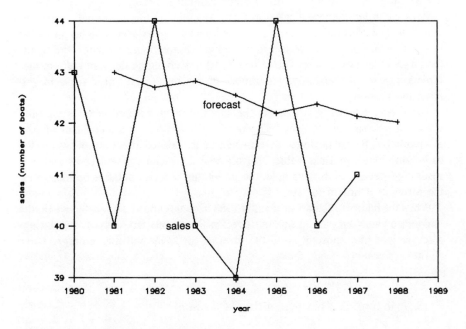

Figure 5.3 Exponential Smoothing

$S_t = aY_t + (1 - a)S_{t-1}$ or

$S_t = a(Y_t - S_{t-1}) + S_{t-1}$

where a is called the 'smoothing constant', Y_t is the observed value for period t,

and $Y_t - S_{t-1}$ is the 'correction'

The worksheet is set out initially to show the impact of an arbitrary smoothing constant of 0.1 (any figure between 0 and 1 will serve as a starting point) which is entered in cell F2 of Table 5.5. The observations are recorded in column B alongside their years and @NA is entered for the two years for which data is 'not available', but for which forecasts will eventually be prepared.

The forecast for the next period is taken as the *smoothed* value for the present period. It is the forecast for the present period, plus the smoothing constant multiplied by the correction.

As shown in Table 5.5 and illustrated in the graph (Figure 5.3), the initial forecast (for 1981) is quite simply the observation for 1980. This gives rise to a 'correction' of -3.00 (actual less forecast), which appears in cell D7 containing the formula $+B7 - G6$, or $+B7 - E7$. This formula is copied from D7 as far as D15. The smoothed value for 1981 is then given by $+G6 + \$F\$2*D7$, which is then copied down column G. The forecast for 1982 is this smoothed value, so E8 takes the formula $+G7$, which is copied down column E.

What we are doing is analogous to firing at a moving target. Initially, we take aim at the last position of the object, but as it moves we adjust our sights *partially* in the direction of the last observed movement. Sometimes, we will actually hit the target as it moves in its varied path, whereas changing our aim *fully* in the direction of the movement would almost always result in a 'miss' if the target is on the move.

The constant which gives rise to the smallest mean squared error is the one chosen to prepare the forecast. The result of variations in the constant of 0.1 entered in cell F2 can be noted, so as to achieve the desired effect. More systematically, one may use Data Table 1 to observe the mean squared error and the resulting forecast. In this example, the smoothing constant of 0.2 is optimal, and the forecast of orders for 1988 is 41.5 boats.

When the number of boats ordered in 1988 becomes known, a new 'correction', 'smoothed value' and 'mean squared error' will be computed, possibly suggesting a revision of the 'constant', and the forecast for 1989 will then emerge.

The expression set out above:

$S_t = aY_t + (1-a)S_{t-1}$

(S_{t-1}, in turn, is a function of S_{t-2}, and so on)

indirectly includes *all* past observations, but with declining influence. For example, with a smoothing constant, a, of 0.5, the observation 4 periods ago would receive

Table 5.5 Exponential Smoothing

	A	B	C	D	E	F	G	H
1						constant		
2						0.1		
3	year	number		correction			smoothed	error
4		of boats					value	squared
5					forecast	+G6+$F$2*D7		
6	1980	43					43	
7	1981	40	+B7-G6 →	-3.00	43.00		42.70	9.00
8	1982	44		1.30	42.70←		42.83	1.69
9	1983	40		-2.83	42.83		42.55	8.01
10	1984	39		-3.55	42.55		42.19	12.58
11	1985	44		1.81	42.19		42.37	3.27
12	1986	40		-2.37	42.37		42.14	5.63
13	1987	41		-1.14	42.14		42.02	1.29
14	1988	NA		NA	42.02← G13		NA	NA
15	1989	NA		NA	NA		NA	NA
16								
17								
18								
19					mean squared error ---->			5.92
20								

29-Oct-88   01:35 PM

	A	B	C	D	E	F	G	H
21								
22					Data table to minimise error			
23					=============================			
24						+H19	+E14	
25					0.05	6.32	42.44	
26					0.1	5.92	42.02	
27					0.15	5.72	41.72	
28				min→	0.2	5.66	41.50	
29					0.25	5.70	41.34	
30					0.3	5.81	41.23	
31					0.4	6.20	41.10	
32					0.5	6.77	41.02	
33					0.6	7.49	40.98	
34					0.7	8.35	40.94	
35					0.8	9.38	40.92	
36					0.9	10.59	40.94	
37								
38								
39								
40								

a weighting of only $0.5(1-0.5)^4$, which is 0.03125. A smoothing constant of 0.1 attaches a weight of 0.06561 to the same observation.

Simple exponential smoothing does not give accurate results if, coupled with the random movement, an upward or downward trend exists. More sophisticated approaches to remedy this problem include 'double exponential smoothing' and a variant of this called 'Holt's method'. (See Jarrett 1987, Chapter 2 for a discussion of smoothing methods.)

Other moving average forecasting methods include ARIMA techniques (Auto-Regressive Integrated Moving Average) which permit greater selectivity in the choice of past observations and their weights. The most widely used ARIMA method is the Box–Jenkins procedure. This uses statistical estimation methods to detect any systematic relationship (autocorrelation) between successive observations, and to build these into the forecast.[6]

5.5 External Forecasts and Indicators

(a) External Forecasts

Although the collection and analysis of primary data[7] is essential for some purposes (e.g. new product forecasting), the investigator will often try to detect relationships, trends and patterns from less costly secondary data sources.

Even business economists employed by major companies are seldom called upon to develop forecasts from first principles. Rather, it is their task to interpret existing forecasts concerning income growth, consumer spending, interest rates, inflation, etc., prepared by bodies such as the Treasury and the Bank of England, the National Institute for Economic and Social Research, and the London Business School, and to assess the impact of anticipated changes on the prospects of their companies.

Such forecasts may be used in conjunction with regression models developed by the company. For instance, if a sales forecasting model includes an income variable as a significant influence on demand, the forecasts for income prepared by the aforementioned bodies can be substituted in the regression equation to yield the required prediction.[8] If conducted through a spreadsheet, a range of external forecasts could feature in a data table exercise (sensitivity analysis).

Forecasts for major industrial sectors of the economy are also available from a variety of sources[9] and these, too, can often be employed to project the sales of an individual company, or of a given brand within a market, based on assumptions about the market share which the company expects to hold. Again, some statistical modelling may be employed by the firm in predicting market shares, but quite often the external forecasts and the internally generated data are used in a simplistic manner, without attempting to measure the influence of predictors.

---

6. See Jarrett (op. cit.) – Chapter 9 of which deals exclusively with Box–Jenkins methods. ARIMA techniques are included in statistical packages such as Minitab, and the procedures are described in various Minitab handbooks – e.g. Miller (1988, pp. 243-68).
7. Primary data is what is acquired through specific investigations, experiments, or market research, while secondary data comprises routinely collected information (e.g. from the MIS) and also data available routinely from external sources. See Kotler (1983, p. 62).
8. The prediction intervals computed in the usual regression procedures are not valid if the independent variables are no longer certain.
9. A useful summary of data sources including economic forecasts, industrial and market surveys can be found in Barron and Targett (1985, Chapter 10).

(b) Indicators

In some circumstances it may be appropriate to consult data or forecasts about various aspects of economic conditions not directed specifically at the business activities of the investigator. For example, changes in share prices are often viewed as an indicator of future prospects for the economy and, indirectly, for the fortunes of its constituent businesses.

Leading indicators, i.e. series or indices which precede changes in economic activity and sales, are hard to come by and do not always lead by the same interval of time. Apart from movements in share prices, changes in the money supply and purchases of durable goods have been tried as leading indicators with mixed success.

The use of this method is an improvement on simple extrapolations of trends because at least one is trying to isolate variables which move together (subject to a time lag). However, the observed relationship between an indicator and a predicted series may be fortuitous, and the identification of indicators is not to be compared to rigorous econometric forecasting.

Nevertheless, the approach is to be commended to the extent that serious data analysis is involved, and that one becomes aware of the multiple factors in the business environment which may have a bearing on a company's activities. Ideally, the performance of indicators should be analysed statistically, to identify correlations, lags, and forecast accuracy. A spreadsheet could be used to examine the performance of the most promising indicators in terms of these attributes.

Useful publications include the *Sunday Times* (Business Section) which contains an 'Economic Data Bank' listing a wide range of domestic and international indicators and also the *Monthly Digest of Statistics* and *Economic Trends* for a more comprehensive range of indicators.

5.6 Impact of the Product Life Cycle

The Product Life Cycle Concept

The product life cycle (PLC) is a widely used concept in the marketing and strategic planning literature (see, for example, Porter 1980 and Kotler 1983). It is a statement of a belief that brands, products, and even whole industries, pass through four main phases: introduction, growth, maturity, and decline, as shown in Figure 5.4. Initially, slow growth may be experienced as a new product proves itself; then rapid growth occurs when success is achieved; eventually, growth levels off as the market becomes saturated, and a period of sales decline may ensue as new products attract consumers' attention.

Evidence about the PLC is inconclusive. Cox (1967) found six different types

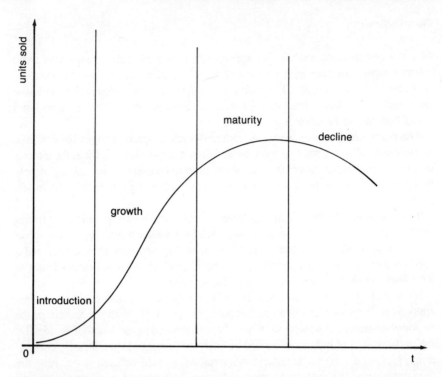

Figure 5.4 Product Life Cycle

of PLC in a study of ethical-drug brands. In many cases, a second 'hump' appeared as a consequence of increased promotional activity to arrest decline. Dhalla and Yuspeh (1976) have expressed reservations about the concept, arguing that in many cases 'the much expected ebullient growth phase never arrives'. They further emphasise that a product's success over time is not predetermined, but very much in the hands of marketing management. Evidence by Doyle (1976), however, showing that most products do follow a cycle similar to the indicated pattern, is more supportive of the PLC. (A useful summary of these, and other, views on the PLC is given in Watkins 1986, Chapter 6.) The concept is useful, in any case, in demonstrating that the choice of forecasting method is dependent on the phase that the product has reached. In particular, econometric methods depend on a long sales history, or extensive market research data being available.[10]

Historical analogy, based on the life-cycle concept, is one method of forecasting

---

10. Two useful articles which evaluate forecasting methods in terms of data requirements/ availability, and age of product, are by Chambers *et al.* (1971) and Georgoff and Murdick (1986).

the sales of new products. Although innovation often changes the product benefits and the consumer appeal, many types of consumer durable have followed a similar product life cycle curve, and it may be possible to identify a predecessor whose sales history might be approximated. If, indeed, a similar pattern emerged over time, it would be appropriate to update statistical investigations carried out for the former product to guide forecasting for its successor.

In many instances, a new product is designed to replace an existing one. For instance, photo-copying machines have largely substituted duplicators. Continuity in trends may be assumed as a working approximation, coupled with some estimate of the proportion of demand which will be transferred to the new product period by period. If the new product offers significant advantages over its older competitor, a value/utility analysis (discussed further in Chapter 6) may assist in determining the shift in demand, and point to an appropriate adjustment to trends in sales.

The Bass Model

Modelling of the PLC to generate an S-curve may be attempted through a number of mathematical forms.[11] The Bass (1969) model is one of the best known attempts to predict sales over time. It requires estimates of three parameters:

r = coefficient of imitation

p = coefficient of innovation

Q = ultimate number of adopters

These may be obtained by historical analogy, from test marketing, or from consumer observations under experimental conditions. Otherwise, if they are to be found from statistical analysis of actual sales, three years' data is required for the procedure laid down by Bass. The model enables one to predict:

the time when sales will reach their peak

the magnitude of peak sales

Success for the model has been claimed in several case studies mainly dealing with consumer durables, including: air conditioners; refrigerators; freezers; cable TV; and power lawnmowers. It has been extended, however, to include retail services, agriculture and industrial technology (see Lilien and Kotler 1983, Chapter 19).

The main problem in the model is the estimation of the three parameters listed

---

11. An excellent survey of sales models for new products is to be found in Lilien and Kotler (1983, Chapter 19).

above. If these are estimated from limited time-series observations, they are very sensitive to small variations in the data, as Bass himself observed.

A Simple Growth Model

It is possible to model the PLC curve up to the flattening portion before peak sales occur by using a logarithmic, reciprocal transformation of the form:

$$\log Y = a - b/X$$

It generates an S-curve with a point of inflexion where

$$X = b/2$$

Putting quantity as Y and time as X, one would regress log quantity on 1/time, to estimate the parameters a and b.[12] A typical fitted curve and the scatter of observations are shown in Figure 5.5. The curve suggests that the product is already approaching maturity as the eighteenth observation is recorded. Attempts to project this curve from a few initial observations would yield unreliable forecasts, although once the point of inflexion (change in slope at around t = 3 in this illustration) is experienced, a guide to b is available given the property stated above.

Pre-Test Market Modelling

The PLC models rely on the availability of some early sales data from which projections can then be made. Other models are available, however, to assist in the evaluation of a new product before it is even test marketed. Notable amongst these is the ASSESSOR model developed by Silk and Urban (1978). The model is based on a market experiment in which consumers are exposed to advertising and invited to purchase a new brand in a simulated retail outlet. Follow-up interviews are conducted to ascertain the potential of the product in attracting repeat purchases. The latter are generally conducted by telephone, and the consumer is given the opportunity to place a repeat order, and is asked to give the new brand a rating (in relation to competing brands where appropriate).

The observations undertaken at the 'laboratory' stage of the investigation do provide measurements suitable for sales modelling but, as Lilien and Kotler suggest:

> ... it is questionable whether repeat rates can be adequately measured by telephone questioning and/or purchasing.'   (op. cit., p. 734)

The derivation of the brand share prediction from the ASSESSOR model is a

---

12. A suitable worksheet for this exercise is given in Jackson (1985, Chapter 10).

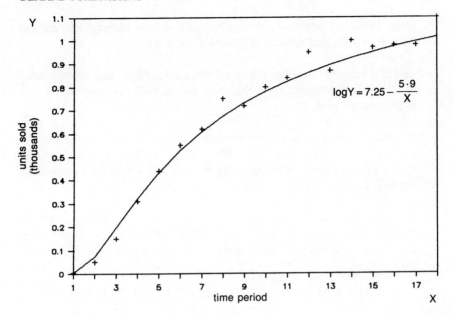

Figure 5.5   S-Curve for Product Life Cycle

complex process, which is beyond the scope of this book. The difficulties of experimental design, in obtaining reliable parameter estimates at this level, are more formidable than the mathematical modelling which is within the capability of modern microcomputer systems.

Concluding Comment

Because of the paucity of reliable data in the new product case, it is unusual to rely on a single forecasting method. Opinions, and assumptions based on managerial judgement combined with assessments of economic trends, tend to play an important part in new product forecasting, although mathematical modelling is making an increasing contribution.

The difficulties in obtaining and generating reliable data at this level make it all the more important that the underlying assumptions and assessments are made explicit, and that sensitivity analysis is conducted. Accordingly, the microcomputer spreadsheet has an important part to play in providing decision support in all aspects of demand forecasting.

Exercises

1. From Table 5.2(c), find the price elasticity of demand at the forecast sales

level. Prepare a new forecast for CMPsales = 300, BUSprof = 125, and PRICE = 100, and again find the price elasticity.

2. In Table 5.3, use linear regression to obtain a trend line, and state the value of the trend as predicted for the third quarter of 1988, together with a 95% prediction interval.

3. In Table 5.3, imagine that the consumption figures for the first three quarters of 1987 were revised to 4,700, 1,800, and 1,050. Prepare a new forecast for the five periods which follow, using the moving averages approach without regression.

4. From the exponential smoothing exercise in Table 5.5, provide a forecast for 1989 if 35 boats are ordered during 1987 (instead of the 41 tabulated) and 35 are also ordered during 1988:

   (a) if a smoothing constant of 0.1 is taken;
   (b) if a smoothing constant is selected to minimise the mean squared error.

5. Compute the mean squared error, and Theil's inequality coefficient for the National Income forecasts prepared by the Downtown Management Centre, and the Citicentre School of Business. (You are now in the year 2003!)

Year	ACTUAL (1990 = 100)	Forecast DMC	Forecast CSB
1995	107	105	106
1996	104	107	107
1997	104	105	104
1998	109	110	104
1999	118	114	109
2000	125	123	118
2001	120	122	125
2002	130	128	123

References and Further Reading

Barron, M. and Targett, D. (1985) *The Manager's Guide to Business Forecasting*, Basil Blackwell.

Bass, F.M. (1969) 'A new product growth model for consumer durables', *Management Science*, pp. 215–27.

Box, G.E.P. and Jenkins, G.M. (1976) *Time Series Analysis, Forecasting and Control*, 2nd edn, Holden-Day, San Francisco.

Chambers, J.C., Mullick, S.K. and Smith, D.D. (1971) 'How to choose the right forecasting technique', *Harvard Business Review*, July–August, pp. 45–74.

Cox, W.E. (1967) 'Product life cycles as marketing models', *Journal of Business*, pp. 375–84.

Dhalla, N. and Yuspeh, S. (1976) 'Forget the product life cycle concept', *Harvard Business Review*, January—February, pp. 102—12.

Doyle, P. (1976) 'The realities of the product life cycle', *Quarterly Review of Marketing*, Summer, pp. 1—6.

Georgoff, D.M. and Murdick, R.G. (1986) 'Manager's guide to forecasting', *Harvard Business Review*, January—February, pp. 110—20.

Jackson, M. (1985) *Creative Modelling with Lotus 1-2-3, John Wiley*.

Jarrett, J. (1987) *Business Forecasting Methods*, Basil Blackwell.

Kotler, P. (1983) *Principles of Marketing*, 2nd edn, Prentice-Hall.

Koutsoyiannis, A. (1977) *Theory of Econometrics*, 2nd edn, Macmillan (repr. 1981).

Kvanli, A.H., Guynes, C.S. and Pavur, R.J. (1986) *Introduction to Business Statistics: A Computer Integrated Approach*, West Publishing Company, St. Paul, Minnesota.

Kyd, C.W. (1986) *Financial Modelling Using Lotus 1-2-3, Osborne McGraw-Hill*, Berkeley, Ca.

Lilien, G.L. and Kotler, P. (1983) *Marketing Decision Making: A Model-Building Approach*, Harper and Row.

Miller, R.B. (1988) *Minitab Handbook for Business and Economics*, PSW—Kent, Boston, Mass.

Porter, M.E. (1980) *Competitive Strategy*, Free Press.

Ryan, B.F., Joiner, B.L. and Ryan, T.A., Jr. (1985) *Minitab Handbook*, 2nd edn, Duxbury, Boston, Mass.

Silk, A.J. and Urban, G.L. (1978) 'Pre-test market evaluation of new packaged goods: a model and measurement methodology', *Journal of Marketing Research*, May, pp. 171—91.

Theil, H. (1962) *Applied Economic Forecasting*, North-Holland.

Watkins, T. (1986) *The Economics of the Brand: A Marketing Analysis*, McGraw-Hill.

Wigley, K.J. and Vernon, K. (1983) 'Methods for projecting UK energy demands used in the Department of Energy' in P. Tempest (ed.) *Energy Economics in Britain*, Graham and Trotman.

Chapter 6

COST AND PRICE RELATIONSHIPS

6.1 Cost−Volume−Profit Analysis

Although it is not always justifiable to assume linearity in the behaviour of revenue or cost functions, there remain many circumstances in which linear relationships provide working hypotheses which are close enough to reality to be practical decision-making aids.

A convenient device for gauging profitability at various production levels is the break-even chart, such as the one described in earlier chapters for the firm making footballs. The analysis of the cost, revenue, and profit functions goes beyond the determination of the break-even point, which occurs where the cost and revenue functions intersect and where the profit line cuts the output axis. It encompasses an examination of the relationships, at all levels, between a changing volume of production, costs, sales revenue, and profits, and the subject is normally called 'cost−volume−profit' (CVP) analysis.[1]

In Figure 6.1 cost, revenue, and profit are all linear functions of output. Each unit produced is sold at a common price which dictates the slope of the revenue function. The total cost line does not pass through the origin because there are fixed costs which still have to be borne when production is zero. The constant slope of the total cost function is dependent on the unit variable cost remaining unchanged.

The profit function is deduced from the other two functions, being the difference between total revenue and total cost. When output is zero, profit will be negative by an amount equal to the fixed costs, and thereafter it will rise by an amount $(s - v)$ for every unit produced, where s and v are the unit selling price and variable cost, respectively. The magnitude $(s - v)$ is called the *contribution* to profit. Initially, the contribution from each unit helps to offset the fixed costs, and no profit

---

1. See, for example, Drury (1985, Chapter 9).

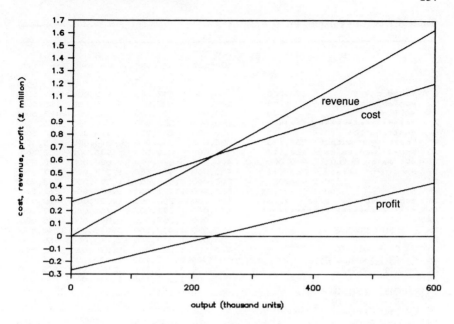

Figure 6.1 Initial Cost–Volume–Profit Chart

overall is made until the break-even output is reached — where total cost equals total revenue, and profit is zero.

If we let f = fixed cost, and Q = output, we can write:

Total cost = $f + Qv$, the sum of fixed and variable costs

Total revenue = Qs

The break-even output occurs where:

$$f + Qv = Qs$$

from which it can be deduced that:

$$Q \text{ (break-even)} = f/(s - v)$$

In the example, the selling price of the footballs was £2.70
the average variable cost was   £1.55

so the contribution was   £1.15

Fixed costs were £270,000, so substituting in the formula:[2]

---

2. The reader may recall that no allowance was made for depreciation in the fixed costs of this example. The break-even quantity would obviously be greater if this item, too, had to be recovered.

Table 6.1 Cost−Volume−Profit Analysis

	A	B	C	D	E	F	G	H	I
1						Output	Cost	Revenue	Profit
2				£					
3						0	270,000	0	(270,000)
4	fixed costs			270,000		50,000	347,500	135,000	(212,500)
5	variable costs			1.55		100,000	425,000	270,000	(155,000)
6	selling price			2.70		150,000	502,500	405,000	(97,500)
7	***************************					200,000	580,000	540,000	(40,000)
8	contribution		£	1.15		250,000	657,500	675,000	17,500
9	break-even output			234,783		300,000	735,000	810,000	75,000
10	break-even sales	£		633,913		350,000	812,500	945,000	132,500
11	estimated output			400,000		400,000	890,000	1,080,000	190,000
12	margin-of-safety			165,217		450,000	967,500	1,215,000	247,500
13			or £	446,087		500,000	1,045,000	1,350,000	305,000
14			or	41.3%		550,000	1,122,500	1,485,000	362,500
15	profit-volume ratio			42.6%		600,000	1,200,000	1,620,000	420,000
16	***************************					650,000	1,277,500	1,755,000	477,500
17						700,000	1,355,000	1,890,000	535,000
18		CELL FORMULAE				750,000	1,432,500	2,025,000	592,500
19						800,000	1,510,000	2,160,000	650,000
20	D8	+D6−D5				850,000	1,587,500	2,295,000	707,500
21	D9	+D4/(D6−D5)				900,000	1,665,000	2,430,000	765,000
22	D10	+D9*D6				950,000	1,742,500	2,565,000	822,500
23						1,000,000	1,820,000	2,700,000	880,000
24	D12	+D11−D9							
25	D13	+D12*D6							
26	D14	+D12/D11							
27	D15	+D8/D6							
28									
29									

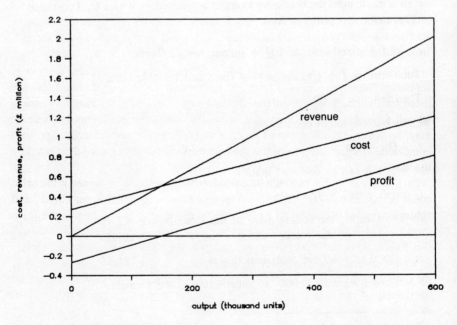

Figure 6.2 Impact of Price Increase

$$Q \text{ (break-even)} = f/(s-v)$$

$$\text{Break-even quantity} = 270,000/(2.70-1.55)$$

$$= 270,000/1.15$$

$$= 234,783 \text{ footballs}$$

If the firm is expected to sell 400,000 footballs each year, this gives a 'margin-of-safety' of 165,217, or £446,087 expressed in sales revenue. These latter figures show how far the units sold would have to fall below the estimated level before losses emerged, and the corresponding fall in sales revenue. Expressed as a percentage, the margin of safety is:

$$\frac{165,217}{400,000} = 41.3\%$$

Another attribute which may be measured through CVP analysis is the 'profit—volume ratio', which is the contribution expressed as a proportion of sales revenue:

On a single unit sold
profit—volume ratio $= (s-v)/s$

$$= \frac{2.70-1.55}{2.70} = 42.6\%$$

This ratio will apply for the range of sales for which s and v remain constant. In this range, every £100,000 increase in sales will be accompanied by an increase in profit of about £42,600 (to be precise, £42,593).

All the ratios and margin-of-safety figures are computed within the worksheet set out as Table 6.1. The cell formulae for these are all straightforward, but are listed for the reader's convenience at the bottom left of the tabulation. There is no cell formula for D11, since the estimated output is not determined here. It may, however, be the output of another worksheet (for sales forecasting), so it is included with the outputs of the present worksheet, in the range delineated by the asterisks.

On the face of it, there would be considerable benefits to be gained if the price could be raised. In Figure 6.2, the firm now breaks even at a lower output, and achieves greater profits at all production levels, as a result of raising the price from £2.70 to £3.35. It enjoys a larger profit—volume ratio and margin-of-safety. It is likely, however, that a price increase would reduce the quantity demanded, so an understanding of the product's price elasticity would seem essential before the CVP analysis could make further progress in assessing whether a price increase (or reduction) would be beneficial to the firm. The need for demand considerations to be made explicit will be a recurring theme in this chapter.

It is apparent from the previous paragraph that the total revenue function will frequently not be linear since price adjustments will generally be required to dispose of additional production, unless the firm operates in a perfect market.[3] Furthermore, total costs may not be a linear function of output, either because unit variable costs are not constant[4] (see Figure 6.3 where they are rising), or because there are costs of a semi-fixed/semi-variable nature (e.g. wages of supervisory staff) which cause a sudden jump in the cost function when the critical output is reached.

Once the revenue and cost curves cease to be linear, there is the possibility of additional break-even points (a second appears in Figure 6.3), with a position of profit maximisation occurring somewhere between the break-even points.

6.2 CVP and Economic Theory

Marginal Analysis

Economic theory relies heavily on marginal analysis in the treatment of output and price determination. Marginal cost is the change in cost brought about by a unit change in output. Since fixed costs are insensitive to output changes, by definition, it is the behaviour of variable cost which is relevant in the application of marginal analysis. One could equally define marginal cost as the change in *variable* cost brought about by a unit change in output.

Marginal revenue is defined similarly as the change in total revenue brought about by a unit change in output. The marginal functions show the slope of their respective total functions at each possible output.

Perfect Competition

In the microeconomic models of the firm, the profit-maximising output is located where marginal cost is equal to marginal revenue. Under conditions of perfect competition, each firm is a price taker, with price being determined impersonally by the interaction of market supply and demand. The firm's marginal revenue is then constant and equal to the market price.

Instead of the usual economist's diagram featuring the marginal functions, we can use the CVP chart (Figure 6.3) to illustrate the profit-maximising output in the short run. The linear revenue function is still appropriate for a given market

---

3. Alternative sales revenue curves are shown in Figures 6.4 and 6.5.
4. The linearity, or otherwise, of cost functions is an issue which has been subject to considerable investigation in 'statistical' and 'engineering' studies. (See the *Managerial Economics* texts by Pappas *et al.* 1983, and McGuigan and Moyer 1986.) Linearity of total cost over the ranges of output experienced in practice has been widely reported (for given scales of plant). Although the subject will not be discussed at length here, it should be explained that the regression techniques described in earlier chapters can be employed to investigate cost behaviour.

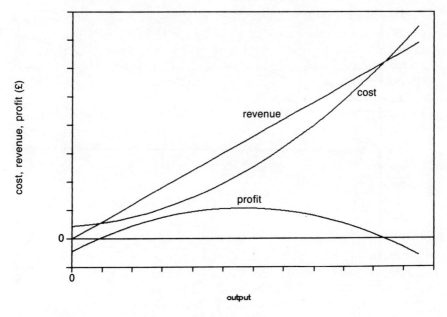

Figure 6.3 Cost Curve with Two Break-Even Points

price. However, if marginal cost is not constant, but rising (in theory because of 'diminishing returns'), total cost will accelerate as shown in Figure 6.3.

The main lesson of CVP analysis is that profits will improve with an expansion of output, so long as there is a positive contribution $(s - v)$. In Figure 6.3, marginal cost rises unit by unit, and the contribution from successive units will fall. In place of the single break-even point, with ever-increasing profit beyond, there are two break-even points shown, with a profit-maximising output lying somewhere between the two. This output may be located through marginal analysis by finding where marginal cost is equal to marginal revenue (= market price, under perfect competition).

Pricing in Less Competitive Conditions

At the other extreme from perfect competition lies the market form known as monopoly.[5] The monopolist can select an appropriate price and quantity, but must ensure that these are consistent (with market demand). In economic theory it is usually assumed that the choice will be made so as to maximise profit.

So long as we restrict our attention to those situations where there is some discre-

---

5. See Koutsoyiannis (1979), Chapters 5 and 6, for a discussion of perfect competition and monopoly respectively.

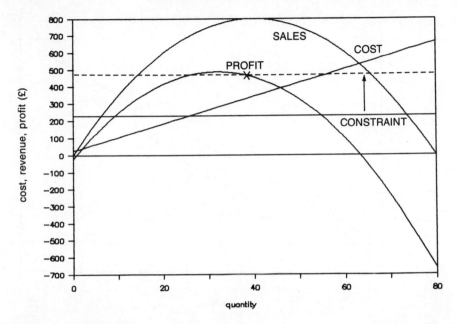

Figure 6.4   Maximisation of Sales and Profit

tion over price and output, the analysis may be loosely extended to cover big-business situations other than monopoly, although there is no accommodation of interdependence in what is exhibited here, and so this facet of oligopoly is not adequately represented.

In the CVP chart drawn in Figure 6.4, a linear cost function is adopted once again for simplicity, with fixed costs of £24, and unit variable costs of £8. However, a new SALES revenue function is introduced. The slope of this function gradually falls until the curve flattens at its peak, beyond which the slope is negative. This sales revenue behaviour is characteristic of a linear demand function for the firm's product, or brand. In this example the equation has been chosen to be:

$$Q = 80 - 2P \quad \text{(as tabulated in Table 6.2)}$$

In this case, the firm adjusts its price (AVERAGE REVENUE) according to the output which it tries to sell. Disposal of 60 units per period requires a price of £10, while 40 units per period could be cleared at a price of £20.

Traditional economic theory proposes a profit-maximising solution, which will occur at a quantity of 32 units and a price of £24. This may be read from the table (or extracted from a Lotus worksheet using the @MAX function). The peak of the PROFIT curve can also be identified from Figure 6.4, which directly confirms the output decision.

Alternatively, the firm may pursue sales—revenue maximisation according to

Table 6.2 Maximisation of Profits and Sales

QUANTITY	AV. REV	SALES	COST	PROFIT
INTERC 80		FIX. COST	24	
SLOPE -2		VAR. COST	8	
80	0	0	664	-664
78	1	78	648	-570
76	2	152	632	-480
74	3	222	616	-394
72	4	288	600	-312
70	5	350	584	-234
68	6	408	568	-160
66	7	462	552	-90
64	8	512	536	-24
62	9	558	520	38
60	10	600	504	96
58	11	638	488	150
56	12	672	472	200
54	13	702	456	246
52	14	728	440	288
50	15	750	424	326
48	16	768	408	360
46	17	782	392	390
44	18	792	376	416
42	19	798	360	438
40	20	800	344	456
38	21	798	328	470
36	22	792	312	480
34	23	782	296	486
32	24	768	280	488
30	25	750	264	486
28	26	728	248	480
26	27	702	232	470
24	28	672	216	456
22	29	638	200	438
20	30	600	184	416
18	31	558	168	390
16	32	512	152	360
14	33	462	136	326
12	34	408	120	288
10	35	350	104	246
8	36	288	88	200
6	37	222	72	150
4	38	152	56	96
2	39	78	40	38
0	40	0	24	-24

the 'managerial' model of the firm proposed by Baumol (1959). In this instance, the peak of the SALES revenue curve would be located at an output of 40 units and price of £20. The sales—revenue maximising (SRM) firm would therefore produce a greater quantity and sell at a lower price than its profit-maximising counterpart.

Economists anxious to defend the profit-maximising assumption have attempted to reconcile it with SRM, by arguing that SRM is a short-run objective consistent with long-run profit maximisation. This is a plausible reconciliation based on the view that the firm may try to build up market share with a competitive price, with the intention of reaping larger profits in the future.

Although Baumol's reasoning will not be explored in detail here, he cites other reasons for SRM based on the fulfilment of managerial objectives. For example, size as measured by sales volume may confer salary benefits, as well as the satisfaction of being associated with a powerful business, more effectively than profitability. SRM as a managerial objective in pricing could then be at odds with shareholders' interests, as suggested in an article by Jobber and Hooley (1987)

An intermediate position, which is neither profit nor sales maximising in an absolute sense, arises if sales revenue is maximised subject to a profit constraint. Thus an absolute sales maximiser would reach the peak of the SALES curve in Figure 6.4, achieving revenue of £800 at an output of 40 units. The profit at this output is below the maximum (£456 as against £488).

In trying to achieve the highest sales level possible without dipping below a profit of £470 (broken constraint line in Figure 6.4), the solution would be to produce at 38 units and enjoy a sales revenue of £798. If the profit requirement were set as low as £230 (solid line in Figure 6.4), the constraint would not be binding on the SRM firm, since sales-maximising profits would comfortably exceed this figure.

To summarise, we have:

Profit maximisation	PRICE £24	OUTPUT 32 units
SRM	PRICE £20	OUTPUT 40 units
Constrained SRM	PRICE £21	OUTPUT 38 units

The form of the SALES revenue curve used in this example may be reconciled with the conventional CVP chart as shown in Figure 6.5. The line marked rev 1 is the total revenue line which would be drawn for a selling price of £20. With the demand function

$$Q = 80 - 2P$$

in operation, it is found that 40 units can be sold at this price. With the line marked rev 2, a price of £15 is taken, at which 50 units may be sold. Finally, rev 3 corresponds to a selling price of £10, at which 60 units are demanded. The shape of the SALES function begins to emerge when these outputs of 40, 50 and 60 are marked on to their respective revenue lines as shown in Figure 6.5.

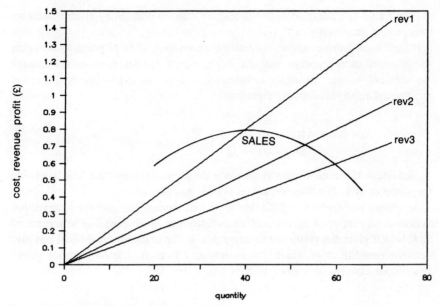

Figure 6.5 Alternative Revenue Assumptions

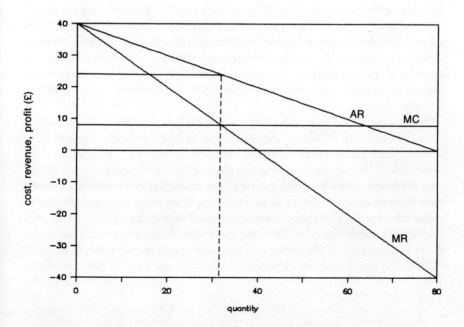

Figure 6.6 Maximisation of Sales and Profit

(The remaining paragraphs in this section may be omitted by readers with no background in economics.)

Before leaving this example, the profit-maximising and SRM positions will also be illustrated using marginal analysis. In Figure 6.6, the MC function is unchanging with output, and is simply a horizontal line drawn at £8. The AR function is obtained from the demand equation:

$$Q = 80 - 2P$$
which gives P (or AR) = 40 - 0.5Q
and   MR = 40 - Q

The linear MR and AR functions share the same intercept, but MR has twice the slope of AR. See Koutsoyiannis (1979, pp. 50−2).

As shown in Figure 6.6, MC intersects MR from below and the intersection occurs at an output of 32 units. This quantity can be disposed of at a price of £24, which gives the profit-maximising price. The unconstrained SRM position occurs where MR = 0, which is at an output of 40 units. The AR function shows this output clearing at a price of £20.

6.3   Cost-Based Pricing Models

The pricing procedure known as full-cost pricing amounts to assessing the direct[6] costs for the product in question, adding a charge for overhead costs, with the aid of a suitable absorption method, and then adding a percentage of the resultant 'full cost' to allow for profit. The practice of this method, with its implicit rejection of marginal analysis, has been the subject of considerable debate between economists and accountants since Hall and Hitch (1939) reported on its use in British industry.

Price is determined relatively easily, even if the firm engages in the production of several products. However, the determination of the overhead element to be borne by each product type is often a source of controversy. A basis has to be chosen which the departments using any joint facilities will regard as a fair reflection of the resources which they appear to consume. Methods frequently adopted involve plant or labour hours as bases for apportionment in manufacturing or construction, and floor space occupied in retail operations.

There is no single correct method, and many accountants, along with economists, doubt the necessity of absorbing all costs when preparing statements for most aspects of decision analysis. However, if the traditional form of full-cost pricing

---

6.   The word 'direct', as used in accountancy terminology, means that costs can be *traced* to specific units, or batches, of production. Direct costs will include materials and most of the variable labour costs, but will, by definition, omit overhead (indirect) costs. Most of the latter will be fixed, but some will be variable. See Drury (1985) for a classification of costs used in accountancy.

Table 6.3(a)   Cost-Plus Pricing

	A	B	C	DE	F	G	H	I
1								
2								
3	Variable cost per unit			£	25.00			
4	Fixed cost per unit			£	15.00			
5	--------------------------				---------			
6	Full cost per unit			£	40.00			
7	--------------------------				---------			
8	Percentage markup		15.00%	£	6.00			
9	--------------------------				---------			
10	Selling price			£	46.00			
11	============================				=========			
12								

Table 6.3(b)   Cost-Plus Pricing

	A	B	C	D	E	F	G	H	I	J
1										
2	Direct materials						£	12.00		
3	Direct labour						£	8.00		
4	Factory overheads:		fixed		8.00					
5			variable		3.00		£	11.00		
6	--------------------------				---------			---------		
7	Total manufacturing cost						£	31.00		
8	--------------------------							---------		
9	Other overheads:		fixed		7.00					
10			variable		2.00		£	9.00		
11	--------------------------				---------			---------		
12	Full unit cost						£	40.00		
13	--------------------------							---------		
14	Percentage markup		15.00%				£	6.00		
15	--------------------------							---------		
16	Selling price						£	46.00		
17	==========================							=========		
18										
19										
20										

is adopted, overhead absorption in some shape or form is implied. In Table 6.3(a), a worksheet has been set up to add variable and fixed costs per unit together, to give full unit cost, and then to add a percentage markup (15%) so as to provide a selling price.

The components of cost are detailed in Table 6.3(b) which shows that only part of the variable cost is to be found in direct materials and labour. Some indirect (overhead) elements will also vary with output even in non-manufacturing costs such as administrative and selling and distribution expenses. The precise nature of the cost-output or cost-throughput relationship is, however, difficult to determine in these non-manufacturing areas, and the separation into fixed and variable overheads is not always practised.

Sometimes the cost-plus is simplified to omit such overheads altogether in a

Table 6.4 Manufacturing Cost-Plus Pricing

```
          A         B         C    D    E      F  G     H         I         J
1
2     Direct materials                             £     12.00
3     Direct labour                                £      8.00
4   . Factory overheads:   fixed      8.00
5                          variable   3.00         £     11.00
6     -------------------------- ---------         ---------
7     Total manufacturing cost                     £     31.00
8     --------------------------                   ---------
9     Percentage markup     50.00%                 £     15.50
10    --------------------------                   ---------
11    Selling price                                £     46.50
12    ============================                 =========
13
```

'manufacturing cost-plus' formula. The cost base is then direct materials and labour together with factory overheads, as shown in Table 6.4. In this case, the percentage markup is designed to cover the omitted overhead components as well as the profit margin, and will therefore be greater than a markup intended to provide for profit alone. In this illustration, a markup of 50% on manufacturing cost gives a selling price of £46.50. Previously, in order to obtain a similar price (£46.00) based on *full* unit cost, a markup of only 15% was required.

Obviously, if firms wish to determine prices according to either of these cost-plus formulae, worksheets can be used to perform the necessary calculations. An obvious extension would be the computation of the fixed cost per unit from the total sum involved divided by the number of units produced.

Although empirical work (for example, Hall and Hitch) undertaken in the inter-war period suggested that markups tend to be governed by trade convention or impressions of what is fair or reasonable, a tendency in more recent years has been to set the markup to achieve a target rate of return on investment.

6.4 Target Rate of Return (TRR) Pricing

The TRR approach has been widely observed in American, British, and European studies of pricing objectives. The article by Lanzillotti (1958) for the USA remains the best-known contribution, but several more recent studies, including Shipley (1981) and Jobber and Hooley (op. cit. 1987), (both UK studies), demonstrate that TRR objectives are widely pursued in pricing, particularly by larger firms. Investigations into investment appraisal practices are also indicative of a target return on investment being sought (see Chapter 3, and the references to Scapens *et al.* 1982 and Pike 1983).

The TRR approach to pricing requires rather more computation than cost-plus with a fixed percentage. The following example describes one way of determining the markup.

Suppose that a firm has capital employed worth £2,500,000, and it sets a target rate of return (TRR) of 20% before taxes. The annual profit requirement is then £500,000. The next stage is to relate this to the total costs anticipated at normal rates of activity — what is called 'standard volume' — which may be taken as 80 to 90% of capacity, depending on past and expected performance. If, for example, annual costs were expected to be £4,000,000 at standard volume, the profit requirement would imply a markup of:

$$\frac{500,000}{4,000,000} \times 100\% = 12.5\%$$

The formula in general for the markup is:

$$\text{markup on cost} = \frac{\text{capital employed}}{\text{annual costs}} \times \text{TRR (as a percentage)}$$

Alternatively, if the company starts with an assumed or forecast sales volume, the markup as a percentage of the selling price may be determined as:

$$\text{markup on sales} = \frac{\text{capital employed}}{\text{sales revenue}} \times \text{TRR (as a percentage)}$$

The markup as a percentage of the selling price naturally differs from that applied to cost, although the two figures are related.

In Tables 6.3(a) and (b) a markup of 15% was applied to costs of £40 to give a profit margin of £6. If the £6 margin is expressed as a percentage of the £46 selling price, the required figure is 6/46 × 100%, or 13.04%. Alternatively, one may calculate:

$$15/(100 + 15)\% = 13.04\%$$

Conversely, a 13.04% markup on sales becomes a markup on cost equal to: 13.04/(100 − 13.04)% — i.e. 15%.

Let us now modify Table 6.3(b) to include a TRR calculation, and to present the markup on *selling price* rather than on cost. The result appears as an enlarged worksheet — Table 6.5. The figures have been chosen to give a markup close to the 13.04% indicated above. In fact, 13.05% is the figure obtained. This percentage markup is translated into the required profit margin (cell H21) by taking: +H19*C21/(1 − C21).

A possible refinement would be the use of an after-tax TRR, which would involve a tax rate factor to determine the required markup. Although the TRR approach to pricing, particularly with such elaboration, appears to offer something rather more sophisticated than cost-plus or manufacturing cost-plus pricing, its only merit is that the impact of different profit targets can be explored more fully. If it starts with cost and works up to price, without considering market conditions, however, there is no guarantee that the assumed volume can be sold at the price which emerges from the formula.

What seems to emerge in practice is a benchmark which corresponds to a long-

Table 6.5 Target Rate of Return Pricing

	A	B	C	D	E	F	G	H	I	J
1										
2	Target rate of return				25.00%					
3	Capital employed			£	4,750,000					
4	Sales forecast			£	9,100,000					
5										
6	Markup on sales				13.05%	←	+E2*E3/E4			
7										
8										
9	Direct materials						£	12.00		
10	Direct labour						£	8.00		
11	Factory overheads:	fixed			8.00					
12		variable			3.00		£	11.00		
13	----------------------------			------------			---------			
14	Total manufacturing cost						£	31.00		
15	----------------------------						---------			
16	Other overheads:	fixed			7.00					
17		variable			2.00		£	9.00		
18	----------------------------			------------			---------			
19	Full unit cost						£	40.00		
20	----------------------------						---------			
21	Markup on sales	13.05%					£	6.00		
22	----------------------------						---------			
23	Selling price						£	46.00		
24	========================						=========			

term aim for pricing across the whole product range. Most firms using TRR show a willingness to vary the markup applied to a specific product, according to competitors' prices in the market, changes in economic conditions, differentiated product features, and life-cycle strategies.

The worksheet displayed in Figure 6.5 can also be used in the reverse direction — i.e. if we know the price which has to be followed in order to maintain the product's position in the market and attain the assumed sales volume, we can work back to unit costs to find out what reductions are necessary to achieve the profit target.

For instance, we have seen that the product cost details suggest a price of around £46 to cover all costs and provide the necessary markup. Competitors' prices may, however, be set at only £45. One item which we might be able to control is the direct materials cost. Through trial and error, or backward iteration (using the supplementary package Goal Solutions), we can show that the unit direct materials cost should be £11.13 if a 25% TRR is required when prevailing prices are £45.00, as shown in Table 6.6.

If a price of only £44.00 were attainable, it could be shown that the 25% TRR would require the direct materials cost to be reduced to £10.26 where no other costs could be controlled. This kind of 'price-minus costing' is a feature of 'value' or 'utility' pricing which is discussed further below.

If a TRR worksheet is used to examine the interaction of costs, price, and rate of return, rather than simply work up to cost plus a markup, then its construction is justified. Basic cost-plus pricing is distinctly at odds with economic principles, and decision makers need to pay heed to the following lessons:

Table 6.6 Cost Control to Achieve a Target Rate of Return

	A	B	C	D	E	F	G	H	I	J
1										
2	Target rate of return				25.00%					
3	Capital employed			£	4,750,000					
4	Sales forecast			£	9,100,000					
5										
6	Markup on sales				13.05%					
7										
8										
9	Direct materials						£	11.13		
10	Direct labour						£	8.00		
11	Factory overheads:	fixed			8.00					
12		variable			3.00		£	11.00		
13	------------------------------				------------			---------		
14	Total manufacturing cost						£	30.13		
15	------------------------------							---------		
16	Other overheads:	fixed			7.00					
17		variable			2.00		£	9.00		
18	------------------------------				------------					
19	Full unit cost						£	39.13		
20	------------------------------							---------		
21	Markup on sales	13.05%					£	5.87		
22	------------------------------							---------		
23	Selling price						£	45.00		
24	============================							=========		
25										

(a) both cost and demand are vital considerations;
(b) marginal rather than average or standard cost needs emphasis;
(c) overhead apportionments seldom reflect the true costs involved in using productive facilities, and the economist proposes that opportunity cost measures be adopted.

The principle of opportunity cost is that the true sacrifice (cost) in using scarce resources is the return or benefit foregone by denying those resources to the best alternative opportunity.

Although we have started to use our worksheet to work back from market conditions to cost, we have yet to modify the cost-plus formula so that opportunity costing and marginal analysis can be made explicit. These issues will be tackled in the two sections which follow.

6.5 Modified Cost-Plus Procedure 1: Processing Charge to Reflect Opportunity Cost

The approach outlined here for incorporating opportunity cost into the pricing decision follows the procedures devised by Baxter and Oxenfeldt (1961). First, though, comes the computation of 'avoidable cost', which is essentially the same as marginal, or incremental, cost − determined by posing the question: 'What will be saved if an extra unit is not produced, or if an additional job is not undertaken?'

Identifying what can be avoided or saved often provides a deeper insight into costing issues than an examination of the additional costs which will be incurred when activity is increased. However, in the simplest cases, the required figure is quite simply the *direct* cost. It may only be a first approximation in some cases — for instance:

(a) direct cost may have been based on past usage, rather than replacement of resources;

(b) some costs classified as indirect, or overhead, for convenience may be incurred/avoided if the production in question is undertaken/not undertaken;

(c) in the long run, most costs, not just direct costs, or short-run variable costs, are strictly avoidable.

However, avoidable cost should be calculable for most products, and it is the next stage which tends to be the more difficult.

This second step is to assess the consequences of displaced opportunities. This involves a consideration of the contribution of other products which are competing for the use of the productive facilities. Quite often this element of opportunity cost will be a function of production time, e.g. man hours if labour is a constraining factor, or plant hours if plant utilisation is at capacity. Thus an additional product involving relatively large amounts of machine time will incur high opportunity costs because of the volume of other profitable production that will have to be displaced when capacity is scarce. This involves a 'processing charge'.

Having determined the product's true cost by combining the avoidable and opportunity cost elements, Baxter and Oxenfeldt stress the need to examine demand and competition before determining the price. No longer is a predetermined mark-up added to the cost figure to yield a price; rather, what the true cost figure offers is an indication of the minimum price at which we can afford to transfer resources from one use to another.

If we were to find that the market cannot bear a price which exceeds full cost in our new sense, it is not worthwhile producing a given item unless it is to be used as a loss leader or as an entry into a market which offers high future profits.

Let us now illustrate these principles, using numerical examples relating to two extreme cases — one where there is no spare capacity at all, the other where ample resources are available to produce any product for which there is a demand.

A. Processing Charge at Full Capacity

Let us first re-examine the cost statement for the single product case (Table 6.5) and modify it to include the calculation of fixed factory overheads per unit. This is set out as Table 6.7, where the existing product is given the name 'PRODEX' to distinguish it from other possibilities which we are going to consider.

Cell B11 shows the annual fixed factory overhead (£1,580,000), comprising

Table 6.7 Pricing with Overhead Recovery

```
          A        B         C    D   E        F        G  H    I     J    K
 1
 2    Target rate of return                      25.00%
 3    Capital employed          £           4,750,000
 4    Sales forecast            £           9,100,000
 5
 6    Markup on sales                       13.05%
 7
 8                        Cost for PRODEX
 9                        ****************
10    Fixed factory overhead              standard utilisation      recovery rate
11         £ 1,580,000                    395,000 hrs/year          £   4.00
12                                                                         ↑
13    Direct materials                                    £  12.00
14    Direct labour                                       £   8.00         +B11/F11
15    Factory overheads:    fixed   2 hrs @
16                                  £ 4.00          8.00
17                          variable               3.00   £  11.00
18    ------------------------------       -----------    -------
19    Total manufacturing cost                            £  31.00
20    ------------------------------                      -------
21    Other overheads:      fixed              7.00
22                          variable           2.00       £   9.00
23    ------------------------------       -----------    -------
24    Full unit cost                                      £  40.00
25    ------------------------------                      -------
26    Markup on sales    13.05%                           £   6.00
27    ------------------------------                      -------
28    Selling price                                       £  46.00
29    ==============================       ============   =======
30
31
32    Contribution to profit                            ⟋£  21.00
33
34    Contribution per hour                             ⟋£  10.50
35                                                        *******
```

+I28−F17−I13−I14−F22

such items as depreciation, periodic maintenance, and other production charges which do not vary with the rate of production. These are charged out to units of output on the basis of machine usage, which is 395,000 hours each year at standard utilisation, shown in cell F11. The charge-out, or recovery rate, for absorption costing purposes is given in cell K11 as +B11/F11, which works out at £4.00 in this instance. This recovery rate also appears in cell E16.

If each unit of PRODEX uses 2 hours of machine time (cell D15), the fixed factory overheads may be computed in cell F16 as +D15*E16. The other overheads appear as before − we shall not probe into the basis on which they might have been derived.

The procedure of charging out overheads as described here is one of the fundamental objections to the cost-plus procedure. It is not the assumption that production costs are consumed at an hourly rate which is unsound, but the failure to identify the opportunity cost which is incurred during each hour of machine time.

In the single product case, the processing charge concept cannot really be applied − it comes into its own when products competing for scarce resources (e.g. machine time) are assessed. What we need to abstract from the worksheet for PRODEX is not the overhead recovery rate, but rather what it will cost the firm each time it diverts one hour of machine time to another use. This will be a crucial consideration once full capacity working is reached, because part of the contribution to profit from PRODEX will be lost if the limited resource is to be made available for any other use.

In order to calculate the value of machine time in terms of the contribution of PRODEX we need to take the selling price less the unit variable costs. Estimation of the latter would entail close scrutiny of all overhead expenditures to check where costs do, in fact, vary with output, and some variable selling and administration expenses may be revealed.

Let us suppose that such searching enquiries have been undertaken, and that the worksheet presented as Table 6.7 offers as accurate a classification of costs as is possible. It is also necessary to assume that the selling price of £46.00 given in cell I28 is actually achievable, and is not just a cost-plus price calculated without reference to the market.

The contribution given in cell I32 is then: $+I28 - F17 - I13 - I14 - F22$ which is £21.00 for the price—cost figures given here. The value of machine time, if allocated to other products, is then £10.50 per hour (cell I34 obtains this from the formula $+I32/D15$). It is this figure which will appear as the 'processing charge' when other products are costed out.

The worksheet shown as Table 6.8 includes this processing charge in costing a new product, 'NEWTEX'. The first stage in the Baxter and Oxenfeldt procedure, however, is to find the avoidable costs: direct materials and labour plus *all* variable overheads. Imagine that these are £10.00, £8.00 and £6.50 respectively. The minimum acceptable price must not only cover these outlays, but also the contribution foregone when production of PRODEX is curtailed to release the necessary machine time. If NEWTEX also requires 2 machine hours for each unit produced, the processing charge will be 2 × £10.50 = i.e. £21.00.

The minimum acceptable price is then the sum of the avoidable and opportunity costs, working out to £45.50 as shown in Table 6.8. Whether or not the new product can attract this price cannot be determined just by cost considerations.

Table 6.8 Processing Charge Based on Opportunity Cost

```
           A        B         C         D        E     F       G       H     I     J
 1
 2                                      Cost for NEWTEX
 3                                      *****************
 4
 5    Direct materials                                    £      10.00
 6    Direct labour                                       £       8.00
 7    Variable overheads                                          6.50
 8    Processing charge        2        hrs @
 9                                      10.50             £      21.00
10    ------------------------------                           ----------
11    Minimum acceptable price                            £      45.50
12    ==============================                           ==========
13
14 .
```

Table 6.9   Changing the Opportunity Cost

```
                              Cost for FILLTEX   - case 1
                              *****************

Direct materials                                £       7.00
Direct labour                                   £       6.00
Variable overheads                                      6.50
Processing charge          3    hrs @
                                0.00            £       0.00
-------------------------------                      ----------
Minimum acceptable price                        £      19.50
===============================                      ==========




                              Cost for FILLTEX   - case 2
                              *****************

Direct materials                                £       7.00
Direct labour                                   £       6.00
Variable overheads                                      6.50
Processing charge          3    hrs @
                                10.50           £      31.50
-------------------------------                      ----------
Minimum acceptable price                        £      51.00
===============================                      ==========
```

If similar products sell for only £35.00, say, and there are no special qualities to justify a premium for NEWTEX, then it is apparent that resources should not be transferred to its production and away from PRODEX.

B.   Processing Charge with Spare Capacity

If the demand for PRODEX were to slacken, one would arrive at a different conclusion. If production of NEWTEX could be sustained in viable quantities without displacing production of PRODEX, the processing charge would become zero, and it would only be necessary to cover the avoidable costs of producing NEWTEX. The minimum acceptable price for the latter would then be just £24.50, so that the selling price of £35.00, suggested previously, would render this a profitable opportunity. Capacity-filling operations, therefore, must be treated differently from those where transfer of resources is necessary, because in the one instance there is zero opportunity cost, while in the other a processing charge must be imputed.

To give another example, consider the choice between PRODEX and FILLTEX – the latter being designed as a capacity-filling product during a slack period. Cost details are given in Table 6.9, and a minimum acceptable price of £19.50

Table 6.10   Reversion to TRR Pricing

	A	B	C	D	E	F	G	H	I	J	K
1											
2											
3											
4	Target rate of return					25.00%					
5	Capital employed		£			4,750,000					
6	Sales forecast		£			9,100,000					
7											
8	Markup on sales					13.05%					
9											
10			Cost for FILLTEX								
11			****************								recovery
12	Fixed factory overhead					standard utilisation					rate
13	£ 1,580,000					395,000 hrs/year					£ 4.00
14											
15	Direct materials								£ 7.00		
16	Direct labour								£ 6.00		
17	Factory overheads:		fixed		3 hrs @						
18					£ 4.00	12.00					
19			variable			5.00			£ 17.00		
20	---------------------------					-----------			-------		
21	Total manufacturing cost								£ 30.00		
22	---------------------------								-------		
23	Other overheads:		fixed			10.00					
24			variable			1.50			£ 11.50		
25	---------------------------					-----------			-------		
26	Full unit cost								£ 41.50		
27	---------------------------								-------		
28	Markup on sales		13.05%						£ 6.23		
29	---------------------------								-------		
30	Selling price								£ 47.73		
31	=============================								=======		
32											

is computed (case 1). On return to normal working, however (case 2), a price
of £51.00 would be needed in order to justify production of FILLTEX. The difference is the 3-hour processing charge of £31.50 which arises when there is no
spare capacity.

In Table 6.10 we revert to TRR pricing for FILLTEX. Some fixed overheads
have been included under two of the headings and the required markup is applied
to full cost. With the figures illustrated, a selling price of £47.73 emerges. As
we have seen, this is not an appropriate guide to profitability under either set
of contrasting circumstances. The price would be too low at full capacity working,
and higher than the minimum necessary as a capacity-filling operation.

6.6 Modified Cost-Plus Procedure 2: Marginal Cost and Elasticity

An attempt to reconcile cost-plus pricing with the economist's marginalist principles results in a formula where the markup is based on the price elasticity of
demand. The derivation is as follows:[7]

---

7. Non-economists may skip the proof and simply note that the required markup is inversely related
    to the numerical value of price elasticity. For further discussion, see Koutsoyiannis (1979, pp
    279–80).

MR (marginal revenue) is related to elasticity as shown here —

$$MR = P(1 + 1/E)$$ where P is the price and E is the price elasticity

or $$MR = P(1 - 1/e)$$ where e is the numerical value of elasticity ignoring the minus sign

For profit maximisation, MC is set equal to MR, so that

$$MC = P(1 - 1/e)$$ which may be rearranged to give

$$P = \frac{MC(e)}{e - 1}$$

or $$P = MC\left(1 + \frac{1}{e - 1}\right)$$

If constant marginal cost is experienced, MC = AVC and we have

$$P = AVC\left(1 + \frac{1}{e - 1}\right)$$

The profit maximising price will be equal to the avoidable costs (unit direct costs plus variable overheads) plus a markup equal to

$$\frac{1}{e - 1}$$

For example, in Table 6.8 our product NEWTEX had unit direct costs of £18.00 and variable overheads of £6.50. AVC is therefore £24.50.

The markup depends on the price elasticity of demand. Suppose a market experiment suggests that this is about -2.88. The value for e substituted in the above formula is, therefore, 2.88 and the resulting markup is $1/(2.88 - 1)$.

This is 1/1.88 or 0.532

i.e.   53.2%

The markup is then just over £13.00, and the price would be

£37.50

At first sight this offers a way of maintaining the simplicity of cost-plus principles, yet bringing elasticity into the markup to satisfy the requirements of economic analysis. Regrettably, elasticity is seldom a known, constant magnitude. If it varies, it is only the elasticity value at the optimal price—output combination which will give the required markup. In such cases, we have to know the optimal position before we can determine the elasticity.

The formula applies to the pricing of a single product. If there are competing uses for available resources, the optimal combination of products will depend on their relative contributions and resource usage (see Chapter 7).

The pricing approaches discussed in this section are summarised in Table 6.11.

Table 6.11   Cost-Based Pricing Formulae

```
Cost-plus              TRR            Processing      Demand elasticity
                                       charge
****************************************************************************
       AVC             AVC              AVC                 AVC
      +AFC            +AFC        +processing charge      +AVC/e-1
      ------          ------      -------------------     ---------------
       ATC             ATC        min. accept. PRICE      prof. max. PRICE
   + percentage    + percentage            !                   !
      markup          markup               !                   !
      ------          ------               !                   !
      PRICE           PRICE                v                   v
      ======          ======        relate to market   compare contrib.
                                    ================   ================

NOTES
=====

Markup based on   Markup based on   Processing charge Formula relates
trade convention  the required TRR  based on oppor-   to single product
or what is seen   on investment.    nity cost, or     - elasticity must
to be satisfactory                  shadow price.     be known in
or fair.                                              required range.
```

6.7   A Pragmatic Approach to Pricing

It is apparent that the elasticity concept needs to be accommodated in pricing decisions, but it does not have to be introduced through the markup, despite the attraction of this method in its attempted reconciliation of economic principles with cost-plus pricing methods. More plausible is the notion that a firm should try to identify a relatively narrow band of prices which will be consistent with its objectives, and then attempt to gauge the responsiveness of quantity to price in this range.

The range of prices to be included in such an exercise may emerge from one of the cost-based methods compared in the previous section. It may, on the other hand, be determined largely by the prices set by competitors, and an important consideration here will be the 'characteristics' of the competing brands or products. Another factor will be the role of pricing in the firm's long-term strategy, and the impact of cost reductions achieved through experience. Further discussion of some of these issues will take place in the sections which follow, but in the present section a pragmatic approach to optimal pricing will be outlined.

A worksheet can be compiled to calculate profit at several price—quantity combinations. This kind of exercise is illustrated in the example shown in Table 6.12, with a given set of price, quantity, and cost figures. For each price in the range considered (52 to 60 pence), the quantity which will be sold is estimated (rows 3 and 4 of the worksheet respectively). In rows 6 and 7, variable costs per unit and fixed costs (in total) are entered. Note that 'fixed' costs are not completely insensitive to output in this example: they amount to £3,500 (per month) when 26,000 to 30,000 units are produced; this rises to £4,000 when output is 30,001 to 35,000 units; and to £4,500 if more than 35,000 units are produced each month.

Table 6.12 Optimal Pricing with Demand and Cost Variations

	A	B	C	D	E	F	G	H
1								
2								
3	PRICE		0.52	0.54	0.56	0.58	0.60	0.62
4	QUANTITY		38500	36000	33500	31000	28500	26000
5								
6	VAR COST		0.39	0.39	0.36	0.36	0.36	0.36
7	FIX COST		4500	4500	4000	4000	3500	3500
8								
9	TOTAL REVENUE		20020	19440	18760	17980	17100	16120
10	TOTAL COST		18465	17490	16060	15160	13760	12860
11	=============		====					
12	PROFIT		1555	1950	2700	2820	3340	3260
13								
14	BREAK-EVEN:							
15		OUTPUT	34615	30000	20000	18182	14583	13462
16		SALES	18000	16200	11200	10545	8750	8346
17								
18	PRICE (top row)		0.52	0.54	0.56	0.58	0.60	0.62
19	=============		====					
20	MAXIMUM PROFIT							
21		3340						
22	PROFIT MAXIMISING							
23	PRICE	0.60						
24	=============		====					
25								

$$+ C6*C4 + C7 - (35000*(C6 - \$E\$6))$$

Unit variable costs also rise with output − 36 pence up to 35,000 units, and 39 pence thereafter. The calculation of cost is straightforward in columns E to H − being the variable cost multiplied by quantity added to the fixed cost.

In columns C and D, where variable cost has risen to 39 pence, it has to be recognised that the first 35,000 units incur the lower variable cost of 36 pence. Thus in cell D10 we start with: $+D6*D4+D7$ to give the cost if all 36,000 units incurred the higher variable cost. It is then necessary to subtract the magnitude: $[35000*(D6-\$E\$6)]$ to allow for the lower cost of the first 35,000 units. So D10 contains the formula:

$$+D6*D4+D7 - (35000*(D6 - \$E\$6))$$

and this is copied to C10.

The top row (price) is replicated in row 18 to facilitate use of the @HLOOKUP function. Before this is invoked, however, maximum profit is identified (in cell B21) by taking the @MAX function. The profit range is C12..H12 and the full entry is thus @MAX(C12..H12). The profit maximising price is then found, by entering in cell B23:

@HLOOKUP(B21,C12..H18,6)

The first cell in the bracket gives the value to be found (the maximum profit). The range C12..H18 locates the first cell from which a horizontal scan is to take place − i.e. across the profit row, and H18 is the last entry in the row where the optimal price is to be located. The last term inside the bracket − the number 6 − is the number of rows, below the profit, where the corresponding price is

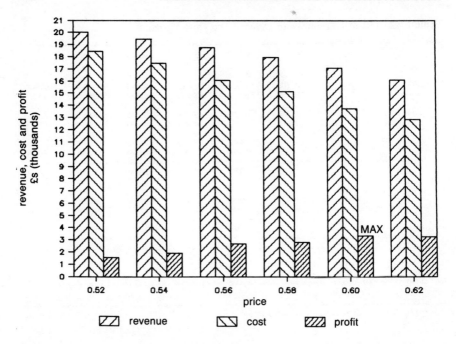

Figure 6.7 Optimal Price with Cost Variations

given.[8] Thus maximum profit of £3,340 is obtained by charging a price of 60 pence (cells B21 and B23 respectively).

A bar chart is exhibited in Figure 6.7 to illustrate the optimal position. Although one is neither at the point of maximum revenue, nor at minimum cost, the difference between the two − i.e. the profit − is maximised at a price of 60 pence.

6.8 Value or Utility Pricing

In direct contrast to cost-based methods of pricing, value pricing aims to achieve prices related to attributes which offer utility to consumers, with the onus then being on the firm to produce at a cost below the value price. While a consumer would obtain no direct value from a firm just because it incurred higher unit costs (perhaps through a heavy loading of overheads onto a particular product group) and would therefore find no rationale for paying a higher price, he might be willing to pay a higher price for a product which is more reliable, which has a better performance, or just a more attractive appearance.

---

8. To be absolutely sure that a table lookup will function correctly, the values in the top row should be in ascending order. As the lookup scans the profits until the maximum is identified in this instance, it will normally provide a correct answer.

Table 6.13 Pricing Based on Product Attributes

	A	B	C	D	E	F	G
1							
2							
3			Engine +	Engine ++	Super-	Sunroof	Sports
4					proof		trim
5		value weight	0.1	0.15	0.02	0.05	0.03
6							
7	Midi S	0.00%	0	0	0	0	0
8	Midi L	10.00%	1	0	0	0	0
9	Midi GL	17.00%	1	0	1	1	0
10	Midi Super	25.00%	0	1	1	1	1
11	Marvel S	0.00%	0	0	0	0	0
12	Marvel L	10.00%	1	0	0	0	0
13	Marvel GL	17.00%	1	0	1	1	0
14	Marvel Super	25.00%	0	1	1	1	1
15							
16	Maxime Extra	18.00%	1	0	0	1	1
17							
18							

The concept and its application is described by Shapiro and Jackson (1978). A similar concept is Product Analysis Pricing (PAP) as described by Brown and Jaques (1964). It is also compatible with Lancaster's (1971) approach to consumer theory, in which the demand for goods arises from their ability to provide 'characteristics' which provide utility to the consumer.

The first step in the value-pricing procedure is for the analyst to describe the significant properties of the product and determine how much value the market ascribes to each property. Significant properties such as cubic capacity, horse power, or some other measure of size, could be one means of classification, so long as the price paid in the market is seen to be related to the attribute in question. If possible, a formula should be devised relating price to each significant property.

In Table 6.13, a car manufacturer's varieties of two models are listed − the Midi and the Marvel − which are sold in S, L, GL, and Super versions. These models are priced to a base for the S version, and percentage value weights are added for superior engines (2 improved types are available marked as engine + and + + in Table 6.13), a 'superproof' extended warranty, a sunroof and sports trim. The 'Super' versions both carry a 25% premium because they comprise the best engine and all the accessories.

Let us suppose that, after several years' experience, the company is content that the value weights indicated in row 5 of Table 6.13 are about right − that the resulting prices enable it to compete effectively against the opposition. It now wants to set a price for a special edition of a new model, the 'Maxime Extra'. How much more should it charge for this version as compared with the basic version?

The worksheet incorporates the relevant weights for engine +, sunroof, and sports trim, which amount to 0.18, or 18% of the basic price. If experience suggests that the weights need to be adjusted, a worksheet of this kind can rapidly compute the appropriate price for every model produced by the company.

Value pricing does not guarantee that costs will be covered by the price, but cost-plus cannot be sure of realising a profit either, despite the addition of a percentage markup. Value pricing aims to show what consumers will pay for a job, or particular product type, as defined by its characteristics. The analyst must then ask whether, at that price, the firm is better off by taking on the opportunity or rejecting it.

The contribution and opportunity cost analysis should be used to check that resources are being used optimally. It is then up to the firm to make sure that it can make a profit at these prices, if necessary by careful control of cost, or by modifying the product's characteristics to give wider consumer appeal.

Although this example is contrived, there is evidence that the principles of value pricing do have practical relevance to the pricing of motor vehicles. In fact, the 'hedonic' technique for evaluating the influence of product characteristics was pioneered by Court (1939) with reference to automobiles.[9]

The hedonic technique involves identification of a set of characteristics, and estimation of an equation in which price, or the log of price, is related to the set of characteristics. The regression coefficients thereby obtained are similar in meaning to the value weights described above.

However, the hedonic technique is often applied as a means of *adjusting* demand relationships for the influence of characteristics, rather than for an insight into the value weights *per se*. For instance, in measuring price elasticities of demand, Cowling (1972) used 'quality-adjusted' prices. In the case of motor vehicles, regressions were run of the price on the following characteristics: brake horsepower, passenger area, fuel consumption, the presence of power-assisted brakes, the presence of four forward gears, and quality of trim (luxury or not).

In a more recent study, Cubbin and Murfin (1987) developed a model focusing on fuel economy (MPG − miles per gallon) as a characteristic, supplementing the traditional hedonic equations with auxiliary equations representing technical and market constraints. This modified approach was necessary because the presence of multicollinearity invalidated the estimates of the individual coefficients in earlier studies, yielding some results with the incorrect sign or shown as insignificantly different from zero. This modified model, however, was able to generate significant positive coefficients on the MPG variable in the price equation.

Harbour (1986) lends support to the notion that price comparisons between models can usefully be made on the basis of attributes. In particular, he explains that it is possible to identify whether a car is over- or under-priced by comparing the actual list price with that 'expected' by reference to its specification.

---

9. For other examples, see Stoneman (1978) on computers, Bajic (1984) on housing, and Leech and Cubbin (1978) on cars again.

6.9 The Product Life Cycle

The concept of 'penetration' pricing as a policy for new products is well established in the pricing literature (see Dean 1950). The idea is to build up a large market share through charging a relatively low price initially, then using the firm's established position in the market as a platform to reap larger profits in the future. In terms of the markup on cost, a firm might be prepared to accept a low markup initially (and even a negative markup on full cost) in the hope that bigger profit margins would accrue in the future.

Thus, although losses might be sustained in the short run, the strategy might enable profits to be maximised in the long run. In principle one could use the investment appraisal rules of Chapter 3 (NPV or IRR) to determine whether the initial sacrifices in profitability would be recovered by the expected stream of future benefits. The 'investment' stage of penetration pricing would be mainly during the *introduction* phase of the PLC, shown in Figure 5.4 in the previous chapter. Benefits would begin to accrue in the *growth* phase, and be maintained through *maturity* until falling sales and erosion of profits in the *decline* phase bring the product to the end of its useful life.

The treatment of price (as well as advertising and other marketing expenditures) in an investment framework is a logical approach in the context of strategic decisions. In an illustration by Palda (1969) a series of marketing proposals is the subject of a capital budgeting exercise. This includes an assessment of the impact on NPV of changes in advertising, market research, price cutting, and rental of trade-fair space. A more recent model dealing specifically with price promotion (in the form of temporary price reductions) by Rao and Sabavala (1980) also treats this issue as an allocation of the marketing budget, thus emphasising that price is just one element of the overall marketing strategy.

Penetration pricing (and the use of price promotions) as a component of strategy is usually regarded as justifiable in the context of longer-term profit aims, and is sometimes cited as an example of inconsistency between short-run and long-run profit maximisation. Thus period-by-period optimisation without considering the dynamics of pricing may produce sub-optimal results.

However, a study by Simon (1979) of pricing strategies in West Germany demonstrates that there could also be a short-run argument for penetration pricing in terms of price elasticity. Simon's examination of 'brand life cycles' for three consumer products, comprising 43 brands in total, revealed that price elasticity was typically high in the introduction and growth stages, lower in maturity, then rising again in the decline phase. The achievement of low profit margins during the relatively elastic introduction phase would therefore be consistent with short-run profit maximisation.

The contrasting alternative to penetration pricing is 'skimming pricing' in which the launch of a new product is at a relatively high price, to take advantage of unique features and the absence of successful imitators. Price elasticity and cross-elasticity may be relatively low, thus permitting high *gross* profit margins, although the skimming strategy may be accompanied by heavy promotional expenditures.

Subsequently, the entry of competitors forces down the price, and reduces the profit margins. The price would therefore tend to be on a downward path over time, possibly accompanied by price discrimination practices − in the form of producing cheaper versions of a basically similar product to cater for groups of purchasers whose demand is more price-elastic.

6.10   Experience Effects

As suggested in the previous section, penetration pricing may help to generate large sales volumes. These, in turn, should enable lower unit costs to be enjoyed. This means that a low penetration price need not be followed by real price increases over time, since lower costs will enable bigger margins to be achieved at a given price.

The lower costs are in part due to economies of scale,[10] and in part to the learning, or experience, effect. Whereas scale economies refer to the lowering of unit costs by constructing large scale production facilities capable of delivering a high annual throughput, the experience effect as defined by the Boston Consulting Group (see Abell and Hammond 1979) refers to cost reduction as a function of *cumulative* output. The experience effect has been observed in almost every sector of manufacturing industry − including aircraft, automobiles, petrochemicals, telecommunications − and also in service industries.

Abell and Hammond cite evidence, accumulated by the Boston Consulting Group and others in the 1960s, which shows that each time the cumulative volume of a product doubles, total value-added costs (including non-manufacturing elements) fall by a 'constant predictable percentage'. The 'experience curve' is the graph of cost per unit drawn as a function of cumulative production, an example of which is given in Figure 6.8(a). The curve shown is for a learning rate of 90%, which means that unit costs fall to 90% of their original level when cumulative output doubles. This is at the less ambitious end of the typical 70% to 90% range claimed by Abell and Hammond, but useful for purposes of exposition. The relevant figures are set out in the worksheet of Table 6.14, where a specified learning rate at cell address C2 generates the column of falling unit costs for cumulative production which doubles from 10 to 20 to 40, and so on. Figure 6.8(a) is based entirely on those cost computations for the stated range of cumulative output.

---

10. Although the presence of scale economies may be an important consideration in strategic decisions, the subject is less amenable to mathematical modelling than is the experience curve. The emphasis given to the latter in this section is for that reason alone, and it is not intended that economies of scale should be seen as unimportant. Suitable references include the *Managerial Economics* texts by Pappas *et al.* (1983) and McGuigan and Moyer (1986).

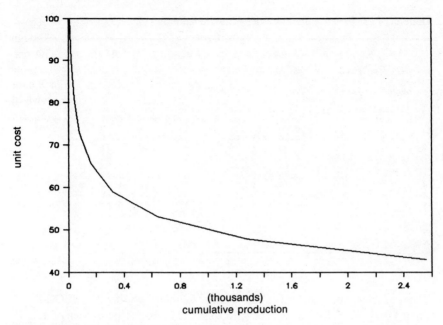

Figure 6.8(a)   The Experience Curve (90%)

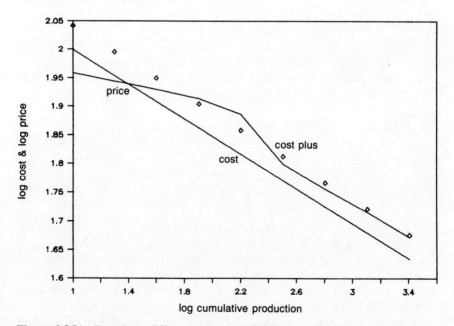

Figure 6.8(b)   Experience Effects on Cost and Price

Source (for both diagrams): derived from the Lotus 1-2-3 worksheet of Table 6.14.

Table 6.14 Experience and the Price–Cost Relationship

	A	B	C	D	E	F	G	H	I
1									
2	learning rate		90.0%						
3									
4	markup on cost		10.0%						
5								log	log
6	cumulative		unit	cost	pricing	log	log	cost	price
7	production		cost	plus	strategy	prod'n	cost	plus	strategy
8		10	100.00	110.00	91	1	2	2.04	1.96
9		20	90.00	99.00	88	1.30	1.95	2.00	1.94
10		40	81.00	89.10	85	1.60	1.91	1.95	1.93
11		80	72.90	80.19	82	1.90	1.86	1.90	1.91
12		160	65.61	72.17	77	2.20	1.82	1.86	1.89
13		320	59.05	64.95	63	2.51	1.77	1.81	1.80
14		640	53.14	58.46	57	2.81	1.73	1.77	1.76
15		1280	47.83	52.61	52	3.11	1.68	1.72	1.72
16		2560	43.05	47.35	47	3.41	1.63	1.68	1.67
17									
18									
19									
20									

The curve may be transformed into a linear function by using the @LOG function of Lotus 1-2-3. In this instance @LOG (which is base 10) has been preferred to the natural logarithms offered by @LN, simply because the example starts with 10 units of output and unit costs of 100, whose logarithms (to the base 10) are 1 and 2 respectively. So columns F and G are created by expressing cumulative production and unit cost as logarithms.

F8 is obtained from @LOG(A8), which is copied down column F. Likewise G8 is computed from @LOG(C8). The transformed data in columns F and G provides the cost line of Figure 6.8(b). The same kind of linear function is exhibited in the Boston Consulting Group diagrams showing the experience curve on log–log scales.

The analysis may be extended to incorporate cost-plus methods of pricing. In Table 6.14 a markup of 10% (at cell address C4) is applied to each unit cost figure in column C to produce column D. Taking logs of these cost-plus figures results in column H, and this is represented by the series of diamond symbols in Figure 6.8(b). A cost-plus pricing policy would therefore result in falling prices whenever experience effects are present.

It can also be shown that the application of marginal analysis, as an alternative to cost-plus, will result in falling prices, as shown by Bass (1980). He argues that 'pricing according to the learning curve', particularly in those industries with high levels of innovative activity, is a well understood concept. In a study of the pricing of consumer durables, Bass found that, although the learning rates were 'substantially lower' than those reported by the Boston Consulting Group for industrial technological innovations, they were 'large enough to have resulted in very substantial price reductions' (Bass, op.cit., p.S60).

In Figure 6.8(b) the 'cost-plus' positions indicate one possible price outcome set from the experience effect. However, an alternative pricing path may emerge, which corresponds to the 'price curve' of Figure 6.8(b). This latter curve is based on the hypothetical 'pricing strategy' figures listed in column E of Table 6.14 (and transformed in column I).

This pattern could emerge from the following events: (1) penetration pricing results in prices which are initially below cost; (2) this strategy then causes costs to fall rapidly, but price expectations do not fall in proportion, particularly if the market leader avoids aggressive price cutting; (3) a phase of rapid price reduction then occurs when a producer tries to take the initiative in raising market share: inefficient producers are consequently forced out of the market; and (4) stability returns when profit margins return to normal and prices follow costs down the experience curve.

These cost—price phases are described by the Boston Consulting Group (1972, p. 21) as: (1) development; (2) price umbrella; (3) shakeout; and (4) stability. The market leader has a choice as to how long he maintains the 'price umbrella' over relatively high-cost latecomers, but if he doesn't run the risk of starting the shakeout phase, a rival may take the initiative and become the dominant firm.

Although the worksheet used here (Table 6.14) has a very simple structure, it can be applied to assess the implications of different assumptions about learning rates, profit margins, and pricing strategies. It offers a framework for the market leader to test expansion strategies − e.g. by precipitating shakeout − and for imitators to determine the rate of growth needed to compete effectively with the market leader.

Whether or not a spreadsheet model is chosen to assist in strategic planning, the need to allow for the experience effect is obvious. Abell and Hammond point to the withdrawal of RCA, Xerox, and GE from the mainframe computer business after suffering losses running into millions of dollars. They suggest that had these firms performed appropriate calculations at the outset, they might never have entered the market.

Exercises

1. If fixed costs in each production period are £30,000, variable costs are £10,000 per item, and the selling price is £15,000, find the break-even output and all the other magnitudes defined in Table 6.1 if the actual output/sales is expected to be 18 units.

   Show how profit and revenue change if only 12, 10, 11, or 9 items are produced and sold, using a graphical presentation, and a data table.

2. A firm's demand function is found to be $Q = 96 - 0.0024P$. If fixed and variable costs are as stated in the previous example, find the profit maximising price and quantity.

3. Using the same figures as provided in exercise 2, find the output at which total revenue will be maximised:

   (a) if there is no profit constraint;
   (b) subject to a profit constraint of £500,000.

4 Find the selling price for PRODEX (Table 6.7) if fixed factory overhead increases by 50%. How many units at the new price will have to be sold in order to achieve the sales forecast of £9,100,000, and what assumption would have to be made about the price elasticity of demand?

5. If the firm is able to reach full capacity working despite increasing the price of PRODEX, what would be the minimum acceptable price for NEWTEX (details of the latter in Table 6.8)?

References and Further Reading

Abell, D.F. and Hammond, J.S. (1979) *Strategic Market Planning: Problems and Analytical Approaches*, Prentice-Hall.
Bajic, V. (1984) 'An analysis of the demand for housing attributes', *Applied Economics*, pp. 597–610.
Bass, F.M. (1980) 'The relationship between diffusion rates, experience curves and demand elasticities for consumer durable technological innovations', *Journal of Business*, July, pp. S51–67.
Baumol, W.J. (1959) *Business Behaviour Value and Growth*, Macmillan.
Baxter, W.T. and Oxenfeldt, A.R. (1961) 'Approaches to pricing: economist versus accountant', *Business Horizons*, pp. 77–90. Reprinted in D. Solomons (ed.) (1968) *Studies in Cost Analysis*, 2nd edn, Sweet and Maxwell.
Boston Consulting Group (1972) *Perspectives on Experience*, Boston, Mass.
Brown, W. and Jaques, E. (1964) *Product Analysis Pricing*, Heinemann.
Court, A.T. (1939) 'Hedonic price indexes with automotive examples', in *The Dynamics of Automobile Demand*, GM Corporation, New York.
Cowling, K. (ed.) (1972) *Market Structure and Corporate Behaviour: Theory and Empirical Analysis of the Firm*, Gray-Mills. This includes Cowling's own study, 'Optimality in firms' advertising policies: an empirical analysis'.
Cubbin, J. and Murfin, A. (1987) 'Estimation of the demand for fuel economy', in G. Rhys and G. Harbour (eds) *Modelling Vehicle Demand: Alternative Views*, Dept of Economics, University College, Cardiff.
Dean, J. (1950) 'Pricing policies for new products', *Harvard Business Review*, November–December, pp. 45–53.
Drury, C. (1985) *Management and Cost Accounting*, Van Nostrand Reinhold.
Hall, R.L. and Hitch, C.J. (1939) 'Price theory and business behaviour', *Oxford Economic Papers*, May, pp. 12–45.
Harbour, G. (1986) 'The price is right', *Company Car*, October, pp. 30–3.
Jobber, D. and Hooley, G. (1987) 'Pricing behaviour in UK manufacturing and service industries', *Managerial and Decision Economics*, pp. 167–71.
Koutsoyiannis, A. (1979) *Modern Microeconomics*, 2nd edn, Macmillan.

Kyd, C.W. (1986) *Financial Modelling Using Lotus 1−2−3*, Osborne McGraw-Hill, Berkeley, Ca.

Lancaster, K.J. (1971) *Consumer Demand: A New Approach*, Columbia University Press.

Lanzillotti, R.F. (1958) 'Pricing objectives in large companies', *American Economic Review*, pp. 921−40.

Leech, D. and Cubbin, J. (1978) 'Import penetration in the UK passenger car market: a cross-section study', *Applied Economics*, pp. 289−303.

McGuigan, J.R. and Moyer, R.C. (1986) *Managerial Economics*, 4th edn, West Publishing Company, St. Paul, Minnesota.

Palda, K.S. (1969) *Economic Analysis for Marketing Decisions*, Prentice-Hall.

Pappas, J.L., Brigham, E.F. and Shipley, B. (1983) *Managerial Economics*, UK edition, Holt, Rinehart and Winston.

Pike, R. (1983) 'A review of recent trends in formal capital budgeting processes', *Accounting and Business Research*, Summer, pp. 201−8.

Rao, V.R. and Sabavala, D.J. (1980) 'Allocation of marketing resources: the role of price promotions', in R.L. Leone (ed.) *Proceedings of the Second Market Measurement Conference*, TIMS College of Marketing and the Institute of Management Sciences, Providence, R.I.

Scapens, R.W., Sale, T.J. and Tikkas, P.A. (1982) *Financial Control of Divisional Capital Investment*, Institute of Cost and Management Accountants, London.

Shapiro, B.P. and Jackson, B.B. (1978) 'Industrial pricing to meet consumer needs', *Harvard Business Review*, November−December, pp. 119−27.

Shipley, D. (1981) 'Pricing objectives in British manufacturing industry', *Journal of Industrial Economics*, pp. 429−43.

Simon, H. (1979) 'Dynamics of price elasticity and brand life cycles: an empirical study', *Journal of Marketing Research*, November, pp. 439−52.

Stoneman, P. (1978) 'Merger and technological progressiveness: the case of the British computer industry', *Applied Economics*, pp. 125−39.

Chapter 7

LINEAR PROGRAMMING

7.1 Background and Applications

The mathematical technique known as linear programming (LP) belongs to the Operational Research (OR) family.[1] LP is also closely allied to the economics of the firm with its emphasis on resource allocation issues. In this chapter, it is the product-mix problem which will be used as a prime illustration of the technique. This is directed to decisions concerning the outputs of several different, though usually technically related, products made by the same firm.

This production problem is normally formulated so as to maximise (contribution to) profit. Other problem types which feature in this chapter are also directed towards maximisation: media selection, in which advertising resources are allocated to achieve maximum 'exposure'; and multi-period capital rationing, where the objective function is expressed in terms of net present value (NPV).

Other applications include:

(a) choice of process − which can help management to select the best combination of production methods from those available;

(b) blending − to find the least-cost mix of ingredients which will meet a given specification (used in the manufacture of animal feed and in petroleum blending);

(c) transportation − to find the minimum cost of routing supplies from a number of warehouses in different locations to various destinations.

These three all have an objective function expressed in cost, which is minimised.

---

1. A useful reference for readers interested in OR applications, is Littlechild (1977). As well as discussing the OR method and its historical background, several industrial case studies are described, including applications at Heinz, Rover, and Cadbury Schweppes.

The computerised procedure for solving for both maximisation and minimisation problems is entirely straightforward, as long as the problem details are entered correctly. However, our attention henceforth will be directed primarily at maximisation cases.

All applications of LP have the following characteristics:

(i) There is a clearly defined objective function, normally profit or cost, which is to be maximised or minimised.

(ii) There are constraints which limit the attainment of the objective.

(iii) The constraints reflect the availability of scarce resources which have alternative uses.

(iv) The value of the objective function changes in response to the parameter values (e.g. a change in the output of one or more of the products will bring about a rise or fall in the contribution to profit).

(v) The problem can be expressed mathematically as a system of *linear* relationships. (Other types of mathematical programming can handle non-linear relationships, but we are dealing here exclusively with the simplest case which has widespread applicability.)

7.2   The Product-Mix Problem

In Chapter 1, and again in Chapter 6, an example was given of a firm which made footballs. Through this example the concept of the 'break-even point' was explained. The firm was initially engaged in the production of a single product, and it was possible to identify the output where costs would be matched by revenue. The analysis suggested that the firm should try to move as far away to the right of the break-even point as possible in the search for increasing profits.

Even in the single-product case, however, one recognises that profits will not be without bounds, since various bottlenecks in production will tend to arise in practice, thereby limiting the output which may be realised. If the firm makes several products with the resources available to it, it has to choose the quantities of each, which are to be produced in order to attain the declared objective.

The LP solution is obtained using the Simplex method, which comprises a set of logical procedures for moving towards the optimal solution. Because a set routine is involved, computer programs can perform the Simplex method, including various add-on programs for Lotus 1-2-3. To illustrate the principles involved, let us consider the following application.

Example

Our firm originally engaged in the production of footballs has recently moved into the manufacture of other sports equipment. The firm can use its new machinery to produce cricket bats, hockey sticks, or both. Production involves two main stages: 'cutting' the wood to the required shapes in a highly-automated workshop; and 'finishing' which entails bonding, polishing, fitting a grip, and labelling.

The available machine time in the cutting workshop and in the finishing section is limited for the foreseeable future to 2,400 and 2,700 minutes per day respectively. The products need the following inputs for each item produced:

cricket bats: 2 minutes cutting and 3 minutes finishing
hockey sticks: 2 minutes cutting and 2 minutes finishing

These requirements are highly inflexible, and the material, labour, and all other inputs into each production process are also predetermined. The contribution to profit after allowing for all the variable costs, but ignoring fixed costs, is £12 for each cricket bat, and £10 for each hockey stick.

The profit-maximising (strictly, contribution maximising) combination of outputs can be determined from the following relationships:

total contribution to profit $= 12X1 + 10X2$

where X1 and X2 are the quantities of cricket bats and hockey sticks to be produced each day. This objective function is to be maximised subject to the constraints:

$2X1 + 2X2 <= 2,400$ (cutting)
$3X1 + 2X2 <= 2,700$ (finishing)

(X1,X2 both non-negative)

In the above system of relationships, the less than or equal to conditions state that the amounts of machine time used in producing X1 cricket bats and X2 hockey sticks (expressed on the LHS of each constraint) must be no more than the quantities available for both scarce resources (expressed on the RHS). In other types of LP problem, equalities, or greater-than or equal-to constraints, may be imposed. The latter, for example, could appear in the blending of foodstuffs to ensure that each pack contained minimum specified contents of vitamins, protein etc.

A complete Simplex program provides for more than two products (or other variables), and for a large number of constraints, even though the application here could be solved using a fairly short listing. (A very brief program for the case with two variables and two constraints, written in BASIC, may be found in Cohen 1985, p. 25.)

A more versatile program is to be found in the *OR* text by Whitaker (1984).[2] The listing is not reproduced here, but the manner in which the program runs will now be described. It is written in BASIC, and the user is prompted to input data by the appearance of a question mark on the screen. Because of this prompting for input, the features of the LP procedure are made more explicit in BASIC

2. The output from Whitaker's program for LP has been modified slightly so that the phrase 'shadow price' appears in place of the expression 'marginal value' used in the original version.

than in the spreadsheet routines, and the former will be used for purposes of exposition. The spreadsheet-based approaches will be described after the principles of the method have been further explained through the medium of a graphical solution.

Operation of Program

Having loaded and run Whitaker's program from within BASIC, and selected option 1 (LINEAR PROGRAMMING) from the suite of available programs, we choose K for Keyboard input first time around, although data may be saved in a file for future revisions of the problem. For product-mix we are going to MAX(imise) the objective function, and we need to accommodate 2 variables (i.e. quantities of the 2 products) and 2 constraints, both of a less-than or equal-to nature. The two variables − i.e. the quantities to be produced − appear as X1 (cricket bats) and X2 (hockey sticks).

Constraint 1: variable coefficients are 2 in each case; RHS value is 2,400.
Constraint 2: variable coefficients are 3 and 2 respectively; RHS value is 2,700.
Objective function: variable coefficients are 12 and 10 respectively.

If the data has been typed in correctly (this may be checked by selecting option 1 from the menu which then appears), the user may elect to end changes and solve (option 10), and the solution appears on the screen, or at the printer, after a few seconds. A full display of the problem is given in Table 7.1.

In addition to the solution for the product mix, and a statement of the maximum profit achieved, this version of the Simplex method summarises the values and shadow prices for the 'slacks'. The significance of these will now be explained briefly.

Shadow prices (usually presented as 'Marginal values' in the output to this program) appear as part of the optimal solution. They indicate the amount by which the value of the objective function will change when a constraint is relaxed by one unit, provided that other constraints permit the expansion of output. The shadow prices may also be interpreted as the opportunity cost (profit foregone) of transferring a resource to an alternative use.

For constraint 1 − cutting machine time − the shadow price is given as 3 (£s), and for constraint 2 − finishing − we have a shadow price of 2 (£s). Both scarce resources are fully utilised in producing the optimal quantities of the two products. This is not always the case: for example, if hockey sticks became relatively more profitable than cricket bats, it would eventually pay the firm to produce exclusively hockey sticks. If this were to happen, the cutting constraint would limit daily production to 1,200 hockey sticks (and no cricket bats) drawing on 2,400 minutes of finishing time, leaving 300 minutes unused (as slack).

However, with the present contributions to profit, and the solution of X1 = 300,

Table 7.1 Product-Mix Problems

(a) Program Input	(b) Program Output

(a) Program Input

```
OR ON THE MICRO
DAVID WHITAKER
C JOHN WILEY & SONS LTD

OPTIONS

    1   LINEAR PROGRAMMING
    2   NETWORK ANALYSIS
    3   CRITICAL PATH ANALYSIS
    4   INVENTORY CONTROL
    5   INVESTMENT APPRAISAL
    6   QUEUEING SIMULATION

OPTION NO.? 1


LP PROGRAM
===========

FILE OR KEYBOARD INPUT? K

MAX OR MIN?MAX

NO. OF VARIABLES?2

NO.OF <=,>=,= CONSTRAINTS?2,0,0



<= CONSTRAINTS
---------------

CONSTRAINT 1

VARIABLE COEFFICIENTS
X 1?2
X 2?2
RHS VALUE?2400

CONSTRAINT 2

VARIABLE COEFFICIENTS
X 1?3
X 2?2
RHS VALUE?2700



OBJ.FUNCTION
-------------

VARIABLE COEFFICIENTS
X 1?12
X 2?10
```

(b) Program Output

```
***AMENDMENT OPTIONS***

    0-SAVE CURRENT PROBLEM
    1-DISPLAY PROBLEM
    2-CHANGE COEFFICIENT OF A CONSTRAINT
    3-CHANGE RHS VALUE OF A CONSTRAINT
    4-DELETE A CONSTRAINT
    5-ADD A NEW CONSTRAINT
    6-CHANGE COEFFICIENT IN OBJ FUNCTION
    7-DELETE A VARIABLE
    8-ADD A NEW VARIABLE
    9-CHANGE SENSE OF OPTIMISATION
    10-END OF CHANGES AND SOLVE
    11-NEW PROBLEM
    12-STOP

OPTION NO? 1

HARD COPY(ONLY WHEN PRINTER IS OPERATIONAL)? Y

CONST  X 1  X 2  CONDIT  RHS
  1     2    2    <=     2400
  2     3    2    <=     2700
 OBJ   12   10    MAX

OPTION NO? 10

SOLUTION TO LP PROBLEM
----------------------
OBJ.VALUE    12600

VARIABLES    VALUE
---------    -----
   X 2        900
   X 1        300

SLACKS              VALUE
------              -----

SLACKS           SHADOW PRICE
------           ------------
CONSTRAINT 1          3
CONSTRAINT 2          2
```

X2 = 900, the constraints are both binding and slacks are zero. That is why the part of the tabulation headed:

  SLACKS   VALUE

is blank. Because the resources are limited, and the firm is unable to expand output and profit beyond the levels stated, it follows that both resources have a scarcity value in their present context. If more resources of both types were available, the company could increase profits by £3 for each additional minute of cutting time and £2 for each additional minute of finishing time which became available.

Conversely, if access to these resources were denied to the firm, or if these resources were transferred to an **alternative use**, profits would fall by these shadow prices. This may be most effectively illustrated by imagining that the company transfers all its machinery to another factory making oars for boats and canoes. Whilst positive profits may well be enjoyed in these other production activities, the firm would have to offset against these the cost in lost profits from its existing lines. Using the shadow prices of the scarce resources, this cost will be:

  2,400 minutes at a shadow price of £3 = £7,200
  2,700 minutes at a shadow price of £2 = £5,400

                        TOTAL   £12,600

This result should come as no surprise since it represents the total contribution to profit indicated at the optimal solution. Cessation of activities, or transfer of resources to alternative uses, naturally involves a loss, possibly made good by profitable use elsewhere. As suggested, this may be regarded as a cost to the firm, defined by economists as an *opportunity* cost.

7.3 The Graphical Method

It is also possible to solve LP problems which involve only two variables using a graphical approach as shown in Figure 7.1. In the diagram, the problem which has been used in the previous section is represented graphically. The most important aspects of this diagram appear as unbroken lines, with those portions appearing as broken lines assuming lesser significance. The quantities of the two products (X1,X2) are represented on their respective axes of the graph. Constraints, and then the objective function, are entered as straight lines (all being linear functions). First, we take the *limiting value* of each constraint:

  $2X1 + 2X2 = 2,400$ (cutting time)
  $3X1 + 2X2 = 2,700$ (finishing time)

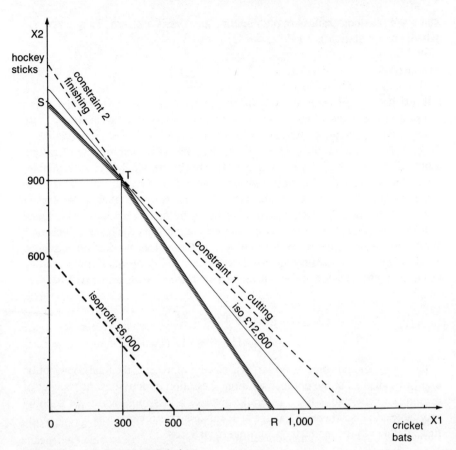

Figure 7.1   LP Graphical Solution

The intercepts for the former constraint are at 1,200 on the X1 axis and 1,200 again on the X2 axis — these being the maximum quantities of either product made in isolation permitted by the 2,400 minutes available. With the second constraint, however, there are differing requirements as between the two products for the scarce resource, and the intercepts (maximum permitted quantities) are unequal, being 900 and 1,350 respectively. The combinations of X1,X2 satisfying each equation may be seen by connecting the intercepts with a straight line in each case.

The *feasible region*, ORTS, has its outer boundary marked by the heavily shaded portions of the constraints. At any point in the feasible region, both constraints must be satisfied *simultaneously*, which means that parts of each constraint (marked with the broken lines) above and below point T are not feasible — in effect being dominated by the other constraint in those particular parts of the diagram.

Having mapped out the feasible region, the impact of the objective function can now be explored. This is a vital part of the graphical method since it shows which corner point R, T or S will be optimal.[3]

In this example our objective function is $12X1 + 10X2$. For instance, by producing *either* 500 cricket bats *or* 600 hockey sticks, a profit of £6,000 could be realised. Alternatively, the same level of profit could be obtained by producing 250 cricket bats *and* 300 hockey sticks.

All points yielding the same level of profit lie on a given ISOPROFIT line. Thus we have isoprofit for £6,000 passing from one intercept to the other ($X1 = 500$ to $X2 = 600$) and through (250, 300). Note that the gradient of the isoprofit line is 600/500 (or 6/5 − strictly *minus* 6/5). This should be apparent from the relative profit contributions of 12:10.

The isoprofit line for £6,000 is just one of many possible profit levels which one may explore in the diagram. All will have the same gradient so long as the contributions to profit remain unchanged. As we move away from the origin, drawing isoprofit lines of common slope (not illustrated), we will reach successively higher levels of profit.

The line chosen as a starting point is convenient because it involves whole numbers of products at the intercepts, and also because it lies entirely within the feasible region. Any point lying on that line could therefore be achieved within the resources available. However, this latter property is a distinct disadvantage other than for expositional purposes, since it means that the firm is not exploiting its scarce resources fully.

In order to identify the optimal solution, it is necessary to attain an isoprofit line as far out as possible from the origin where there is just one point[4] on the feasible region which lies on that extreme isoprofit line. Here, it is the isoprofit line passing through point T which is seen to be optimal, since even a minor shift outwards would result in an isoprofit line which lay *entirely* outside the feasible region.

As we have seen already, this corresponds to a daily production of 300 cricket bats and 900 hockey sticks resulting in a profit contribution of £12,600. The reader should check his understanding of the isoprofit concept by demonstrating that all points on the ultimate isoprofit line would yield (if feasible) profits of £12,600.

It should be emphasised that the optimality of point T hinges critically on the slope of the isoprofit line. If this were to change from 1.2 to 1.6 (in fact anything greater than 1.5), point R would become optimal. Conversely, if the slope were to fall to 0.9 (in fact anything less than 1.0), point S would become optimal. In each case the critical ratios are the gradients of the constraints which bound the feasible region.

---

3. Whilst, in general, an optimal solution will prevail at one of the corner points of the feasible region, it is also possible for a complete segment of the boundary to be optimal − e.g. all points along ST, or all points along TR. A unique optimal solution does not obtain under such circumstances, although the computer program will still tend to indicate one or other corner point at either end of the relevant segment.
4. Or one segment − see the previous footnote.

7.4 Sensitivity Analysis

Sensitivity analysis is conducted after an optimal solution has been derived from a given set of values. For example, one might ask, 'if the profitability of one of the products changes, will it necessitate a change in the product mix?'

Already, in commenting on the possibility of other corner points in the graphical solution being invoked, we have started to test the first optimal solution for sensitivity to changes in relative profit contributions (bringing about changes in the slope of the isoprofit lines). Another term for the same kind of approach is 'post-optimality' analysis which conveys its role more effectively, perhaps, than the word 'sensitivity'.

In fact, sensitivity analysis may be used to examine the result of changes in any parameter — e.g. resource usage, or resource availability — although, for purposes of illustration, reference will continue to be made to the profit contributions. The graphical solution shows that corner point R will emerge as optimal if the slope of the isoprofit line exceeds the slope of constraint 2.

Thus, if the profit contribution from cricket bats rises to £16 while the profitability of hockey sticks remains unchanged, the isoprofit line will be of slope 1.6, and this will leave the feasible region at point R, giving an optimal solution of 900 cricket bats (profit = 900 × £16 = £14,400) with no hockey sticks being produced. This result is confirmed by the computer solution, which is now:

OBJ.VALUE	14400

VARIABLES	VALUE
X 1	900

SLACKS	VALUE
CONSTRAINT 1	600

SLACKS	SHADOW PRICE
CONSTRAINT 1	0
CONSTRAINT 2	5.3

The above summary also demonstrates, for constraint 1, that 600 minutes remain unused, with opportunity cost (shadow price) being zero.

If we now move to the other extreme corner, S, this would emerge as optimal with a fall in the profit contribution from cricket bats to £9. The slope of the isoprofit line would now be only 0.9, which is less than the slope of constraint 1. The computer solution now shows that production is exclusively of hockey sticks, with £12,000 profit resulting from 1,200 items. 300 minutes of the second resource (finishing time) remain unused and these have an opportunity cost of zero. To summarise:

OBJ.VALUE	12000
VARIABLES	VALUE
X 2	1200

SLACKS	VALUE
CONSTRAINT 2	300

SLACKS	SHADOW PRICE
CONSTRAINT 1	5
CONSTRAINT 2	0

The original optimal product mix (300 : 900) is *insensitive* to changes in the profitability of cricket bats in the range £10 to £15.[5] (Assuming that the profitability of hockey sticks remains constant at £10.) This may be confirmed by choosing option 6 from the menu — change coefficient in objective function — and experimenting with various profit contributions until the optimal production levels are seen to change.[6]

The other options in the menu, which include addition/deletion of constraints, changes to RHS of constraints (typically resource availabilities), addition/deletion of variables (products), etc., provide the means to re-examine the results of the LP far more conveniently and rapidly than with any manual solution — algebraic or graphical. The latter, of course, is limited to two products, so that its usefulness is directed to illustration of the technique rather than to practical application.

The opportunity costs, or shadow prices, which appear with each computer solution enable sensitivity tests of a rather different character to be carried out. These values give an indication of the cost of using resources for another purpose, or the value of additional resources being made available in terms of profits foregone, or profits to be enjoyed, respectively. Thus, if one knows the resource requirements of a new product, one can find out whether it is worthwhile introducing that product, before going to the computer solution to determine how much should be produced. This type of sensitivity issue will be considered at the end of the next section.

7.5 Spreadsheets in Linear Programming

It would appear that the solution could be obtained through the medium of the spreadsheet, given the latter's ability to recalculate profit for any combination

---

5. In the computer solution the range indicated is £10 to £14.99.
6. A given product mix will not yield a constant level of profit when objective function coefficients are being changed, but at each stage the Simplex method will ensure that whatever profit is indicated is the best that can be obtained under the circumstances.

of variables, once the initial data about the products has been entered. Whilst this view of the spreadsheet's capabilities has some validity, experimentation without a logical sequence could involve considerable time and effort as soon as a problem with several products and constraints had to be tackled.

In order to take advantage of the spreadsheet's versatility in assembling and analysing data, various software devices have been designed to interface with Lotus 1-2-3. One such product is **What's***Best*!™ − so called because its purpose is to solve optimisation problems such as have been described. The initial position and optimal solution are presented in spreadsheet form in Tables 7.2(a) and (b) respectively.[7]

Users of the Lotus spreadsheet who construct their models through that medium will undoubtedly find it advantageous to be able to call up the **What's***Best*! LP routine while the spreadsheet is still in view. Optimisation can take place, and the user may then return to his spreadsheet model, undertake any revisions which appear desirable, and optimise again.

As can be seen, the initial solution (Table 7.2a) leaves all resources unused by taking zero production and, obviously, it achieves zero profit. At the optimal solution (Table 7.2b), 300 cricket bats and 900 hockey sticks are produced. All resources are fully utilised.

The add-on package **What's***Best*! should be stored in the same directory as the main Lotus program. If the main purpose of the session is to construct worksheets for linear programming, the supplementary package will be made available at the outset by typing **WB**. After some disk activity, the user will be informed that the program has been installed successfully, and will be advised how much memory is free. When the screen prompt re-appears, the procedure for starting the Lotus session is the same as usual − i.e. **123** will be keyed in to commence.

The user can then proceed to construct worksheets in the normal way without actually having to employ the **What's***Best*! facility. It will only be activated if the asterisk key with the PRT SC is depressed (unshifted).

To prepare the product-mix worksheet for LP solution we set up Table 7.2(a) with appropriate headings for the product names or identifying numbers, resources, profits, etc. The problem data for input requirements, resource availability, and profit contributions are entered in the cells selected. All this is done as if a normal worksheet were being prepared.

In the opening position, no production will take place, so the numbers zero will be placed in the cells reserved for the quantities produced [B7 and C7 in Table 7.2(a)].

Total usage of resource is entered as a formula in each case. Starting with the 'cutting' resource, the amount used will be found by multiplying the quantity produced by the requirement of each product:

---

7.   **What's***Best*! is a registered trademark of General Optimization Inc. If used with Lotus Release 2, a mathematical co-processor (8087) can be supported. The latter considerably reduces computational time, and is a highly desirable facility if large-scale problems are to be solved.

Table 7.2(a)   Problem Structure — Initial Solution

	A	B	C	D	E	F	G	H	I	J
1										
2										
3		cricket	hockey							
4	Product	1	2							
5										
6	Profit/Unit	12	10							
7	Quantity	0.00	0.00 ← adjustable cells KEY f3							
8	produced									

10	Resource requirements			Total	Resources	Amount		Shadow
11		cricket	hockey	usage	available	unused		price
13	cutting	2	2	0 <	2,400	2,400	leave	0.00←KEY
14	finishing	3	2	0 <	2,700	2,700	blank	0.00 f7

16		+B13*$B$7+C13*$C$7	
17			************
18		FORMULA	TOTAL PROFIT:	KEY f5 to MAX
19		+B6*B7+C6*C7 → 0 ←	(or f6 to MIN)
20			************

Table 7.2(b)   LP Output — Optimal Solution

	A	B	C	D	E	F	G	H	I	J
1										
2										
3		cricket	hockey							
4	Product	1	2							
5										
6	Profit/Unit	12	10							
7	Quantity	300.00	900.00							
8	produced									

10	Resource requirements			Total	Resources	Amount		Shadow
11		cricket	hockey	usage	available	unused		price
13	cutting	2	2	2,400 <	2,400	0		3.00
14	finishing	3	2	2,700 <	2,700	0		2.00

16			
17		************
18		TOTAL PROFIT:
19		£ 12,600
20		************

+B13*$B$7+C13*$C$7

which goes in cell D13, giving a zero value at this stage.

This may be copied to cell D14, to give the total usage of the other resource. The other formula required is for total profit in cell F19, which is:

+B6*B7+C6*C7

At this point, while the cursor is still at cell address F19, **What'sBest!** is called up by pressing the asterisk key (the one whose shifted form is PRT SC) followed by the function key 5, which then designates cell F19 as 'Maximize!' (Function key 6 enables 'Minimize!' for those problems where the objective function is expressed as cost.)

The cursor is then moved to B7 (the first of the quantity cells). Asterisk followed by function key 3 is used to indicate the range of cells:

B7..C7

which are 'adjustable' − i.e. the variables whose values are to be adjusted until optimisation occurs (after marking this range to be 'unprotected', the *RETURN* or *ENTER* key must be pressed).

Apart from the shadow prices, which are an optional part of the problem structure, the remaining task is to enter the constraints in the manner required by **What'sBest!**

Column E, which has been set to a width of just 3 characters, lies *between* the 'Total usage' and 'Resources available' columns, and is used to indicate the nature of the constraints.[8]

Having moved the cursor to cell E13, the **What'sBest!** procedures are invoked again with the asterisk, and this time the appropriate keystroke which follows is < (less than). This will automatically place the 'less than' symbol in cell E13, and deliver an output to cell G13 (always two cells to the right) equal to the resources available less the total usage − i.e. amount unused.[9] The same task must be performed for the next constraint (finishing), but copying the < entry from cell E13 will only copy the symbol. If copying is employed to replicate the nature of the constraint, it is also necessary to copy the formula which has been delivered to cell G13.

In the opening position, quantities produced are zero, as are resources used, and total profit is also zero. Amounts of resources unused are equal, therefore, to the amounts available.

If shadow prices are required in the optimal solution, another function key must be activated. The cursor should already be placed in the cell which will receive the shadow price (cell I13) and, when the asterisk followed by function key 7 ('dual value') is employed, the user is prompted for the cell address referring to the appropriate variable.[10] Here the appropriate cell address is the 'slack' for the constraint (amount unused). Hence G13 is indicated for 'cutting', followed by *return* or *enter*, and the other shadow price entry may be obtained by copying from I13 to I14.

Finally, after saving the worksheet if desired, **What'sBest!** is recalled once

---

8. Although the precise column width is unimportant, it is essential that a single column be left between the 'Total usage' and 'Resources available' columns, and that a further column for the 'slack' (labelled 'Amount unused' here) be left free to the right of 'Resources available'.
9. 'Greater than' (>) constraints are entered with the appropriate keystroke, and the excess value, or 'slack', is delivered two cells to the right of the symbol.
10. At this point the screen displays: @IF(0= and the program waits for the appropriate cell address to be typed or pointed, followed by *return* or *enter*.

again, with the asterisk, followed by function key 1, and optimisation proceeds. After a variable period of time during which screen displays offer some impression of the progress being made in solving the problem, the optimal solution is revealed, as illustrated in Table 7.2(b). Quantities produced, profits created, and resources used/unused, are indicated, together with any shadow prices for which provision has been made.

Note on Integer Solutions

If the adjustable cells are treated as described above, fractional solutions will be presented if these offer the optimal result. In some cases, however, including the capital rationing problem tackled in a later section of this chapter, fractional solutions may not be feasible. This integer restriction can be accommodated by using the sequence: asterisk, function key 8. The range of adjustable cells to receive integer answers must be indicated, followed by *RETURN*, or *ENTER*. The display for integers is '+' for a value of one, or '.' for a value of zero.

Use of the Shadow Prices in Sensitivity Analysis

Let us return to the optimal solution where the sports-goods factory is working at full capacity. In this solution, shadow prices are given for the two limiting factors: cutting machine time £3.00; finishing machine time £2.00. These will be included as opportunity costs when testing for the viability of any other product which would draw on these resources.

As an example, imagine that the firm intends to make billiard cues. Each cue requires one and two minutes respectively of these resources. Variable costs for materials and labour are estimated to be £20 and the opportunity cost, based on machine requirements, will be:

    cutting   − 1 @ £3.00 = £3.00
    finishing − 2 @ £2.00 = £4.00

which gives a total of £7.00. This means that, unless the firm can sell each cue for £27.00 (allowing for the £20 variable costs), it cannot justify transferring resources from its existing production plan to this new product.

If a contribution of more than £7.00 could be obtained from this new use for the resources − e.g. if each cue could command a price of £28.00 (contribution £8.00) − then production would be justifiable.

In Table 7.3(a) **What's*Best*!** is run again with this third product included in the worksheet model. If the contribution for the new product is only £6.00, the previous solution featuring hockey sticks and cricket bats is repeated − i.e. quantity of billiard cues = 0, as shown in Table 7.3(b).

Table 7.3(a) Problem Structure for Three Products

	A	B	C	D	E	F	G	H	I
1									
2									
3		cricket	hockey	billiards					
4	Product	1	2	3					
5									
6	Profit/Unit	12	10	6					
7	Quantity	0.00	0.00	0.00					
8	produced								
9	--								
10	Resource requirements				Total		Resources	Amount	Shadow
11		cricket	hockey	billiards	usage		available	unused	price
12	---								
13	cutting	2	2	1	0	<	2,400	2,400	0.00
14	finishing	3	2	2	0	<	2,700	2,700	0.00
15	---								
16									
17					************				
18					TOTAL PROFIT:				
19					0				
20					************				

Table 7.3(b) LP Output — Unchanged Optimal Solution

	A	B	C	D	E	F	G	H	I
1									
2									
3		cricket	hockey	billiards					
4	Product	1	2	3					
5									
6	Profit/Unit	12	10	6					
7	Quantity	300.00	900.00	0.00					
8	produced								
9	--								
10	Resource requirements				Total		Resources	Amount	Shadow
11		cricket	hockey	billiards	usage		available	unused	price
12	---								
13	cutting	2	2	1	2,400	<	2,400	0	3.00
14	finishing	3	2	2	2,700	<	2,700	0	2.00
15	---								
16									
17					************				
18					TOTAL PROFIT:				
19					£ 12,600				
20					************				

If the contribution for these cues is raised to £8.00, a new optimal solution results, with the number of cues = 300. Cricket bats are no longer produced since it is now more profitable to transfer resources to the production of the new product. Profits improve from £12,600 to £12,900 as a consequence of the change.

7.6 Data Matrix Commands in Linear Programming

Let us suppose that the graphical solution for the original 2-product, 2-constraint case has been attempted, showing that the optimal solution occurs at corner point

Table 7.3(c)   New Optimal Solution for Three Products

```
          A       B       C       D      E    F    G       H      I
 1
 2
 3                cricket hockey  billiards
 4      Product     1      2        3
 5
 6      Profit/Unit 12     10       8
 7      Quantity   0.00 1050.00  300.00
 8      produced
 9      ----------------------------------------------------------------
10      Resource requirements                  Total   Resources Amount Shadow
11                cricket  hockey  billiards    usage   available unused price
12      ----------------------------------------------------------------
13      cutting       2       2        1       2,400  <   2,400     0    2.00
14      finishing     3       2        2       2,700  <   2,700     0    3.00
15      ----------------------------------------------------------------
16
17                                          *************
18                                          TOTAL PROFIT:
19                                          £  12,900
20                                          *************
```

T in Figure 7.1. This result means that both resources are fully utilised so that:

$$2X1 + 2X2 = 2,400 \text{ (cutting time)}$$
$$3X1 + 2X2 = 2,700 \text{ (finishing time)}$$

Note that these are now equalities, and not less-than or equal-to conditions. It is possible to check the accuracy of the graphical solution, without having to invoke a linear programming routine, by solving the pair of simultaneous equations.

They may be solved using the Data Matrix commands of Lotus 1-2-3 (release 2.0 and above). The procedure is as follows with reference to Table 7.4, dealing first with the section of the worksheet headed PRIMAL.

Ensure that the variable coefficients form a square matrix, occupying adjacent cells of the worksheet. Cells B9..C10 are used here for that purpose, and the rest of the problem data is assembled around that matrix. Although headings for the inverted matrix and SOLUTION can be placed in the worksheet, there will be no values below row 14 until the problem is solved. Line up the RHS values of 2,400 and 2,700 in adjacent cells. To lend some structure to the worksheet, cells E9 and E10 have been selected for these values. The matrix operations now commence:

Matrix inversion
type **/DM**   (Data Matrix)
choose Invert
enter the Range address which is B9..C10
enter the Output range which is B15 here (address of the top left corner)

The inverted matrix is delivered as the output in cells B15..C16. It is then multiplied by the matrix of RHS values:

Table 7.4 Linear Programming Using Matrices

	A	B	C	D	E	F	G	H	I	J	K
1											
2											
3		PRIMAL						DUAL			
4		******						******			
5											
6	Product	1	2				Resource	C	F		
7		cricket	hockey								
8											
9	cutting	2	2 =		2,400			2	3 =		12
10	finishing	3	2 =		2,700			2	2 =		10
11											
12	Profit/Unit	12	10								
13											
14		inverted matrix						inverted matrix			
15		-1	1					-1	1.5		
16		1.5	-1					1	-1		
17											
18	SOLUTION						SHADOW PRICES				
19											
20	cricket	300					cutting	3			
21	hockey	900					finishing	2			
22											
23					PROFIT						
24				£	12,600 ◀─── +B20*B12+B21*C12						
25					=========						

Matrix multiplication

type /DM

choose Multiply

enter the First range (range address of the inverted matrix) which is
    B15..C16

enter the Second range (range address of RHS values) E9..E10

enter the Output range which has been chosen as B20.

The numbers 300 and 900 appear in cells B20 and B21 as the output of this procedure. Labels may be placed alongside to identify the variables.

This yields the solution to the pair of simultaneous equations. The profit may then be computed as shown in cell E24 of Table 7.4. It provides the optimal solution to the PRIMAL LP problem, i.e. the problem as originally stated. However, if the simultaneous equations:

$2C + 3F = 12$ (resource usage coefficients for cricket bats, contribution to profit on RHS)

$2C + 2F = 10$ (resource usage coefficients for hockey sticks, contribution to profit on RHS)

are solved, the solution, in this special case, will be the shadow prices of the scarce resources. This transformed problem is called the DUAL. It is set out alongside the PRIMAL, and follows the same matrix operations. The shadow prices are computed as £3 for each unit of cutting and £2 for finishing.[11]

It is important to observe that the above method only applies when the optimal solution has been identified at a particular corner point, so that equations, rather than inequalities, are operative. Additionally, the matrix inversion procedure can only be employed with square matrices. In this illustration, with optimality occurring at the intersection of two constraints, and with the number of variables also being two, these requirements are met. However, the range of applications where such conditions prevail is strictly limited, and a spreadsheet solution would normally require an add-on product such as **What'sBest!**

7.7 Media Selection

The media selection problem concerns the deployment of an advertising budget. It is not a means of determining how large that budget should be, although the implications of relaxing or tightening any constraint in the model may be examined in the ensuing sensitivity analysis.

The choice of advertising media − television, local radio, daily and evening newspapers, etc. − is a problem which is tackled in several management science/operational research (MS/OR) texts as an illustration of LP in marketing (see, for example, Anderson, Sweeney and Williams 1985, Chapter 5, section 5.2).[12]

The principal feature of the media selection application is the objective function, which is set in terms of 'exposure units'. For each medium, the effectiveness of a single advertisement is placed on a scale between 0 and 100, or any other convenient range. Such factors as audience profile, expected number of responses, image quality and other relevant factors − most of which are judgemental in character − are built into the exposure unit assessment.

The number of potential consumers reached is another possible objective. This may appear alongside the exposure objective in a 'goal programming' formulation of the problem − requiring specialised treatment to handle multiple objectives. Otherwise the number of potential customers is treated as a constraint which must be obeyed in the attempt to maximise total exposure units.

A complication which is recognised in some formulations of the model is that diminishing returns are likely to set in if too much advertising is allocated to a

---

11. In this worksheet, the DUAL has only been partially specified. In its full form, the equations would be replaced by *greater*-than or equal-to constraints and one would be attempting to *minimise* 2,400C + 2,700F. If the reader requires a fuller account of the dual problem, a suitable reference is Eppen *et al.* (1987, pp. 184−95).
12. Also treated as a marketing application in the same source is the allocation of advertising and sales force effort between a number of market segments.

particular medium (see Eppen *et al.* 1987, pp. 323—7). Whilst linear programming cannot cater for situations in which the marginal effectiveness of advertising, measured in exposure units, is falling continuously, it is possible to accommodate one or more falls in the exposure unit rating of each advertising medium, as will be shown in the following example, which adopts the Eppen approach.

Example

Suppose that a brand of instant coffee, INSCO, has been improved, and an advertising budget of £49,000 has been set aside for the first five weeks' campaign, which is to take place in an area of the UK served by a local radio station, a commercial television region, and a regional newspaper.

The budget may be allocated to local radio at a cost of £625 for 90 seconds of adverts each day, to the regional commercial TV where the unit cost is £1,200 for a 10-second spot, or to a regional newspaper at a cost of £700 for each small display. The number of families reached by each placement is expected to be 16,000, 30,000, and 20,000 respectively. The effectiveness of each medium in exposure units is judged to be as follows:

	exposure units	
RADIO	32	for each of 10 placements, only 21 thereafter
TV	42	for the first 12 adverts, then falling to 28
NEWSPAPER	36	for the first 10 inserts, then only 18 per insert

We start in the usual way by defining our variables in the LP model:

X1 is the number of radio adverts up to 10
X2 is the number of radio adverts beyond 10
X3 is the number of TV adverts up to 12
X4 is the number of TV adverts beyond 12
X5 is the number of newspaper adverts up to 10
X6 is the number of newspaper adverts beyond 10

Constraints may be imposed of the following kind:

(i) limits on the number of advertisements to appear in a particular medium
 — here we set 25 as the upper limit for radio and 30 for the other media;
(ii) a condition that at least so many potential consumers or families are reached
 — here, a figure of 1.2 million families is chosen;
(iii) logical conditions relating to levels achievable before diminishing returns set in;
(iv) the budget constraint — expenditure on this advertising campaign for INSCO is restricted to £49,000.

The usual non-negativity conditions should also be specified for completeness, although they will not affect the computer solution in this case.

Table 7.5(a)   Media Selection — Initial Solution

	A	B	C	D	E	F	G	H	I	J
1	*************									
2	TOTAL EXPOSURE:									
3	0									
4	*************									
5	Variable	1	2	3	4	5	6			
6	Exposure	32	21	42	28	36	18			
7										
8	Value	0	0	0	0	0	0			
9	— —									
10	CONSTRAINTS							LHS total		RHS
11	— —									
12	1	1	1	0	0	0	0	0 <		25
13	2	0	0	1	1	0	0	0 <		30
14	3	0	0	0	0	1	1	0 <		30
15	4	1	0	0	0	0	0	0 <		10
16	5	0	0	1	0	0	0	0 <		12
17	6	0	0	0	0	1	0	0 <		10
18	7	625	625	1200	1200	700	700	0 <		49000
19	8	16000	16000	30000	30000	20000	20000	0 >		1200000
20	— —									

Cell H12	$+B12*\$B\$8 + C12*\$C\$8 + D12*\$D\$8 + E12*\$E\$8 + F12*\$F\$8 + G12*\$G\$8$

The structure of the problem is as follows (see Table 7.5(a)):

OBJECTIVE function MAXIMISE total exposure units =

$$32\ X1 + 21\ X2 + 42\ X3 + 28\ X4 + 36\ X5 + 18\ X6$$

subject to CONSTRAINTS:[13]

1   $X1 + X2 <= 25$ (we impose a restriction that no more than 25 placements should be on radio)

2   $X3 + X4 <= 30$ (a restriction we impose on TV advertising)

3   $X5 + X6 <= 30$ (a restriction on newspaper advertising)

4   $X1 <= 10$ (i.e. maximum no. for radio before returns diminish)

5   $X3 <= 12$ (i.e. maximum for TV before returns diminish)

6   $X5 <= 10$ (i.e. maximum for newspaper before returns diminish)

7   $625\ X1 + 625\ X2 + 1200\ X3 + 1200\ X4 + 700\ X5 + 700\ X6 <= 49000$ (£49,000 is the allocation for the first campaign)

8   $16000\ X1 + 16000\ X2 + 30000\ X3 + 30000\ X4 + 20000\ X5 + 20000\ X6 >= 1200000$
(this is the constraint which imposes a minimum number of families that are to be reached, i.e. 1.2 million)

---

13. The LHS values, comparing level attained with level permitted for each constraint, all have the same structure in the worksheet, and the long formula shown for cell H12 may be copied to produce entries for all the cells affected in column H.

Table 7.5(b) Media Selection — Optimal Solution

	A	B	C	D	E	F	G	H	I	J
1	**************									
2	TOTAL EXPOSURE:									
3	1807									
4	**************									
5	Variable	1	2	3	4	5	6			
6	Exposure	32	21	42	28	36	18			
7										
8	Value	10	15	12	0	10	17.1			
9	--									
10	CONSTRAINTS							LHS total		RHS
11	--									
12	1	1	1	0	0	0	0	25 <		25
13	2	0	0	1	1	0	0	12 <		30
14	3	0	0	0	0	1	1	27.1 <		30
15	4	1	0	0	0	0	0	10 <		10
16	5	0	0	1	0	0	0	12 <		12
17	6	0	0	0	0	1	0	10 <		10
18	7	625	625	1200	1200	700	700	48995 <		49000
19	8	16000	16000	30000	30000	20000	20000	1302000 >		1200000
20	--									

The **What's*Best*!** solution is as indicated in Table 7.5(b):

> X1 and X2 together give the radio advertising level: 25
> X3 and X4 together give the TV advertising level: 12
> X5 and X6 together give the newspaper advertising level: 27.1

Assuming that fractional solutions are not possible, the latter figure will be rounded down to 27 newspaper adverts.

The maximum total exposure is 1807 units (1805 units if the 27.1 is rounded down), and the advertising campaign for this improved version of INSCO is expected to reach 1.3 million families (row 19 of Table 7.5b), which is comfortably in excess of the 1.2 million specified as a minimum.

The main difficulties in applying the LP technique to the media selection problem lie partly in the assumptions of linearity − not only in the effectiveness of each medium, which can be partially remedied − but also in the unit costs. In practice, a structure of discounts for advertising rates is usually operated, and this can be quite complex. Another major problem is inevitably the determination of reliable exposure unit measures for each medium.

The LP approach to media selection has evolved over the years through more sophisticated methodologies, typically involving dynamic programming. Notable in this context is the work of Little and Lodish (1966, 1969, 1981).

7.8 Multi-Period Capital Rationing

In looking at Table 7.6, we return to the earlier single-period capital rationing problem discussed in Chapter 3. The reader should refer back to that subject to

Table 7.6   Appraising Several Projects with the NPV Function

	A	B	C	D	E	F	G	H	I	J	K
1											
2	Project	A	B	C	D	E	F				
3									FINANCE AVAILABLE		
4	Flow 0	-75	-75	-30	-15	-75	-30		225		
5	Flow 1	-75	-105	-150	-30	0	-75		(£ thousand)		
6	Flow 2	-40	150	-45	75	300	-150				
7	Flow 3	300	225	450	-150	150	450				
8	Flow 4	150	75	375	150	150	150				
9	Flow 5	150	0	0	150	0	150				
10											
11	disc rate	10.0%									
12											
13	NPV	244.7	173.8	390.7	102.6	388.1	311.5				
14											
15	prof index	3.3	2.3	13.0	6.8	5.2	10.4		**********		
16									TOTAL NPV:		
17	projects	1	0	1	1	1	1		1437.6		
18	selected								**********		
19	CAPITAL	75	0	30	15	75	30	FINANCE	225		
20								USED	**********		

be reminded of the context in which this problem occurs. With a single financing restriction it is possible to rank capital projects according to NPV per £ invested in year 0.

In Table 7.7, however, there are financing limits for three further years: two more of £225, and one of £150 (thousand). As Table 7.7 stands, there is no solution entered at present — no projects selected, and no NPV generated.

Because there is no longer a single limiting factor to provide a unique profitability index ranking, the only logical way of handling the multiple constraints is through linear programming. What the technique sets out to do in this context is to maximise NPV, subject to the multiple financial constraints which place limits on the freedom to choose.[14]

The constraints are entered in the lower half of the worksheet, and have the general structure indicated in Table 7.7. The copying facilities of Lotus 1-2-3 enable the list of 'Total Usage' to be produced speedily, once the long formula has been established for one constraint (shown at the bottom of the worksheet).

The 'fraction' restrictions prevent more than one project A, or more than one project B, etc. from being selected, but do permit fractional parts of a project to appear in the optimal solution. The headings for columns J and K do not apply to these constraints.

The solution to the problem, as computed by **What's*Best*!**, is set out in Table 7.8. Optimality requires the adoption of projects A, D, E and F in their entirety and 0.3 of project C.

One may instruct the package to provide integer solutions only — i.e. accept

---

14. It was Weingartner (1963) who provided the first comprehensive LP treatment of the capital rationing problem. A less direct procedure had been described earlier by Lorie and Savage (1955).

Table 7.7   Capital Rationing — Initial Solution

	A	B	C	D	E	F	G	H	I	J	K
1											
2	Project	A	B	C	D	E	F			FINANCE REQUIRED	
3										(£ thousand)	
4	Flow 0	-75	-75	-30	-15	-75	-30			225	
5	Flow 1	-75	-105	-150	-30	0	-75			225	
6	Flow 2	-40	150	-45	75	300	-150			225	
7	Flow 3	300	225	450	-150	150	450			150	
8	Flow 4	150	75	375	150	150	150				
9	Flow 5	150	0	0	150	0	150				
10											
11	NPV	244.7	173.8	390.7	102.6	388.1	311.5			************	
12										TOTAL NPV:	
13	Quantity	0	0	0	0	0	0			0.0	
14	Adopted									************	
15											
16											
17	--										
18		Project	Financing	Requirements				Total	Start	End	
19		and <=1	restrictions					Usage	Fin'ce	Fin'ce	
20	--										
21	Year 0	75	75	30	15	75	30	0 <	225	225	
22	Year 1	75	105	150	30	0	75	0 <	225	225	
23	Year 2	40	0	45	0	0	150	0 <	225	225	
24	Year 3	0	0	0	150	0	0	0 <	150	150	
25	fraction a	1	0	0	0	0	0	0 <	1	1	
26	fraction b	0	1	0	0	0	0	0 <	1	1	
27	fraction c	0	0	1	0	0	0	0 <	1	1	
28	fraction d	0	0	0	1	0	0	0 <	1	1	
29	fraction e	0	0	0	0	1	0	0 <	1	1	
30	fraction f	0	0	0	0	0	1	0 <	1	1	
31	--										
32											

Cell H24   +B24*$B$13+C24*$C$13+D24*$D$13+E24*$E$13+F24*$F$13+G24*$G$13

whole projects only. In **What's***Best*!, this is executed by invoking the command sequence with the asterisk (on the PRINT SCREEN Key). On pressing Function key 8, the user is requested to state the range to format, which is B13..G13 in the original worksheet (Table 7.7). Optimising in the usual way yields the solution shown in Table 7.9.

With **What's***Best*! the quantity adopted in the integer solution normally appears either as a plus sign (+) or a dot (.) to indicate inclusion or exclusion respectively.

Table 7.8 Capital Rationing — Optimal Solution

Project	A	B	C	D	E	F	FINANCE REQUIRED (£ thousand)
Flow 0	-75	-75	-30	-15	-75	-30	225
Flow 1	-75	-105	-150	-30	0	-75	225
Flow 2	-40	150	-45	75	300	-150	225
Flow 3	300	225	450	-150	150	450	150
Flow 4	150	75	375	150	150	150	
Flow 5	150	0	0	150	0	150	
NPV	244.7	173.8	390.7	102.6	388.1	311.5	************* TOTAL NPV:
Quantity Adopted	1	0	0.3	1	1	1	1164.2 *************

	Project Financing Requirements and <=1 restrictions						Total Usage	Start Fin'ce	End Fin'ce
Year 0	75	75	30	15	75	30	204 <	225	21
Year 1	75	105	150	30	0	75	225 <	225	0
Year 2	40	0	45	0	0	150	203. <	225	21.5
Year 3	0	0	0	150	0	0	150 <	150	0
fraction a	1	0	0	0	0	0	1 <	1	0
fraction b	0	1	0	0	0	0	0 <	1	1
fraction c	0	0	1	0	0	0	0.3 <	1	0.7
fraction d	0	0	0	1	0	0	1 <	1	0
fraction e	0	0	0	0	1	0	1 <	1	0
fraction f	0	0	0	0	0	1	1 <	1	0

However, to clarify the output, these signs have been reformatted to register as either 1 or 0. The integer solution is to adopt projects C, E and F.

Even without the linear programming package, it should be possible for the reader to set out a worksheet which computes the NPV offered by combinations of the various projects and which provides a check on the finance used period by period. By trial and error, it is relatively easy to find the maximum possible NPV achievable without violating the constraints.

The result should, of course, correspond to that obtained above through linear

Table 7.9 Capital Rationing — Integer Solution

Project	A	B	C	D	E	F	FINANCE REQUIRED (£ thousand)
Flow 0	-75	-75	-30	-15	-75	-30	225
Flow 1	-75	-105	-150	-30	0	-75	225
Flow 2	-40	150	-45	75	300	-150	225
Flow 3	300	225	450	-150	150	450	150
Flow 4	150	75	375	150	150	150	
Flow 5	150	0	0	150	0	150	
NPV	244.7	173.8	390.7	102.6	388.1	311.5	************* TOTAL NPV:
Quantity Adopted	0	0	1	0	1	1	1090.3 *************

	Project Financing Requirements and <=1 restrictions						Total Usage	Start Fin'ce	End Fin'ce
Year 0	75	75	30	15	75	30	135 <	225	90
Year 1	75	105	150	30	0	75	225 <	225	0
Year 2	40	0	45	0	0	150	195 <	225	30
Year 3	0	0	0	150	0	0	0 <	150	150
fraction a	1	0	0	0	0	0	0 <	1	1
fraction b	0	1	0	0	0	0	0 <	1	1
fraction c	0	0	1	0	0	0	1 <	1	0
fraction d	0	0	0	1	0	0	0 <	1	1
fraction e	0	0	0	0	1	0	1 <	1	0
fraction f	0	0	0	0	0	1	1 <	1	0

programming. A larger, more complex, problem would be less amenable to the trial-and-error approach, and the LP add-on would be a highly desirable accessory.

Exercises

1. Find the optimal product mix for a furniture manufacturer producing chairs and desks, whose unit contributions are £5 and £3 respectively.

The constraints are as follows:

	chairs	desks	resources available
	requirements		
shaping	2 min	3 min	3,600 min
veneering	4 min	2 min	2,800 min

2. Using the product-mix example featured in the chapter, change the profit contributions from cricket bats and hockey sticks to £16 and £12 respectively, and calculate the increase in total profit if the product mix shown in Table 7.2(b) is maintained.

   Can this profit be improved by a change in the product mix?

   Repeat this exercise but keep the profit contribution from hockey sticks at the original £10.

3. Would the solution to the capital rationing problem set out in Table 7.8 be affected by a rise in the cost of capital from 10% to 15%?

4. Find the improvement to NPV (integer solution from Table 7.9) achieved by relaxing the year-1 financing restriction by £105,000 and the year-2 restriction by £10,000.

References and Further Reading

Anderson, D.R., Sweeney, D.J. and Williams, T.A. (1985) *An Introduction to Management Science*, 4th edn, West Publishing Company, St. Paul, Minnesota.

Cohen, S.S. (1985) *Operational Research*, Edward Arnold.

Eppen, G.D., Gould, F.J. and Schmidt, C.P. (1987) *Introductory Management Science*, 2nd edn, Prentice-Hall. (Eppen *et al.* includes a complete chapter on spreadsheet models, focusing on the **What'sBest!** add-on.)

Lev, B. and Weiss, H. (1982) *Introduction to Mathematical Programming*, Edward Arnold.

Little, J.D.C. and Lodish, L.M. (1966) 'A media selection model and its optimisation by dynamic programming', *Industrial Management Review*, Fall, pp. 15–23.

Little, J.D.C. and Lodish, L.M. (1969) 'A media planning calculus', *Operations Research*, pp. 1–34.

Little, J.D.C. and Lodish, L.M. (1981) 'Commentary on judgement based marketing models', *Journal of Marketing*, Fall, pp. 24–9.

Littlechild, S.C. (ed.) (1977) *Operational Research for Managers*, Philip Allan.

Lorie, J.H. and Savage, L.J. (1955) 'Three problems in rationing capital', *Journal of Business*, pp. 229–39.

Makower, M.S. and Williamson, E. (1981) *Operational Research*, 7th impression, Hodder and Stoughton.

Weingartner, H.M. (1963) *Mathematical Programming and the Analysis of Capital Budgeting Problems*, Prentice-Hall.

Whitaker, D. (1984) *OR on the Micro*, John Wiley.

Capital Rationing References cited in Chapter 3

Levy, H. and Sarnat, M. (1986) *Capital Investment and Financial Decisions*, 3rd edn, Prentice-Hall.

Lumby, S. (1984) *Investment Appraisal*, 2nd edn, Van Nostrand Reinhold.

Chapter 8

ISSUES IN PUBLIC SECTOR ANALYSIS

8.1 Cost–Benefit Analysis

A recurring theme in this book has been the need to take a long-term view in decision making. Although investment appraisal was treated as a subject in its own right, it has been emphasised that the discounting of cash flows over time is appropriate to any decision which has a long-term impact.

Cost–benefit analysis (CBA) can be regarded as a kind of investment appraisal designed for application in the public sector, or any other sphere of activity, where the benefits arising from an outlay of resources are not directly measurable in financial terms. Indirect measures of benefit are frequently derived in monetary units, although other types of utility indices are also used. Another characteristic of CBA is that the appraisal usually includes social costs and benefits both within the organisation's prime area of concern and those which are *external* to it.

Social benefits and costs are normally excluded from commercial appraisals, which tend to be restricted to an assessment of cash in as against cash out. In a CBA for a state industry, the conventional form of investment appraisal might be supplemented by an attempt to identify benefits received by users, but not fully paid for, and by an assessment of the wider impact of a project on society: inconvenience/pollution suffered by communities, as well as benefits received indirectly in the form of improved infrastructure, reduction in congestion, and so on.

British Rail, for example, could examine a major electrification scheme purely in commercial terms. It would need to estimate the capital outlays and loss of revenue during the period of modification, and then calculate the changes in future returns — improved receipts from sales of tickets and lower operating costs. The results of the appraisal could then be expressed in terms of NPV or IRR, as described in Chapter 2.

A CBA approach to the same problem could include the same (private) inflows and outflows if the consumer were paying an economic price for the service, but suppose that fares were not raised to reflect the value received by the passengers enjoying faster and more reliable travel. It would then be necessary to place a value on these improvements — typically by quantifying the annual time saved by users of the service and costing out time on the basis of average hourly wage rates. One would also enumerate and evaluate external social elements such as improving urban and rural life by the easing of congestion on the roads, on the one hand, and spoilage of the landscape following the erection of power lines on the other.

It is not always possible to place a monetary value on all the social factors but, in making comparisons, it is useful to list them and either make a qualitative assessment, or ascribe utility values through opinion sampling.

In many instances, however, projects are put forward on essentially commercial considerations. Indeed, the government's emphasis on self-financing and management within cash limits tends to reduce the importance of social costs and benefits. Certainly, under such a regime, organisations are motivated to focus on the costs which they will have to bear, and on the benefits accruing to their primary client groups, rather than to include spillover effects impinging on the activities of other agencies. Whether the inducement to greater efficiency compensates for the narrowing of vision is a moot point, but if managements and their paymasters dictate the adoption of commercial criteria, CBA will tend to resemble conventional investment appraisal.

Sometimes the reduction of the problem to financial inflows and outflows will be appropriate even in traditionally problematic areas of benefit measurement. For example, even in the health service, some projects are designed to save money, typically in the use of energy, chemical reagents and equipment maintenance. Taking a hard-headed 'commercial' approach to such issues — to determine whether such schemes are genuinely 'revenue saving' — is entirely in the patients' interests since the surpluses resulting from the investment can be ploughed back into patient care.

The use of the term 'project' carries the implication that the decision alternatives to be appraised involve outlays of capital. This is not necessarily the case, for a redistribution of expenditure on manpower, or other current items, may have long-lived effects which can only be properly evaluated by discounting the inflows and outflows according to the time periods in which they arise.

The discounting procedure is still relevant even if benefits are not calculable in financial terms. Suppose that the education of sixteen- to eighteen-year-olds is to be modified by a local education authority by introducing sixth-form colleges. Whilst it may be difficult to ascribe monetary figures to the quality of output as between the present and proposed systems, it should be possible to compare expenditure patterns over time for the two alternatives. The cash outflows in each case can be discounted to give the 'present cost', and the lower cost option identified.

Knowledge of the present cost of competing projects is particularly useful when the alternatives offer broadly similar outputs. Under such conditions, the mode of appraisal is often termed 'cost-effectiveness analysis' (CEA). In cases where identical performance in achieving the desired ends is anticipated, the recommended option is the one offering the lowest present cost. Otherwise, when options offer different degrees of effectiveness, appropriate criteria for relating cost to effectiveness have to be devised. For example, in a study by Klarman (1968), kidney transplantation was compared with dialysis on a kidney machine. His results may be summarised as follows:

Effectiveness

   (i) Life expectancy gain for individual on dialysis   9.0 yrs
  (ii) Life expectancy gain for individual with transplant   13.3 yrs
       (plus time on dialysis after failure of transplant)   3.9 yrs

Cost

  (i) (a)   Present cost of hospital dialysis (at 6%) $104,000
      (b)   Present cost of home dialysis $ 38,000
 (ii) (a)   Present cost of transplantation $ 44,500
         (including cost of dialysis after failure of transplant)

Although dialysis in the patient's home offers the cheapest therapy, it does not offer the same life expectancy as transplantation. The latter emerges as the cost-effective choice on a criterion of life years gained per dollar present cost. It would score even more highly if differential weightings were applied to the years of life expectancy to allow for the superior mobility and quality of life offered by transplantation.

Although Klarman's study was published in 1968 the relative economic inefficiency of dialysis is still a topical issue. At the British Association for the Advancement of Science Conference in 1986, Alan Williams advocated the adoption of quality-adjusted life years (QALYs) to measure effectiveness, not just for comparing treatments of kidney failure, but for establishing health care priorities across the board. Since hospital dialysis on the basis of his figures cost £14,000 per QALY gained, compared with £750 for a QALY gained through hip replacement, there was a case for a redistribution of resources in favour of the lower cost therapy. Williams stated that we should not shrink from following where the logic of that approach led us — that hospital dialysis should be restrained and total hip replacement expanded.

Differences in life expectancy are also a complicating factor in another sense, namely the length of time over which an option is expected to perform a service. Such differences arise when comparing the upgrading of old facilities with the construction of completely new ones. Whilst an upgrading may offer a cheaper solution in the short term, it may be false economy in the long term. In order

Table 8.1   Present Value and Annual Equivalent Cost

Year -->	0	1	2	3	4
cost --> (£'s)	0.00	300.00	300.00	300.00	300.00

discount rate
10.00%

present cost
£ 950.96

   AEC
£ 300.00

to make valid comparisons, costs need to be ascertained on an annualised basis, a need which can be served by the *Annual Equivalent Cost* (AEC) variant of discounted cash flow.

The AEC is directly available as a financial function in several spreadsheets. We have already examined the Lotus 1-2-3 version in Chapter 2, in the context of capital projects in a commercial setting. The function is entered as @PMT(S, R, T) for a sum S capitalised to year 0, at a discount rate R and a period of years T. To remind us of its meaning let us consider a simple illustration which utilises the worksheet in Table 8.1.

In this illustration, expenditures of £300 starting one year hence are anticipated annually for four years. At a discount rate of 10%, the present cost of this series is £950.96, revealed by using the @NPV function over the range of the worksheet containing those flows. One way of interpreting this result is that, in order to finance those four annual expenditures, an individual would need to set aside only £950.96 now, if interest of 10% were receivable on funds remaining invested.

If, indeed, we started from year 0 and posed the question as to what level of annual payment would be equivalent to a present sum of £950.96, the @PMT function of Lotus 1-2-3 would give us the answer of £300, for 10% over 4 years. The same function can be used to find mortgage repayments — the three terms which go inside the bracket are the principal, the rate of interest, and the term in years. In Table 8.1 we are expressing the relationship between a present cost and a series of annual equivalent costs.

Annual equivalent cost (AEC) normally processes a series of expenditures, including initial capital outlays, and varying costs over time. The first step is to discount all these back to the present using @NPV at the chosen discount rate. The present cost, thus obtained, is then annualised using @PMT to give the AEC of the entire series.

In Table 8.2(a), an initial capital outlay of £1,000 is followed at yearly intervals by further expenditures of £300. (In practice the latter need not be constant.) The

Table 8.2(a) Appraisal by NPV and AEC

Year -->	0	1	2	3	4
cost --> (outflow)	1000.00	300.00	300.00	300.00	300.00
rev --> (inflow)		620.00	620.00	620.00	620.00
net cash flow-->	-1000.00	320.00	320.00	320.00	320.00
discount rate 10.00%					

present cost
£ 1950.96

    AEC
£ 615.47

    NPV
£   14.36

Table 8.2(b) Appraisal by NPV and AEC

Year -->	0	1	2	3	4
cost --> (outflow)	1000.00	300.00	300.00	300.00	300.00
rev --> (inflow)		615.47	615.47	615.47	615.47
net cash flow-->	-1000.00	315.47	315.47	315.47	315.47
discount rate 10.00%					

present cost
£ 1950.96

    AEC
£ 615.47

    NPV
£   0.00

present cost at 10% of this series is £1,950.96, and the annual equivalent cost is £615.47. If this latter figure were offset each year by revenue of exactly £615.47, the NPV would be zero, as shown in Table 8.2(b).

8.2 The Choice of Discount Rate

In any assessment which involves the calculation of NPV (or present cost), or AEC, a discount rate has to be selected. The choice of discount rate in public sector appraisal is not a straightforward issue since the private sector rules involving shareholders' expectations are not directly relevant, even though an opportunity cost connection is one way of relating the discount rates between the sectors.

The opportunity cost principle lies behind the test discount rate (TDR), which is set by the Treasury for nationalised industries and public services in the UK. It is currently set at 5% in real terms and, according to HM Treasury guidance (1984):

> In choosing this rate as the opportunity cost of capital, consideration was given to pre-tax real returns achieved by private companies, the likely growth in income and consumption, and other factors affecting or indicative of the appropriate time preference for government.

The TDR is more of a baseline rather than a hard-and-fast rule. For instance, it has been advocated that for riskier projects in the health sector, a 2% premium be added — making 7% in total for discounting under such conditions. Nationalised industries consult with their respective government departments in setting individual discount rates consistent with achieving a 5% required rate of return (RRR) on the industry's investment programme as a whole.

8.3 Option Appraisal

Option appraisal as defined in the NHS is an economic evaluation of proposals in which the costs and benefits are estimated and compared with those anticipated for alternative ways of meeting similar ends. It has been advocated as a means of appraising all capital development in the NHS, although a considerable part of the activity seems to be at regional level for schemes requiring expenditures in excess of £500,000.

Ideally, option appraisal should be an integral part of the decision-making process in which the objectives of the service are pre-eminent, and the choice of option follows a full comparison of a range of feasible courses of action designed to achieve these objectives. In practice, it is evident that the technique is often used after a provisional choice has been made, but even then it can still serve as a useful control device by enforcing a check against at least one alternative. Given the possibility of bias in estimation to justify a preferred option, it is important that the final arbiters are able to comprehend the assumptions made and the bases of calculation.

It should be noted that the technique is equally valid for developments or reallocations of resources, which mainly involve changes in revenue, with or without accompanying capital expenditure. There is evidence of its application to such diverse issues as patient administration systems, catering arrangements, screening services, and contracting-out of laundry services.

Stages in Appraisal[1]

The steps involved in option appraisal are:

  (i) statement of the strategic planning context;
  (ii) setting objectives, constraints and performance criteria;
  (iii) formulating options;
  (iv) evaluating options — to include a preliminary sift, and for the shortlisted options:
    (a) a detailed description of each option;
    (b) assessment of benefits;
    (c) assessment of revenue costs;
    (d) assessment of capital costs;
    (e) an estimate of discounted costs (NPV or AEC at 5%);
    (f) an assessment of costs and benefits falling outside the NHS;
    (g) sensitivity analysis;
  (v) selection of the preferred option — presentation of results.

The discounting process and sensitivity analysis are obvious candidates for spreadsheet treatment, but the manipulation of data in all its aspects will be facilitated. In particular, the recording, analysis, and presentation of benefit measures can be greatly assisted by a spreadsheet combined with graphics facilities.

8.4 Indicators and Qualitative Factors in Benefit Assessment

Although there are many instances in public sector appraisals of benefits which arise in the form of cash generated, or cash saved, the enumeration and evaluation of non-financial benefits is usually seen as a prime characteristic of such appraisals, and one of the most tricky aspects for the analyst.

The quantification of outputs is an issue which arises in all aspects of management in the public sector.[2] Despite the difficulties which are inherent in measuring how much service is provided, and how well the services are performed,[3] some performance measures are required if decision making, planning and control are to be practised by management.

---

1. The steps listed here refer specifically to the procedures laid down in the NHS Option Appraisal guidance (1987). However, all types of public investment are required to go through such stages as: objective setting; option consideration; evaluation of costs and benefits; discounting; allowance for risk and uncertainty; and presentation of results in an appropriate manner — sometimes in a standard format.
2. For a full discussion of this subject, see Anthony and Herzlinger (1980).
3. In health care the maintenance of quality is usually termed *quality assurance*.

The difficulties are compounded by the presence of multiple objectives in most non-profit-making organisations. Nevertheless, attempts have been made to develop quantitative performance indicators which can assist managers and planners to compare performance and to set targets for planning purposes. In many public services, particularly those controlled by local government, 'value for money' initiatives have been promoted which rely on the availability of such output and productivity measures.

In the health service, performance indicators include average lengths of stay in hospital for in-patient treatments and waiting lists — issues which will remain topical so long as wide variations in these indicators are experienced between Health Regions, Districts, and even between hospitals in the same District. Despite the volume of data which is entailed in maintaining records for each Health District in England, the DHSS has managed to devise a system linked to Lotus and Symphony packages (using primarily the database and graphics facilities), which can run on an IBM compatible with 10 (ideally, 20 or more) megabyte hard disk storage capacity. Further description of this package is given in the final section of this chapter.

Although performance indicators are often useful in establishing 'desiderata' for option appraisal purposes, these tend to relate to efficiency considerations and are seldom adequate on their own for comparing the performance of one alternative against another. For instance, the construction of a new health centre might be expected to have an impact on service provision and institutional-care rate indicators which would hardly vary with the precise location. The construction costs might also be broadly similar in each of the possible sites under consideration. However, each site might have different qualities in terms of accessibility by public transport, convenience for practitioners and therapists, and the layout of the building permitted by the location. A qualitative factor rating could be established as follows:

   (i)   prepare a list of relevant factors after consultation with professional groups and potential users;
  (ii)   assign a common scale (say, 0 to 10 points);
 (iii)   score each option on the chosen scale;
 (iv)   assign a weight to each factor to indicate its relative importance, and set the weights so that they add up to unity (1.0):
  (v)   multiply the scores by the weights;
 (vi)   combine the results into a weighted 'utility' measure;
(vii)   test the results for robustness to variations in the scores and the attached weights.[4]

This kind of multi-attribute approach may also find a place in establishing prefer-

---

4. 'Robustness' here refers to *consistency* of the rankings in the face of modified subjective values for the attributes, and their perceived relative importance.

ences for the location of commercial production facilities. It is based on the Churchman–Ackoff (1951) model for handling multiple objectives.

More complex models described by Hertz and Thomas (1983) require an examination of trade-offs, revealed by interviewing decision makers, before collapsing the scores into a single utility measure. The simpler Churchman–Ackoff approach, though lacking in technical sophistication, is more practical when the views of a wide range of professional and different interest groups have to be taken into account. Surveys can be undertaken to establish the scores for each option and the perceived importance of each factor, but detailed interviews to establish the trade-offs between each attribute would be too time-consuming for most applications in the public sector where the number of participants in a decision tends to be large.

An example of the approach described above is given in Table 8.3(a) which summarises the points awarded for four possible sites for a day-hospital (W, X, Y and Z). There are four attributes that are regarded as important:

A.   proximity to general hospital diagnostic facilities;

Table 8.3(a)   Points for Shortlisted Sites

	A	B	C	D	E	F
1						
2						
3						
4						
5			A	B	C	D
6	Hospital		Diagnostic	Ease of	Available	Design &
7			Facilities	Access	Expansion	Environ.
8			==
9	W		10	7	7	4
10	X		8	8	1	5
11	Y		6	8	6	2
12	Z		4	6	7	8
13						
14						
15						

Table 8.3(b)   Combined Utility Measures

	A	B	C	D	E	F	G
1							
2							
3							
4							
5			A	B	C	D	
6	Hospital		Diagnostic	Ease of	Available	Design &	weighted
7			Facilities	Access	Expansion	Environ.	utility
8			==
9	W		10	7	7	4	8.2
10	X		8	8	1	5	6.3
11	Y		6	8	6	2	6.0
12	Z		4	6	7	8	5.4
13							
14							
15		weight	0.50	0.20	0.20	0.10	

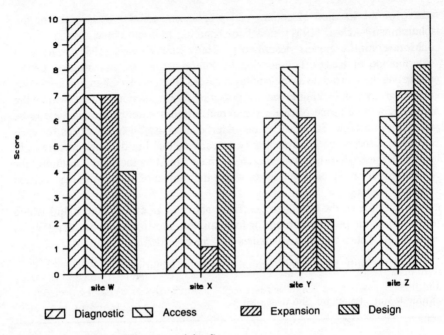

Figure 8.1   Points for Sites (unweighted)

B. ease of access to patients and staff;
C. space available for expansion as the catchment population increases;
D. potential of the site in designing an environment which is attractive to staff, and comfortable for patients.

In Table 8.3(a) the average scores from a survey are recorded, and the results are displayed in graphical form in Figure 8.1. Clearly, site W is going to be a strong contender (ignoring cost for the moment) unless the design/environment attribute is regarded as particularly important.

As it happens, this attribute (D) is seen as being the least critical, while attribute A — proximity to diagnostic facilities, in which this site scores highly — is perceived as being most important. The chosen weights are 0.5, 0.2, 0.2 and 0.1 respectively, for attributes A to D. The weighted 'utility' may be calculated within the worksheet (in column G) and re-appraised for any other set of weights.

8.5   Note on the Delphi Method

One method of arriving at a score for each attribute of an alternative was suggested above — namely, conducting a survey and taking the average. However, the recommendations which result from this process will tend to be a compromise rather than a consensus. Also, by recording the ratings of individuals taken in isolation, there is no scope for the interaction of expert opinion, which might contribute to mutual understanding and enhance the prospect of a consensus.

On the other hand, group interaction may allow the more articulate, forceful members to gain ascendancy at the expense of others whose expertise might have an equal contribution to make. In order to resolve this dilemma, the Delphi technique was devised by the RAND Corporation, primarily for forecasting purposes, but subsequently for other issues in which expert opinion was to be distilled.

The procedure entails the recording of opinions, analysis and summary by the investigator, and subsequent requisitioning of each expert combined with feedback concerning the responses of the other experts.

Emphasis is placed on the median score, and the inter-quartile range (of the middle 50% of answers), with any expert whose score lies outside this range being required to explain his response. Normally, some of the experts will revise their estimates, and the consensus narrows as a result.

In successive rounds, the investigator may modify his original question in the light of the feedback which he receives, and this may remove certain ambiguities and further narrow the range of response. Five or six rounds may be necessary, although the investigator may judge that a close enough consensus has been achieved at an earlier stage.

8.6   Analysis of Costs and Benefits

Suppose we have used a spreadsheet to evaluate the financial consequences of the four day-hospital sites under consideration. The non-financial benefit scores have been obtained from Table 8.3(b), and brought together with the costs into a single worksheet which is presented as Table 8.4. The capital costs of construction depend on the location, as does the expected useful life of the project in each case. To simplify matters, let us suppose that, over the life of a construction on a particular site, the annual recurrent (revenue) costs in real terms will remain approximately constant, although the anticipated level of revenue costs will vary from site to site. These are recorded in column E of the worksheet.[5]

The AEC at 5% for the capital outlays is computed in column F using the @PMT function of the Lotus package. With a constant recurrent expenditure for a given option, the total AEC may be found by adding this magnitude to the capital AEC, and the results are shown in column G. The rather awkward capital figures from column C yield (deliberately!) much more convenient AECs (all cost figures in £s).

---

5. Many construction projects in the public sector are subject to life-cycle costing exercises in which options with rather different expenditure profiles are compared. There is no great difficulty in computing the present cost when revenue expenditure varies and then converting the result to an AEC basis for comparing projects with different working lives.

Table 8.4 Benefit-Cost Ratios for Options

	A B	C	D	E	F	G	H	I
1								Benefit
2	Site	Capital	Life	Annual	AEC	AEC	Benefit	/cost
3		(£'s)	(yrs)	Revenue	Capital	Total		(x 100,000)
4	W	1,715,910	40	50,000	100,000	150,000	8.2	5.47
5	X	1,630,113	40	35,000	95,000	130,000	6.3	4.85
6	Y	1,761,744	25	40,000	125,000	165,000	6.0	3.64
7	Z	1,904,659	40	35,000	111,000	146,000	5.4	3.70
8								

Table 8.5 Sensitivity to Life and Revenue

11	DATA TABLE 2				revenue (£'s)		
12							
13	+I4		35,000	40,000	45,000	50,000	55,000
14		20	4.75	4.61	4.49	4.37	4.26
15	l	25	5.23	5.07	4.92	4.77	4.64
16	i	30	5.59	5.41	5.24	5.07	4.92
17	f	35	5.87	5.66	5.47	5.30	5.13
18	e	40	6.07	5.86	5.66	5.47	5.29
19		45	6.23	6.01	5.79	5.60	5.41
20		50	6.36	6.12	5.90	5.69	5.50

An option can only be regarded as dominant if it entails the lowest cost, and scores most highly for each attribute. In practice such dominance seldom occurs, but an initial guide to the rankings may be obtained from benefit/cost ratios which are computed in column I of Table 8.4.

The suggested order of preference is then W, X, Z, Y, although this would only tend to be an initial ranking before applying judgement as to whether the superiority of site W over site X is worth an extra £20,000 annually over the life of the projects. Because of uncertainty and/or imprecision in estimation, and possible contention surrounding the measures and weightings for desiderata in the benefit measures, it is standard practice to ask questions such as those which follow:

What if the cost of option W has been underestimated? Would different financial estimates affect the cost differentials?

What if the benefits have been over/under stated for any of the options, or the weights are inappropriate?

What if the measure of benefit is controversial — would the ranking change if alternative measures were employed?

Would a change in the TDR influence the ranking?

What would be the annual equivalent cost of option W if its expected life were only 25 years?

Revised worksheets would then be obtained to reflect these and other modified assumptions. Changing the assumed life of option W, for example, from 40 to 25 years would add £21,750 to the annual equivalent cost, changing the above results as follows:

Option	Life	Annual Equiv. Cost	Benefit	Benefit/Cost (X 100,000)
Site W	25	171,750	8.2	4.77

Thus, if option W were regarded as vulnerable to early termination, it would fall from its elevated position in the rankings. A more detailed exploration of the impact of expected life and revenue estimates is given in Table 8.5 which utilises the Lotus 'Data Table 2' facility. Site W maintains a favourable benefit/cost ratio except for the highlighted range of estimates.

There is no *optimal* solution in project appraisal when qualitative factors are being viewed against financial projections. Certainly, it would be wrong to base a decision purely on a simple benefit/cost ratio, such as that applied here. Nevertheless the attention of management can be directed to the most critical issues in the appraisal, and the spreadsheet's strength in recalculation harnessed to re-assess the relative merits of any set of options.

8.7 Specialised Software Applications

The Department of Health and Social Security (DHSS) Operational Research Service has developed microcomputer systems for Performance Indicators (PI) and Balance of Care (BOC) utilising the Lotus Symphony package in conjunction with IBM compatible computers. The PI package is also available to run with Lotus 1-2-3 version 2, and data (without the supporting package) is also provided for use with the earlier version, 1A, again on IBM compatibles. Another version runs on the BBC microcomputer fitted with a Torch Z80 second processor (or in conjunction with a Torch Z80 disk pack).

For the user who intends to use *both* packages, the following items will be required:

IBM compatible microcomputer with at least 640K RAM (preferably 1000K), and a hard disk with 20 megabytes or more storage capacity;

Lotus Symphony version 1.1 or 1.2, which must be already installed;

Epson FX80, or similar, dot matrix printer.

We shall start with a discussion of the PI package.

Performance Indicator System

Although the use of Symphony gives access to both of the DHSS packages, the PI system (its full title is 'Advanced User Performance Indicator System') has been adapted for Lotus 1-2-3 version 2, and there is no real advantage in acquiring Symphony for this particular application if this version of 1-2-3 is already installed. In this discussion it will be assumed that the 1-2-3 version 2 adaptation is in use.

The explanatory literature which comes with the package explains that the main contribution of the indicators is in the assessment of economy and efficiency, rather than outcome and quality. There are some outcome PIs, however, and there are checklists of questions about the quality of service in the accompanying manual.

The services covered by the indicators are those for the elderly, children, mentally ill, mentally handicapped, acute services, manpower, support services, and estate management. Most users would probably make comparisons between health authorities at a particular point in time. However, data for consecutive years can be retained, so comparison over time is possible.

Each PI is held in a separate worksheet file, which is structured as follows:

Row 4   England average;
Rows 5–18   regional values in a fixed order;
Remaining rows   district, unit, local authority, *values* (as appropriate) in one
                 column and *ranks* in the adjacent column.

On entering the PI system, the user may elect to compare data for the available years as a time series. Alternatively, a choice can be made to access data for one of the years shown in the menu of choices.[6]

The next menu offers data presentation in the form of a *HISTOGRAM* for any PI, *SCATTERGRAM* of one PI against another, a *LIST* containing selected ranges of values, an *ADHOC* selection of PIs, or a graphic *DISPLAY* of district, regional, and England values for a given PI.

Let us suppose that the *HISTOGRAM* option is chosen for a given PI. Figures 8.2(a) and (b) illustrate two indicators for the elderly: E1A, which is the Institutional Care Rate Hospital;[7] and E10, the Percentage of Geriatric Beds in Acute Hospitals. The differential shading highlights the range of values into which a chosen district, X, falls.

District X is at the lower end of the range for Institutional Care Rates, and at the upper end of the range for Percentages of Geriatric Beds in Acute Hospitals. One might expect there to be some connection between the two — for example, where facilities for care and rehabilitation of the elderly are closely integrated

---

6. The illustrations given in this section utilise 1984 data, although data for later years is now available.
7. Defined as the annual number of in-patients aged 75 years and over who were discharged from, or died in, the District Health Authority's hospitals after a length of stay exceeding 6 months, expressed as a percentage of the district's total resident population aged 75 years and over.

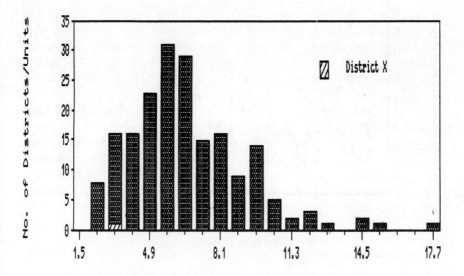

Figure 8.2(a) Institutional Care Rate Hospital (E1A)

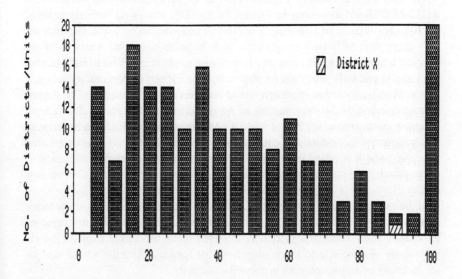

Figure 8.2(b) Percentage of Geriatric Beds in Acute Hospitals (E10)

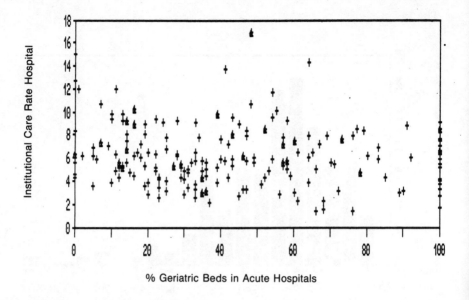

% Geriatric Beds in Acute Hospitals

Figure 8.2(c)   Scattergram of Two PIs (E10 and E1A)

in acute hospitals, patients are likely to return to their homes more quickly, and less likely to become long-stay cases.

The relationship between the two PIs can be investigated with the aid of a *SCATTERGRAM* as shown in Figure 8.2(c). This shows no obvious pattern, despite the presence of relatively low rates of institutional care in those districts with more than 80% of their geriatric beds in acute hospitals. Analysis of the relationship is likely to be complex. It would necessitate inclusion of such factors as total bed and staff provision for this sector. The levels of community services and local authority accommodation would also need to be considered. The degree of collaboration in the organisation of services, too, is important, although no indicator exists to measure this variable. For those attributes which can be reduced to performance indicators, the data can be analysed with the aid of all the Lotus functions, and it is possible to carry out regression and correlation exercises in the exploration of such relationships. (This assumes that the Lotus 1-2-3 version of the PI system is in operation.)

In the main, health authorities are expected to use the indicators to show those aspects of their services which lie at the extremes of the national distribution of PI values. In essence, the system is intended to be used as a diagnostic aid. Potentially, it may help to shape objectives for forward planning which may be set in terms of improvements in related indicators.[8]

The Balance of Care System

As stated in the previous sub-section on performance indicators, the care of the elderly is a complex issue which involves collaboration between health services and local authority social services. There is also a large and growing role played by the private sector.

In planning the care of the elderly, it is necessary to consider the following:

1. the health-care needs of the elderly population;
2. the preferred styles of provision for meeting those needs;
3. the resource implications of the desired patterns of care for the Health Authority, Local Authority, and other relevant agencies;
4. the costs and benefits of alternative patterns of care.

A mechanism for the analysis of needs, priorities, and their resource implications is the DHSS microcomputer-based Balance of Care (BOC) system, which runs in conjunction with Lotus Symphony. The BOC approach operates at a strategic planning level, and enables the resource consequences of providing long-term care of the elderly to be assessed according to their level of dependency. Dependency groups are defined in terms of physical and mental disability, incontinence characteristics, and, in a simple fashion, levels of informal support from family and friends.

The components of the BOC microcomputer system are:

A. The Population Model: the dependent population is either estimated from the projected elderly population for an area using information contained in the model from previous dependency surveys, or supplied by the user directly from a local survey.[9]

The estimation procedure is there because few districts have undertaken such surveys of their own. As dependency characteristics are essentially age−sex linked, data from the previous surveys can be directly applied to elderly population figures elsewhere. The model enables the user to define relevant localities within the planning area as required, and estimates a dependent population automatically for use in the care options model.

---

8. To assist in the analysis of indicators an 'Expert System' is now available which produces a rapid assessment of the data, highlighting extreme values and examining related combinations of PIs to detect possible underlying causes. This system, however, does not operate in conjunction with Lotus software. Instead, it uses the 'Crystal™ Expert System Shell' although, once again, it does use IBM or compatible hardware.
9. The dependency surveys available within the model are Dudley, East Sussex and Wiltshire, and the planner may choose one of these, with the aid of background information supplied in the Technical Guide.

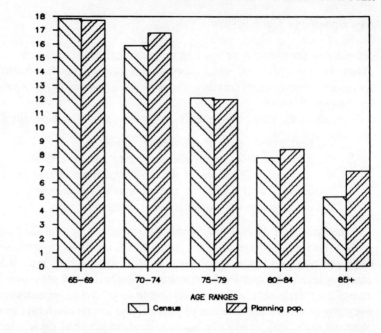

Figure 8.3(a)   Population Comparison — Census/Planning Populations

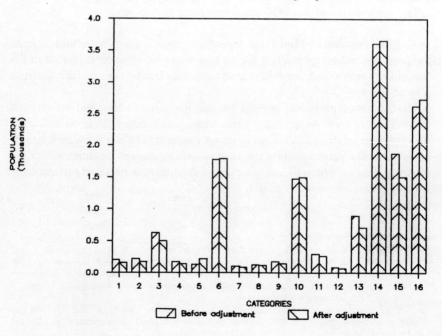

Figure 8.3(b)   Estimated Category Populations (before/after informal support changes)

A variety of outputs in the form of tables and graphs is readily available, and may be printed with the aid of the usual facilities of Symphony. An example is given in Figure 8.3(a), comparing the census and planning populations.

The estimated category populations may be displayed as in Figure 8.3(b). Sixteen dependency categories are defined, and each category population, before and after local informal support adjustments, is estimated.

B. **The Care Options Model**: the investigator is provided with an initial set of options which may be adjusted or replaced as desired. The model incorporates cost data to enable resource usage to be translated into expenditure requirements, so that minimum cost solutions can be explored alongside preferred, but perhaps higher-cost, solutions for meeting dependency group needs. It also provides estimates of the quantities of resources required.

In the light of the results, care options and allocations can then be re-examined, and the procedure repeated until a satisfactory outcome has been reached. It is important to note that the services, care options, and costs supplied are there as a starting point, and can easily be changed to accommodate local circumstances.

Table 8.6 gives an illustration of options for caring for patients with a high level of physical incapacity. The possibilities considered in this table are: hospital care in a long-stay ward; care at home with intermittent hospital care, and a package of community nursing, home help, and other community services; or care entirely within a private nursing home.

When options have been set for all dependency groups, or existing options from a base district have been selected, the model will translate this into allocations for the district's dependent population on one of three selected bases:

1.   minimum cost;
2.   preference indicators chosen by the user;
3.   as allocated in the base district.

The results can be examined in detail, group by group, but summaries and graphic output are also provided as aids to interpretation. For instance, the net cost by *agency* may be summarised (NHS, Private Services, and Social Services). The pie-chart given in Figure 8.4(a) is of net cost by *dependency*, in which groups are allocated to three broad categories of dependency.

Figure 8.4 (b) presents histograms for population and dependency, showing that, despite the relatively small numbers in the high dependency categories (about 11% in this illustration), they cost far more than the others to maintain (almost 50% of the total as shown here).

The trade-offs between cost and quality can be explored with the aid of a 'global allocation table', or a cost/quality diagram. An example of the latter is shown in Figure 8.5. It shows that, if the district's population were allocated in the same manner as in the base district (C1), the total cost for the planning area would be £25.5 million, and the quality indicator (based on preference ratings for options

Table 8.6   Care Options for a Dependency Group

SERVICE	UNIT OF MEASURE	CAT 1 HOSP	PHYS:5 HOME	MENT:- PNRS	INCO:-	SUP:-
Long stay ward	wks pa	52	12			
Psychiatric LS	wks pa					
Day hospital	days pw					
Psych. day hospital	days pw					
Community nurse	hrs pw		14			
Comm. psych. nurse	hrs pw					
Health visitor	hrs pa					
Domiciliary physio.	hrs pm		6			
Private res. home	wks pa					
Private nursing home	wks pa			52		
LA residential home	wks pa					
Sheltered housing	wks pa					
Day centre	days pw					
Home help	hrs pw		10			
Dom. care assistant	hrs pw					
Night sitter	nts pm		8			
Dom. occ. therapy	hrs pa		4			
Meals on wheels	mls pw		3			
Domiciliary laundry	sets pw		6			
Service A	Units					
Service B	Units					
Service C	Units					
Category population						
Annual cost per person		11,180	10,212	9,360	0	0	0
Base district allocation		47%	53%	0%	0%	0%	0%
Preference indicator		2	1	0	0	0	0
Fixed allocation (%)		0%	0%	15%	0%	0%	0%
Allocation used - number		0	170	30	0	0	0
- percent		0%	85%	15%	0%	0%	0%

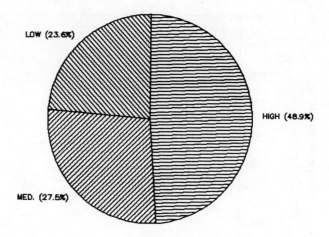

Figure 8.4(a)   Net Cost by Dependency

previously entered by the planner) would be 94%. If the planner allocated the whole population for each category to the first preference care option (subject to any fixed, constraining allocation specified by the planner), the quality indicator would become 100% (C2). The cost would actually fall in this example to £23

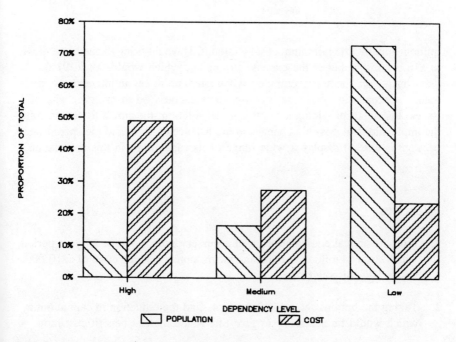

Figure 8.4(b)   Net Cost by Population and Dependency

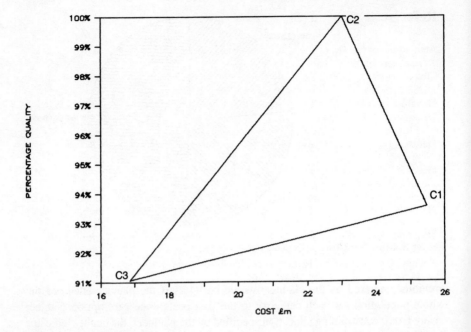

Figure 8.5 Cost/Quality Diagram

million. Finally, the minimum cost solution (C3) would bring expenditure down to £16.9 million, but at the expense of quality, which would fall to 91%.

In conclusion, the microcomputer BOC system promotes an interactive experimental approach in which the investigator is encouraged to explore 'what if?' issues. Instead of providing a single optimal solution, the aim is to demonstrate the implications of possible changes to the balance of care, and the spreadsheet package is able to display a wide range of its capabilities in this application.

Exercises

1. Find the annual equivalent cost of a nursery school over a 20-year period which costs £4 million to build and incurs annual running costs of £210,000. Use a 10% discount rate.

2. Taking the options set out in Table 8.4, find the reduction in capital outlay which would be necessary to give Site X the highest benefit/cost ratio.

References and Further Reading

Anthony, R.N. and Herzlinger, R.E. (1980) *Management Control in Nonprofit Organisations*, Richard D. Irwin.

Churchman, C.W. (1951) *Introduction to Operations Research*, John Wiley.

DHSS (1987) *Option Appraisal: A Guide for the National Health Service*, HMSO.

Donabedian, A. (1985) 'The epidemiology of quality', *Inquiry*, pp. 282–92.

Drummond, M.F., Stoddart, G.L. and Torrance, G.W. (1987) *Methods for the Economic Evaluation of Health Care Programmes*, Oxford University Press.

Gardner, E.S. (1987), 'Analyzing subjective decisions with a spreadsheet', *LOTUS*, January, pp. 68–71.

Gudex, C. (1986) *QALYS and their Use by the Health Service*, Discussion Paper 20, Centre for Health Economics, University of York.

Henderson, J. (1984) *Appraising Options*, SOAP No. 2, HERU, University of Aberdeen.

Hertz, D.B. and Thomas, H. (1983) *Risk Analysis and its Applications*, John Wiley (repr. 1984).

HM Treasury (1984) *Investment Appraisal in the Public Sector: A Technical Guide for Government Departments*, HM Treasury, London.

Keeney, R.L. and Raiffa, H. (1976) *Decisions with Multiple Objectives: Preferences and Value Tradeoffs*, Wiley, New York.

Klarman, H.E., Francis, J.O'S. and Rosenthal, G.D. (1968) 'Efficient treatment of patients with kidney failure', *Medical Care*, pp. 48–54, reprinted in M.H. Cooper and A.J. Culyer (eds) *Health Economics*, Penguin Books, pp. 230–40.

Linstone, H.A. and Turoff, M. (eds) (1975) *The Delphi Method: Techniques and Applications*, Addison-Wesley.

McGuire, A., Henderson, J. and Mooney, G. (1988) *The Economics of Health Care: An Introductory Text*, Routledge and Kegan Paul.

Mishan, E.J. (1975) *Cost Benefit Analysis*, George Allen and Unwin.

Mooney, G.H. (1977) *Planning for Balance of Care of the Elderly*, Discussion Paper No. 2/77, HERU, University of Aberdeen.

Sugden, R. and Williams, A. (1987) *The Principles of Practical Cost–Benefit Analysis*, Oxford University Press.

ANSWERS

Chapter 1

1. $(3.5^2 \times 2.3 \div 5) + (4 \times 3) - 2.5^3 = 2.01$

2. (a) £262.50   (b) 80 tickets

3. 9.642857

4. Variance = 10.51530; standard deviation = 3.242731

5. (a) £4173   (b) 20.57%   (c) −£141

Chapter 2

1.

0	0	300	−300
10	75	337.5	−262.5
20	150	375	−225
30	225	412.5	−187.5
40	300	450	−150
50	375	487.5	−112.5
60	450	525	−75
70	525	562.5	−37.5
80	600	600	0
90	675	637.5	37.5
100	750	675	75
110	825	712.5	112.5
120	900	750	150
130	975	787.5	187.5
140	1050	825	225
150	1125	862.5	262.5

+E9	3	3.25	3.5
250	425	387.5	350
260	415	377.5	340
270	405	367.5	330
280	395	357.5	320
290	385	347.5	310
300	375	337.5	300
310	365	327.5	290
320	355	317.5	280
330	345	307.5	270
340	335	297.5	260
350	325	287.5	250

2. £23,635

3. $Y = 811.67 + 20.95\ X$ (Std Err of Coef. = 3.65 and R Squared = 0.80)

4.   Regression output:

Constant	211.14
Std Err of Y Est	8.05
R Squared	0.994
No. of Observations	10
Degrees of Freedom	5

X Coefficient(s)	9.07	0.011	−96.45	0.010
Std Err of Coef.	0.47	0.009	18.41	0.007
	X1	X2	X3	X4

Suggests possible elimination of X2 and X4

5.   Regression output:

Constant	202.67
Std Err of Y Est	8.94
R Squared	0.99
No. of Observations	10
Degrees of Freedom	7

X Coefficient(s)	9.49	−73.15
Std Err of Coef.	0.46	12.40

visitors	price	prediction
15	1.2	257.29

Chapter 3

1. £24,895 (perpetuity would be £25,000; i.e. error of 0.42%)

2.

	NPV	IRR	ARR	payback
A	140	15.3%	12.5%	4
B	238	23.1%	12.5%	2
C	816	35.9%	35.0%	3

B offers a more rapid payback, but is otherwise inferior to C.
Prefer C to the alternatives since it has the highest NPV.

3. (a) Initial cost   Maintenance   £120.00
       of timeshare   £6,500   +VAT @ 15%
       Cost of capital 4.0%   = £138,00
       Term (in
       years)   80   Membership
                                       fee   £ 40.00
                                       Equivalent cost
                                       of timeshare   £271.79

                    Total annual equivalent cost £449.79

   (b) Rental is preferable since its annual cost is only £400.

4. Select all projects except A. NPV is now £1,516.90 thousand which is an increase
   of £79.30 thousand.

5. NPV at 10% is now −£87 and IRR is approximately 10%.

Chapter 4

1. CONS = 71276 + 0.203 PDI − 372.13 RELPR

2. Elasticities are:
   (a) income 0.502; price − 0.604
   (b) income 0.463; price − 0.276

3. Advertising to sales ratio is 0.16, which is approximately equal to the ratio of the
   advertising and price elasticities.

   Advertising will rise by £5,250 and sales by £5,595
   (NB: production costs will also rise).

4. Profits: turnover = 7.37%

   PROFIT = − 1060 + 0.12 TURNOVER

   Correlation coefficient = + 0.95

Chapter 5

1. Price elasticity   = − 0.267

   New forecast sales = 194.73
   New price elasticity = − 0.262

2. Trend is 2511.

3. 3197; 4484; 2004; 1133; 3335.

4. (a) 40.78   (b) 36.51

5. DMC forecast has $U = 0.367$ and MSE $= 5$
    CSB forecast has $U = 0.906$ and MSE $= 30$

Chapter 6

1. Contribution   £5,000.00
    Break-even output   6
    Break-even sales   £ 90,000
    Estimated output   18
    Margin-of-safety   12
                   or   £ 180,000
                   or   66.7%
    Profit−volume ratio   33.3%

    Profits are   £30,000,   £25,000,   £20,000   and £15,000
    Revenues are   £180,000,   £165,000,   £150,000   and £135,000

2. £25,000 and 36 units per period.

3. (a) £20,000 and 48 units per period.
    (b) £22,917 and 41 units per period (to the nearest unit).

4. Price would be £50.60 and quantity 179,829.
    To achieve the same total revenue, despite a price change, elasticity would have to
    be unitary (i.e. $= -1$).

5. Price for NEWTEX would be £50.10.

Chapter 7

1. Chairs 150; desks 1,110.

2. Profit improves by £3,000; no change in product mix needed.
    Profit falls to £14,400; no hockey sticks produced, 900 cricket bats are made.

3. No change in the allocation.

4. NPV improves by £347.3 thousand.

Chapter 8

1. £679,830.

2. Reduction of £254,494 to an outlay of £1,375,619.

AUTHOR INDEX

Abell, D.F., 164−7
Ackoff, R.L., 1n, 205
Alter, S., 4, 8
Anderson, D.R. (with Sweeney, D.J. and Williams, T.A.), 187
Anthony, R.N., 203n

Bajic, V., 162n
Barron, M., 128n
Bass, F.M., 131−2, 166
Baumol, W.J., 144−6
Baxter, W.T., 151−2
Blight, C., 94−5
Box, G.E.P., 127−8
Broadbent, S., 91
Bromwich, M., 76
Brown, W., 161

Chamberlin, E.H., 87
Chambers, J.C. (with Mullick, S.K. and Smith, D.D.), 130n
Churchman, C.W., 205
Clutterbuck, D., 74
Cohen, S.S., 172
Court, A.T., 162
Cowling, K., 97, 98, 162
Cox, W.E., 129
Cretien, P.D., (with Ball, S.E. and Brigham, E.F.), 53
Croome, P., 88, 91
Cubbin, J., 162, 162n

de Pace, M., 9n
Dean, J., 163
Dhalla, N., 130
DHSS, 203n

Dobbins, R., 59
Dorfman, R., 97−8
Doyle, P., 130
Drury, C., 136n, 146n

Eppen, G.D. (with Gould, F.J. and Schmidt, C.P.), 187n, 188

Finlay, P.N., 9

Georgoff, D.M., 130n
Goldsmith, W., 74
Grushcow, J., 19n

Hall, R.L., 146−8
Hammond, J.S., 164−7
Harbour, G., 162
Hertz, D.B., 76, 79n, 205
Herzlinger, R.E., 203n
Hirst, I.R.C., 65n, 80n
Hitch, C.J., 146−8
HM Treasury, 202
Hooley, G., 148
Horsfall, J., 88, 91

Jackson, B.B., 161
Jackson, M., 119n, 132n
Jaques, E., 161
Jarrett, J., 127, 128n
Jenkins, G.M., 127−8
Jobber, D., 148

Keen, P.G.W., 3
Klarman, H.E. (with Francis, J.O'S and Rosenthal, G.D.), 199
Kotler, P., 128n, 129, 131, 132

Koutsoyiannis, A., 94, 102, 122, 141n,
    156n
Kvanli, A.H. (with Guynes, C.S. and
    Pavur, R.J.), 37, 94, 101, 102
Kyd, C.W., 119n

Lage, G.M., 96
Lancaster, K.J., 87, 161
Lanzillotti, R.F., 148
Leech, D., 162n
Levy, H., 80n
Lilien, G.L., 131n, 132
Lintner, J., 80n
Little, J.D.C., 190
Littlechild, S.C., 170n
Lodish, L.M., 190
Lorie, J.H., 191n
Lotus Development Corporation, 31

McCosh, A., 3
McGuigan, J.R., 140n, 164n
Markowitz, H.M., 77n
Massie, J.L., 1n
Merrett, A.J., 57
Miller, R.B., 112, 128n
Moyer, R.C., 140n, 164n
Murdick, R.G., 130n
Murfin, A., 162
Myers, S.C., 80n

Nugus, S., 28n

Oxenfeldt, A.R., 151–2

Palda, K.S., 163
Pappas, J.L. (with Brigham, E.F. and
    Shipley, B.), 140n, 164n
Piercy, N., 97
Pike, R., 52, 59, 148
Pokorny, M., 39n
Porter, M.E., 129

Quinn, J.B., 1

Rao, V.R., 163
Rea, J.D., 96
Reekie, W.D., 94–5
Remenyi, D., 28n
Robinson, J., 87
Ryan, B.F. (with Joiner, B.L. and
    Ryan, T.A.), 112

Sabavala, D.J., 163
Sarnat, M., 80n
Savage, L.J., 191n
Scapens, R.W. (with Sale, T.J. and
    Tikkas, P.A.), 52, 148
Schofield, J., 19n
Scott-Morton, M.S., 3
Shapiro, B.P., 161
Sharpe, W.F., 80n
Shipley, D., 148
Silk, A.J., 132
Simon, H., 163
Simon, H.A., 3n
Steiner, P.O., 97–8
Stone, R., 88, 91
Stoneman, P., 162n
Sykes, A., 57

Targett, D., 128n
Theil, H., 122–4
Thomas, H., 76, 79n, 205
Turnbull, S.M., 80n

Urban, G.L., 132

Vernon, K., 119n

Watkins, T., 87, 130
Weingartner, H.M., 191n
Whitaker, D., 172–5
Wigley, K.J., 119n
Williams, A., 199

Yuspeh, S., 130

Other authors appear in the references and further reading at the end of each chapter.

SUBJECT INDEX

Absolute cell address, *see* Address, absolute cell
Absorption costing, *see* Costing, absorption
Accounting:
classification of costs, 146, 146n
models, 4−6
profit, 47
rate of return, 62
Addition, 14
Advertising:
in demand analysis, 88, 90−1, 96−8
see also Elasticity, advertising and Media selection
Annual Equivalent Cost (AEC), 60−1, 71−4, 200−1
Annuities, 47n, 61−2
Autocorrelation, 101−3, 127−8
Average, moving, 118−23
rate of return, 62−5
@AVG function in Lotus 1-2-3, 16, 39, 122
Avoidable cost, *see* Cost, avoidable

Backward iteration, 28−30, 68, 150
Balance of care (BOC) system, 213−8
Bar charts and histograms, 17, 160, 206, 210−11, 214, 217
BASIC program for linear programming, 172−5
Beer, demand for, 88−9, 91−6, 101−3
Boston Consulting Group, *see* Experience curve
Brands, 87−8
Break-even analysis, 4−6, 23, 136−46, 171

CALC in Lotus 1-2-3, 13n
Capital Asset Pricing model (CAPM), 80−2
Capital:
budgeting, *see* Investment appraisal
developments in the NHS, 202
expenditure, 44
rationing, 74−6, 190−4
Cash flow, *see* Discounted Cash Flow
Cell addresses: absolute, relative, mixed, 10, 15
Certainty equivalent, 78−9
Column width, 11
Commands in Lotus 1-2-3:
Copy, 14−15
Data, 23−38
File, 16
Graph, 17−18
Print, 17
Competition, perfect, 86−7, 140−1
Compound interest, compounding process, 47−8
Confidence interval:
for regression coefficients, 93−4
in prediction, 106, 107−8, 117
Constant in Lotus 1-2-3 regression output, 34
Constant, smoothing, 126−7
Constraint, profit, 142−4
Constraints in linear programming, 171
Contributions to profit, *see* Profit, contribution
Control panel in Lotus 1-2-3, 13
Control systems, 2−3
Copying in Lotus 1-2-3, 14−15
Corporation tax, 65−8

226

Correlation:
  coefficient, 99−100
  matrix, 100, 116
Cost:
  annual equivalent, see Annual
    Equivalent Cost
  avoidable, 151−2
  -based pricing models, 146−58
  direct, 146, 152
  fixed, 136, 140
  marginal, see Marginal cost
  opportunity, see Opportunity cost
  overhead, see Overheads
  variable, 136, 140
Cost and price relationships, 136−69
Costing, absorption, 146
Cost−Benefit Analysis (CBA), 197−8
Cost-effectiveness, 8, 199−201
Cost−Volume−Profit (CVP) analysis,
  4−6, 23, 136−46

Data:
  cross-section, 91, 99, 100
  primary and secondary, 128
  time series, see Time-series data
Databases, 3, 37
Data commands in Lotus 1-2-3:
  Fill, 38
  Matrix, 38, 184−7
  Regress, see Regression
Data Table commands:
  Data Table 1, 23−5, 68−70
  Data Table 2, 25−6, 69−70, 208
Decision making process, 1−4
  strategic, 1−2
Decision Support System (DSS), 3−8
Default:
  file extension in Lotus 1-2-3, 16−17
  setting for worksheet display, 11
Delphi Method, 206−7
Demand:
  analysis, 85−103
  curve, 86−7, 98−9
  determinants of, 85−6
  estimation, 88−103
  forecasting, 106−135
  functions, 88−96
Depreciation, 46−7, 65−8, 137n
Diminishing returns:
  in advertising, 187−8
  in production, 141
Direct cost, see Cost, direct

Discounted Cash Flow (DCF), 7,
  45−62, 64−8, 71−9
Discounting:
  in investment appraisal, 16, 47
  in option appraisal, 203
Dividend policy, 65−7
Division, 14
Dorfman−Steiner theorem, 97−8
Dual and primal in linear programming,
  185−7
Durbin−Watson statistic, 101−3, 117

Econometrics, problems of, 98−103
Economic life of equipment, 71−4
Economies of scale, 164, 164n
EDIT mode in Lotus 1-2-3, 15
Elasticity, 88−98
  advertising, 90−1, 96−8
  arc, 89−90
  cross, 96
  income, 92
  in markup calculation, 156−7
  point, 89
  price, 89−92, 139
Error:
  measurement in forecasting, 122−4
  standard, see Standard error
Evaluation of alternatives, 8−9
@EXP function in Lotus 1-2-3, 16, 92
Expected value, 76
  see also Mean−variance rule
Experience curve, 164−7
Exponential smoothing, 125−8
Exponentiation, 14

Feasible region, 175−6
Feedback, 2, 4
Financial functions, 16, 47, 49−52,
  60−1
Firm:
  managerial model of the, 144
  microeconomic models of, 140
Fixed cost, see Cost, fixed
Forecasting, 106−35
Format commands in Lotus 1-2-3:
  Comma, 11
  Fixed, 11
  General, 11
  Percentage, 11
  Text, 23
  Worksheet Global, 12
Formulae in Lotus 1-2-3, 13−15

Full-cost pricing, *see* Cost-based pricing
models
Function keys:
— in Lotus 1-2-3,
f2 EDIT, 15
f3 NAME (named ranges), 18
f4 ABS (absolute cell address), 15
f5 GOTO, 10
f8 TABLE (data a table
recalculation), 35
f10 GRAPH, 19
— in What'sBest!, 180−3
Functions in Lotus 1-2-3, 15−16
Functions of Management, 1
Future value, 47

Gas, forecasting consumption of,
118−23
General format, *see* Format commands
in Lotus 1-2-3, General
Goal Solutions, 28−30, 68, 150
Graph commands, 17−18

Hardware requirements:
for Lotus 1-2-3 and Minitab, x
for DHSS applications, 209
Health services, 202−18
@HLOOKUP function in Lotus 1-2-3,
159−60
Heteroscedasticity, 100−1
Hypothesis testing, 94

IBM PC and compatibles, x, 209
Identification problem, 98−9
@IF function in Lotus 1-2-3, 63
Indicators:
leading, 129
performance, 210−13
Inflation, allowing for in investment
appraisal, 46, 48−9
Integer solutions, 183, 191−4
Internal Rate of Return (IRR), 7,
51−60, 64−5
Investment:
appraisal, 6−7, 44−83
characteristics of, 44−5
determinants of, 44
sensitivity analysis in appraisal, 26−8,
68−70
traditional methods of appraisal, 62−5
@IRR function in Lotus 1-2-3, 16,
27−8, 51−2

Keys used in Lotus 1-2-3, 10
see also Function keys

Labels, 12−13, 19
Learning curve, *see* Experience curve
Linear Programming (LP), 170−96
Linear regression, *see* Regression
Line graph, 17−18
@LN function in Lotus 1-2-3, 16, 92,
166
@LOG function in Lotus 1-2-3, 16,
92n, 166
Logarithmic functions, 89, 91−6,
132−3, 166
Long-run profit maximisation, 144, 163

Management:
functions of, 1
Information System (MIS), 2−3, 6
process, 2
systems, 2−4
Margin of safety, 4−5, 138−9
Marginal cost, 140, 146
Marginal revenue, 140, 141, 146
Marginal value, *see* Shadow price
Marketing, 87−8, 163
Markup in pricing, 147−51
Mathematical functions in Lotus 1-2-3,
16
Mathematical programming, 171
Matrix, *see* Data matrix
@MAX and @MIN functions in Lotus
1-2-3, 16, 159
Mean Squared Error (MSE), 122−7
Mean−variance rule, 77−9
Media selection, 187−90
Menus, 13
Minitab, 100, 101, 109−18, 128n
Models:
accounting, 4−6
managerial, 144
microeconomic, 140
optimisation, 6−7
representational, 4
suggestion, 4
Modes in Lotus 1-2-3, 13
Monopoly, 87, 141
Moving averages, 118−23
Multicollinearity, 99−100
Multiple regression, *see* Regression,
multiple
Multiple solutions with IRR, 55−7
Multiplication, 14

Mutually exclusive projects, 57—8

@NA function in Lotus 1-2-3, 119—20
Net Present Value (NPV), 7, 49—51,
   64—70
@NPV function in Lotus 1-2-3, 16,
   27—8, 50, 200—1

Objective:
   profit maximisation, 140—1
   sales revenue maximisation (SRM),
   142—4
   setting, 1
Objective function in linear
   programming, 171, 173, 189
Operational research (OR), 170
Operators in Lotus 1-2-3, 14
Opportunity cost, 151—6
   see also Shadow price
Opportunity cost of capital, 28, 47
Optimal solutions, 171, 181, 184, 185,
   190, 193—4
Optimisation models, 6—7
Option appraisal, 202—3
Output range for regression, 33
Overheads, 146—8, 152—4

Payback period, 7, 63—4
Perfect competition, 86—7, 140—1
Performance Indicators (PI) system,
   210—13
Perpetuities, 61—2
Pie charts, 17, 215, 217
Planning, 1—2, 88, 167
Planning in the public sector, 203
@PMT function in Lotus 1-2-3, 60,
   71—4, 200—1
POINT mode in Lotus 1-2-3, 13, 17
Portfolio theory, 80—2
Prediction, 95—6, 103—4, 106—13
Prediction interval, 108—9
Predictors, 30, 111—12
Present value, 47—8
   see also Net Present Value and
   @NPV function
Price, 136—69
   under perfect competition, 87
   shadow, see Shadow price
Pricing strategy, 167
   penetration and skimming, 163—4
Print commands in Lotus 1-2-3:
   File, 17
   Graph, 18

Printer, 17
Screen, 17
Product Life Cycle (PLC):
   in demand forecasting, 129—33
   in pricing, 163—4
Product-mix problem, 171—87
Profit:
   accounting, see Accounting profit
   contribution, 136—9, 172
   maximisation, 141—6, 163, 171
   —volume ratio, 138—9
Profitability index, 75—6
Protecting in Lotus 1-2-3, 19—20
Public sector analysis, 197—219
@PV function in Lotus 1-2-3, 61

Quality Adjusted Life Year (QALY),
   199

R squared, 34—5, 93, 99—100
Range Name Create in Lotus 1-2-3, 18
Ranking of projects, see Capital
   rationing and Mutually exclusive
   projects
Regression:
   linear, 30—7
   linear in logs, 33n, 89
   multiple, 36—8, 113—18
   template for 2-variable, 38—40
Releases of Lotus 1-2-3:
   2.0 and 2.01, x, 10, 16, 31, 38
   earlier releases, 16, 209
   3.0, ix, 20
Rent-or-buy decision, 58—60
Replacement, see Economic life of
   equipment
Risk and uncertainty in investment
   appraisal, 76—82

S curve, 131—2
Sales Revenue Maximisation (SRM),
   142—4
Saving and retrieving files, 16—20
Scatter diagrams, 31—2, 212
Sensitivity analysis, 9, 23—8, 68—70
   in linear programming, 178—9
   in option appraisal, 203
Shadow price, 172n, 173, 178—9,
   181—4
Short-run profit maximisation, 140—5,
   163
Significance tests, 35, 93—4
Simplex method, 171

Simultaneous equations:
  in demand estimation, 98—9
  solved with Data Matrix, 184—7
Software,
  in decision support systems, 4
  for Health Service Applications,
    209—18
  statistical, 100, 101, 102
Spreadsheets:
  characteristics of, 9—13, 19
  origins of, 9—10
@SQRT function in Lotus 1-2-3, 108
Standard deviation, 16
  see also @STD function
Standard error:
  of coefficient, 35, 93
  of Y estimate, 35, 108—9
Statistical functions, 16
@STD function in Lotus 1-2-3, 16, 76
Subtraction, 14
@SUM function in Lotus 1-2-3, 11, 16
Supply curve, 86—7, 98—9
Symphony (Lotus), ix, 209

t-distribution, 35, 93—4
Target Rate of Return (TRR) pricing,
    148—51
Template for 2 variable regression,
    38—40
Test Discount Rate (TDR), 202
Theil inequality coefficient, 122—4

Time series:
  analysis, 6, 118—23
  data, 6, 30
  decomposition, 119
  seasonal variation in, 119—21

Uncertainty, see Risk and uncertainty
Utility:
  in consumer theory, 87
  multi-attribute, 204—5
  pricing, 160—2

Value pricing, 160—2
@VAR function in Lotus 1-2-3, 16, 39
Variable cost, see Cost, variable
Variables:
  dependent and independent, 30
  lagged, 103
Variance, 16, 39, 76—8
Visicalc, 9

What if?, see Sensitivity analysis
What'sBest!, 180—4, 187—94
Worksheet Global Protection command
    in Lotus 1-2-3, 19—20
Writing down allowance, 65—8
  see also Depreciation

X coefficient in Lotus 1-2-3 regression
    output, 34
XY graphs, 17—18